T0311909

Consumer Financial Vulnerabilities in Malaysia

This book examines four aspects of Malaysian consumers' financial vulnerabilities. First, it discusses the issue of over-indebtedness due to excessive reliance on consumer financing. Second, the book investigates why Malaysians are ill-prepared for their golden years in terms of retirement planning and savings. Third, it delves into the problem of financial fraud victimisation among Malaysian consumers. Fourth, the book analyses the reasons why Malaysians are underinsured despite the distinct benefits of life insurance.

Drawing on secondary data from government agencies such as Bank Negara Malaysia, Employees' Provident Fund, Royal Malaysian Police, and the Department of Statistics Malaysia, each chapter presents statistical trends reflecting the four financial vulnerabilities. In-depth analyses of the literature reveal three broad psychological domains (cognition, motivation, and disposition) and specific psychological factors (e.g. over-confidence, self-control, social norms, and financial literacy) that significantly influence consumers' financial decisions. The four financial vulnerabilities investigated in this book directly address the strategic outcomes of the Malaysian National Strategy for Financial Literacy 2019–2023 (MNSFL), a five-year plan to elevate the financial literacy of Malaysians. Finally, the book presents strategic recommendations that are believed to be useful guidelines for relevant policymakers to promote positive financial behaviours and rational attitudes among consumers.

It will be a useful resource for policymakers and researchers interested in economic psychology and behavioural finance.

Nurul Shahnaz Ahmad Mahdzan is associate professor and the current Head of Finance and Banking Department, University of Malaya, Malaysia. She obtained her PhD from University of Nottingham, United Kingdom. With ten years' experience working in financial services, she has published numerous articles on personal financial behaviour.

Mohd Edil Abd Sukor teaches finance and Islamic finance at Faculty of Business and Accountancy, University of Malaya, Malaysia. He holds a PhD in finance from the University of Melbourne, Australia. He has led several research grants including Vulnerabilities in Malaysian Consumer Finances.

Izlin Ismail is associate professor and the former Head of Finance and Banking Department, University of Malaya, Malaysia. She obtained her PhD from Nottingham University Business School, Malaysia Campus. Her research interests include international finance, microfinance and fintech. She also recently completed a financial literacy handbook for primary schools.

Mahfuzur Rahman works at Finance and Banking Department, University of Malaya, Malaysia. He obtained his PhD from University of Malaya, Malaysia. His research interest includes financial decision-making behaviour and financial risk management. He has managed several research grants and published several research articles.

Routledge Advances in Management and Business Studies

Public Management and Vulnerability
Contextualising Change
Edited by Gareth David Addidle and Joyce Liddle

Sustainability Assessments
Insights from Multinational Enterprises Operating in the Philippines
Hermann Lion, Jerome D. Donovan, Cheree Topple, Rowan Bedggood and Eryadi K. Masli

Cross-Cultural Leadership
Being Effective in an Era of Globalization, Digital Transformation and Disruptive Innovation
Ahmad Muhamad Salih

Tourism in Bangladesh
An Introduction
Azizul Hassan

Transforming Relationship Marketing
Strategies and Business Models in the Digital Age
Edited by Park Thaichon and Vanessa Ratten

Affirmative Action in Malaysia and South Africa
Preference for Parity
Hwok-Aun Lee

Consumer Financial Vulnerabilities in Malaysia
Issues, Trends and Psychological Aspects
Nurul Shahnaz Ahmad Mahdzan, Mohd Edil Abd Sukor, Izlin Ismail and Mahfuzur Rahman

For more information about this series, please visit: www.routledge.com/ Routledge-Advances-in-Management-and-Business-Studies/book-series/ SE0305

Consumer Financial Vulnerabilities in Malaysia

Issues, Trends and Psychological Aspects

Nurul Shahnaz Ahmad Mahdzan, Mohd Edil Abd Sukor, Izlin Ismail and Mahfuzur Rahman

Routledge
Taylor & Francis Group

LONDON AND NEW YORK

First published 2021
by Routledge
2 Park Square, Milton Park, Abingdon, Oxon OX14 4RN

and by Routledge
52 Vanderbilt Avenue, New York, NY 10017

Routledge is an imprint of the Taylor & Francis Group, an informa business

British Library Cataloguing in Publication Data
A catalogue record for this book is available from the British Library

Library of Congress Cataloging in Publication Data
Names: Nurul Shahnaz Ahmad Mahdzan, author. | Mohd Edil Abd Sukor, author. |
Izlin Ismail, author. | Rahman, Mahfuzur (Professor of finance), author.
Title: Consumer financial vulnerabilities in Malaysia: issues, trends and psychological
aspects / Nurul Shahnaz Ahmad Mahdzan, Mohd Edil Abd
Sukor, Izlin Ismail and Mahfuzur Rahman.
Description: Abingdon, Oxon ; New York, NY : Routledge, 2021. |
Series: Routledge advances in management and business studies |
Includes bibliographical references and index.
Identifiers: LCCN 2020026728 (print) | LCCN 2020026729 (ebook) |
ISBN 9780367148874 (hardback) | ISBN 9780429054358 (ebook)
Subjects: LCSH: Malaysians–Finance, Personal. | Finance,
Personal–Malaysia–Psychological aspects. | Financial
security–Malaysia–Psychological aspects.
Classification: LCC HG179 .N89 2021 (print) | LCC HG179 (ebook) |
DDC 332.024009595–dc23
LC record available at https://lccn.loc.gov/2020026728
LC ebook record available at https://lccn.loc.gov/2020026729

ISBN: 978-0-367-14887-4 (hbk)
ISBN: 978-0-429-05435-8 (ebk)

Typeset in Galliard
by Newgen Publishing UK

Contents

Figures

Tables

Preface

Often, we encounter devastating news about individuals who struggle in their lives due to their own financial misconduct. Whether it is a default on loans, bankruptcy, falling prey to financial fraud, having insufficient retirement savings, or being left behind penniless due to the death of a breadwinner, all these problems lead to distressing effects on one's financial, emotional, and mental state of affairs. Recognising the stark reality of these pressing issues, we were impelled to explore the issues of consumer financial vulnerability in the context of Malaysia to better understand the current scenario of these issues, and to investigate, based on theories and past studies, the underlying reasons behind these problems.

The book consists of four major consumer financial vulnerabilities – consumer over-indebtedness, retirement savings inadequacy, financial fraud victimisation, and underinsurance. Each chapter describes the scenario of each situation in the context of Malaysia by providing statistical evidence and trends on the issues. Each chapter will also provide readers a description of each of the issues, for example, a description on the types of consumer debt, retirement plans, financial scams, and life insurance/takaful policies. The theories underlying each of the issues will be discussed, and past studies that have been conducted on the issues will be reviewed. Each main chapter will also deliberate on the main psychological aspects influencing each financial vulnerability. The conclusion of each chapter ends with recommendations for the relevant stakeholders such as the relevant government agencies, policymakers, and financial services institutions.

We hope that the book will help increase awareness among consumers on the occurrence and enormity of the subject matter that may make them financially vulnerable. By reviewing the psychological aspects related to each financial vulnerability, readers may be able to relate each issue to their own situation to better understand their financial positions and to take charge of their finances. Policymakers and the relevant government authorities may find the book useful as it will provide insights on the factors that influence their policymaking decisions on the various financial aspects discussed.

While writing each chapter of the book, we have become more aware of how crucial financial education is to elevate consumers' understanding and knowledge of financial matters. Financial education increases financial literacy and will allow individuals to take control of their own finances in a responsible and forward-looking manner. Financial knowledge that is translated into positive financial behaviour will ultimately lead to higher financial well-being and lower levels of financial distress, especially in the event of financial shocks.

During the final stages of writing this book, the world was suddenly hit by the Covid-19 pandemic. Such situation has indeed aggravated the financial vulnerability of a large number of individuals across the world. The movement restriction order that lasted around three months in Malaysia (and across the globe) has also challenged the livelihood of many working individuals, especially business owners, self-employed individuals, and employees of small and medium enterprises (SMEs). This situation has amplified the importance of good financial behaviour to enable households to withstand future financial uncertainties.

The book is a useful reference to scholars and postgraduate/final year undergraduate students in the area of behavioural finance, economic psychology, consumer behaviour, and personal finance. Nonetheless, it is suitable for readers of any background since consumer finance is a topic that relates to all individuals. The book may also be of interest to policymakers, particularly Bank Negara Malaysia, Securities Commission, financial planning associations, financial advisors/planners, and consumer educators as it will provide insights on consumers' financial vulnerabilities from a psychological perspective. Hence, the book may help policymakers and practitioners to understand the behaviour of consumers deeper and explore ways to nudge them into becoming more financially capable and responsible. In addition, the book will also offer suggestions to consumers on ways to take charge of their finances in a more effective manner.

Nurul Shahnaz Ahmad Mahdzan, Mohd Edil Abd
Sukor, Izlin Ismail and Mahfuzur Rahman
Department of Finance and Banking,
Faculty of Business and Accountancy,
University of Malaya,
Kuala Lumpur, Malaysia
June 2020

Acknowledgements

The authors would like to thank the University of Malaya under the University of Malaya Research Grant Programme (Book) for providing the financial resources that assisted in the process of writing this book (Research Grant No. SG004-19SAH). The authors are also grateful to all family members and colleagues who had given support and encouragement throughout the completion of this book.

Abbreviations

AKPK	Credit Counselling and Debt Management Agency
ASEAN	Association of Southeast Asian Nations
B40	Bottom 40 percent of households according to income
BBA	Al-Bai' Bithaman Ajil
BLCH	Behavioural life-cycle hypothesis
BLR	Base lending rate
BNM	Bank Negara Malaysia
CCRIS	Central Credit Reference Information System
CEIC	Census and Economic Information Center
CETP	Child Education Takaful Plan
CFP	Certified Financial Planner
CGAP	Consultative Group to Assist the Poor
CLR	Consumer leverage ratio
CTOS	Credit Tip-Off Service
DB	Defined benefit
DC	Defined contribution
DOSM	Department of Statistics Malaysia
DSR	Debt service ratio
DVD	Digital versatile disc
EPF	Employees' Provident Fund
EU	European Union
FM	Financial margin
FPAM	Financial Planning Association Malaysia
GDP	Gross domestic product
GNI	Gross national income
HHD	Household debt
HP	Hire purchase
HPA	Hire purchase Amendment
IMC	Integrative marketing communication
IMF	International Monetary Fund
IRB	Inland Revenue Board
KRI	Khazanah Research Institute
KWAP	Retirement Fund (Incorporated)

LCH	Life-cycle hypothesis
LIAM	Life Insurance Association of Malaysia
LIFE	Life insurance and family takaful framework
LTAT	Armed Forces Fund Board
M40	Middle 40 percent of households according to income
MASB	Malaysian Accounting Standards Board
MAT	Motor, aviation, and transit
MCMC	Malaysian Communications and Multimedia Commission
MDTCA	Ministry of Domestic Trade and Consumer Affairs Malaysia
MITBA	Malaysian Insurance and Takaful Brokers Association
MNC	Multinational Corporation
MFPC	Malaysian Financial Planning Council
MLM	Multi-level marketing
MNSFL	Malaysian National Strategy for Financial Literacy
MOH	Ministry of Health Malaysia
MOE	Ministry of Education Malaysia
MRTA	Mortgage Reducing Term Assurance
MTA	Malaysian Takaful Association
MyCERT	Malaysia Computer Emergency Response Team
NAV	Net asset value
NAMLIFA	National Association of Malaysian Life Insurance Fieldforce and Advisers
NBFI	Non-bank financial institutions
NCD	Non-communicable disease
NGO	Non-government Organisation
OECD	Organisation for Economic Co-operation and Development
OPR	Overnight Policy Rate
P2P	Peer-to-peer
PA	Personal accident
PIN	Personal identification number
PPA	Public Pension Administrator Malaysia
PRS	Private Retirement Scheme
PSD	Public Service Department
PT	Prospect theory
PTPTN	National Higher Education Fund Corporation
RAS	Retirement Advisory Service
RBCT	Risk-Based Capital Framework for Takaful Operators
RCT	Rational choice theory
RFP	Registered Financial Planner
RM	Ringgit Malaysia
SEC	U.S. Securities and Exchange Commission
SC	Securities Commission Malaysia
SMS	Short message service
SOCSO	Social Security Organization
SP	Strategic priorities

T20	Top 20 percent of households according to income
UK	United Kingdom
US	United States
USD	United States Dollar
VCD	Video compact disc
WDI	World Development Indicators
ZPTI	Zimbardo Time Perspective Inventory

1 Overview

Consumer financial vulnerabilities in Malaysia

1.0 Introduction

Personal finance is an issue that is relevant to all individuals. It is about the behaviour and practices of money management and encompasses a spectrum of financial aspects such as spending, saving, investing, borrowing, and protection. Financial management skills are normally gained from past experiences and sources such as books, magazines, the Internet, newspapers, social media, and advice from friends and family. In addition, people sometimes follow their emotions and gut feelings in their money-related decisions. Due to the limitations in financial knowledge and skills, not everyone succeeds in managing their finances and are at times, vulnerable to financial shocks and uncertainties that may occur over their lifetime.

In traditional economic theories, people are assumed to be rational. These theories hypothesise that individuals base their decisions in a perfect world with complete information and would always seek to maximise utility and wealth. However, the reality is that humans are imperfect beings living in an imperfect world. In this line of reasoning, proponents of new behavioural economic theory argue that the field of economics and finance cannot be separated from the discipline of human behaviour, cognition, and psychology. Analysing individuals as true homo sapiens rather than "homo economicus" beings should therefore provide a more accurate picture of individuals' financial behaviour. Scholars from the behavioural finance paradigm suggest that individuals who make decisions based on emotions and instincts are prone to behavioural biases, hence leading them into making "sub-optimal" financial decisions. The irrationalities related to the behaviour and choices that people make, thus, explain why the outcomes achieved may sometimes be unexpected and undesirable in the pursuit of financial goals.

Recognising that behaviour and emotions are central in people's decision-making, this book focuses on exploring the common financial vulnerabilities that consumers face over their life cycle, and the behavioural and psychological causes of these vulnerabilities will be analysed. There are four financial aspects that will be covered in this book, namely *over-indebtedness, retirement savings inadequacy, financial fraud victimisation*, and *underinsurance*. While debt may be considered inevitable, especially in the early part of the life cycle, *over-indebtedness* could be a major problem and could possibly lead to delinquency and bankruptcy if left uncontrolled. Such financial problems may also lead to other psychological and social problems such as deteriorated physical health, stress, depression, and strained relationships.

Retirement savings inadequacy is another issue that has been long discussed and debated by policymakers across the globe. Countries that are experiencing population ageing, such as Malaysia, will have an increasing portion of elderly population in the future, hence, ensuring that they have sufficient retirement savings is eminent. Despite mandatory contribution plans enacted, retirees' savings usually fall significantly below the adequate level to be able to sustain pre-retirement lifestyles.

The third aspect discussed in this book relates to *financial fraud victimisation*. Numerous incidents of victimisation cases have been reported to authorities over the past several years, and many cash-rich individuals have lost big sums of their hard-earned money to the scrupulous hands of fraudsters. Thus, understanding the cause of this consumer financial vulnerability is vital in implementing effective control measures.

The last issue to be examined in this book relates to *underinsurance* among Malaysian consumers. Despite numerous consumer education and awareness campaigns, it remains perplexing as to why many Malaysians do not have any form of insurance and Shariah-compliant insurance (takaful) protection. Are Malaysians overconfident about their earning abilities? Do they lack the self-control when it comes to taking on debts and preparing for the future? Are they naïve in their investment decisions, or are they too trusting? Are they innocently ignorant or are they simply greedy? These are questions that the book tends to explore, with a focus on the Malaysian scenario.

This book aims to achieve four objectives. The *first* objective is to examine the current state and trends of various consumer financial vulnerabilities in Malaysia, namely, (i) over-indebtedness, (ii) retirement savings inadequacy, (iii) fraudulent financial and investment victimisation, and (iii) lack of protection using insurance and takaful products. Each of these vulnerabilities will be examined and discussed in four (4) separate chapters, namely, Chapters 2 to 5, respectively. The *second* objective is to explore the causes of consumer financial vulnerabilities from the perspective of behavioural theories and empirical evidence. The *third* objective is to discuss the various policies that have already been implemented to influence consumer financial behaviour in Malaysia. Lastly, the *fourth* objective is to propose additional strategies to policymakers on ways to nudge consumers in the right way in regards to their finances.

1.1 Background of Malaysia

1.1.1 Economic status

Malaysia is an emerging economy, located in the heart of Southeast Asia, and aspires towards becoming a high-income nation. According to the Global Competitiveness Report 2018, out of 140 economies, Malaysia ranks 25th

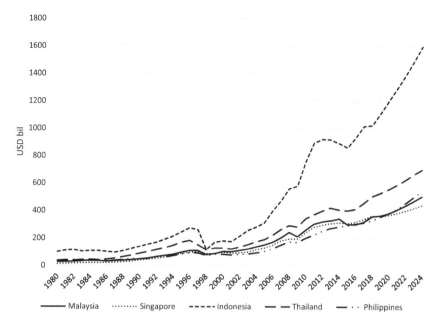

Figure 1.1 GDP of the top five ASEAN economies (in billions of USD).
Source: International Monetary Fund (2019).

globally in terms of national competitiveness and productivity (World Economic Forum, 2018). Among the ten Association of Southeast Asian Nations (ASEAN) countries, Malaysia ranks fourth in terms of gross domestic product (GDP) size, after Indonesia, Thailand, and Philippines (International Monetary Fund, 2019). As at 2020, the Malaysian GDP at current prices is estimated to be USD381.52 billion. Figure 1.1 shows the trend of GDP (current prices) of the top five ASEAN economies.

Meanwhile, Figure 1.2 shows the annual percentage change of real GDP in Malaysia from 1980 to 2020. There are notable downward shocks noted in this illustration, particularly in years 1985, 1998, and 2009. These shocks are due to the financial crises, namely the 1985 commodity shock triggered by the high-interest rate regime in the United States (the Volker shock), the 1998 Asian financial crisis triggered by the floating of the Thai baht, and the 2008 global financial crisis caused by the subprime mortgage crisis in the United States. As can be seen from the graph, these crises had obvious effects on Malaysia's economic growth. The Malaysian GDP growth rate averages at 5.25% annually from 2010 to 2020.

1.1.2 Population

Malaysia's population as of 2019 is estimated to be 32.6 million of which 29.4 million (90.2%) are Malaysian citizens, while the remaining 3.2 million

Figure 1.2 Malaysia's real GDP growth (annual percentage change).
Source: International Monetary Fund (2019).

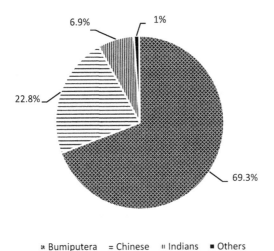

* Bumiputera   = Chinese   ‖ Indians   ▪ Others

Figure 1.3 Population composition of Malaysian citizens according to ethnicity in 2019.
Source: Department of Statistics Malaysia (2019).

(9.8%) are non-citizens. The country is a multi-ethnic nation with four main ethnic groups – Bumiputeras, Chinese, Indians, and others. The Bumiputera group holds the largest majority of citizens (69.3%), followed by the Chinese (22.8%), Indians (6.9%), and others (1.0%) (Department of Statistics Malaysia, 2019). Figure 1.3 illustrates the composition of ethnic groups in Malaysia as of 2019.

Table 1.1 Percentage population by age group

Age group	2018	2019
0–14 years	23.8	23.3
15–64 years	69.7	70
65+ years	6.5	6.7

Source: Department of Statistics Malaysia (2019).

Table 1.2 Median income, mean income, and poverty rate

Median income		Mean income		Poverty rate	
2014	2016	2014	2016	2014	2016
4,585	5,228	6,141	6,958	0.6%	0.4%

Source: Department of Statistics Malaysia (2016).

In terms of age group, Table 1.1 presents the percentage of population according to age group in year 2018 and 2019. The statistics show that the percentage of the elderly population (aged 65 and above) is increasing, while those in the lowest age group (0–14 years) is decreasing. This trend is expected to persist as Malaysia evolves into becoming an aged population.

1.1.3 Household income

According to the Malaysian Household Income and Expenditure Survey 2016, the median income in Malaysia increased by 6.6% per annum between years 2014 and 2016. In 2014, the median income was RM4,585, increasing to RM5,228 in 2016. Meanwhile, the mean income increased from RM6,141 to RM6,958 from 2014 to 2016, which is an increase of 6.2% per year. The incidence of poverty was reduced from 0.6% in 2014 to 0.4% in 2016. These statistics are presented in Table 1.2.

The median and mean household income by the household income group also showed an increment from 2014 to 2016 for household income groups. The Malaysian government refers to the high-income household groups as T20 (reflecting the proportion of 20% of households falling in this group), the middle-income households as the M40 group (reflecting the proportion of 40% of households falling into this group), and the low-income households as the B40 group (reflecting the 40% proportion of households falling within this group).

The median income for the T20 group increased from RM11,610 in 2014 to RM13,148 in 2016, while the mean household income for the same group increased from RM14.305 to RM16,088 between the same period. For the M40 group, the median household income increased from RM5.465 in 2014 to RM6,275 in 2016. During the same period, the mean household income

Table 1.3 Income share, median and mean household income for the T20, M40, and B40 groups

Household income group	Income share (%)		Median household income (RM)		Mean household income (RM)	
	2014	2016	2014	2016	2014	2016
T20	46.1	46.2	11,610	13,148	14,305	16,088
M40	37.1	37.4	5,465	6,275	5,662	6,502
B40	16.8	16.4	2,629	3,000	2,537	2,848

Source: Department of Statistics Malaysia (2016).

increased from RM5,662 to RM6,502. Lastly, for the B40 group, the median household income increased from RM2,629 to RM3,000 in 2014 and 2016, respectively. The mean household income for the B40 group increased from RM2,537 to RM2,848 within the same period. These statistics are shown in Table 1.3. Overall, the figures show that the median and mean income are increasing for all household income groups.

Having discussed the brief background of Malaysia in terms of economy, demography, and household income, the following section delves into the consumer finance issues that will be the focus of this book.

1.2 Consumer finances

1.2.1 Issues in consumer finances

As agents who actively participate in the economy, consumers face a myriad of choices and must make numerous decisions related to their finances. Among the decisions that require thought and deliberation are those related to spending, saving, investing, and protection. These financial decisions are depicted in Figure 1.4.

The main aspects of consumer finances can be extremely challenging due to the increasingly complex financial landscape in today's modern society. Consumers are faced with a wider selection of financial products and services, which are also more sophisticated and complex in nature. Deregulations of financial markets, innovations in financial technology, and easier access to credit make consumers more vulnerable in financial markets.

Referring to Figure 1.4, closely related to the issue of spending is *debt-taking*, which is indeed a complex decision to make as it involves evaluating the interest rates and repayment period. Taking on debts means that there is interest to bear on the loan, therefore suggesting that the cost of the item purchased using the loan is higher due to the cost of interest. It also means that people are committing part of their future income as future instalments, hence depleting the amounts of future disposable income. Consequently, too much debt may cause a strain on one's personal life, self-esteem, and financial well-being.

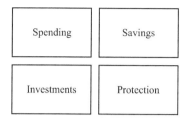

Figure 1.4 Main aspects of consumer finances.

Saving for retirement is also a complex process as there are a number of important decisions to be made, for example, the amounts to save and saving vehicles in order to achieve retirement goals. This decision is complex as it requires knowing how much is required to maintain a comfortable standard of living during retirement and how much is required to be saved in order to achieve that objective. Thus, not having the skills to appropriately plan for retirement will cause consumers to be financially vulnerable, particularly during the retirement phase and may result in inadequate retirement savings.

Consumers also face risks when putting their money into investments. Investing money with the aim of obtaining higher returns comes with risks. While there are many legal investments in the market, consumers are also faced with the risk of fraudulent investments. Thus, the risk of *financial fraud victimisation* is another area that consumers should be aware and remain vigilant of. Finally, everyone is exposed to personal risks such as accidents, illnesses, disabilities, and death. However, it remains puzzling that consumers leave themselves exposed to these risks and remain *underinsured*. Figure 1.5 depicts the consumer financial vulnerabilities that will be discussed in this book.

1.2.2 *Background of consumer financial vulnerabilities in Malaysia*

1.2.2.1 *Over-indebtedness*

Malaysia has one of the highest household debt-to-GDP ratio in Asia. Household debt levels reached a peak of 86.9% of GDP in 2015 but has moderated somewhat since then. As at June 2019, household debt stood at 82.2% of GDP. This is significantly higher when compared to high-income nations such as United States (at 75%) and Japan (at 58.2%).

The main component of household debt is made up of housing loans, and one of the key drivers of this is rising house prices. A cultural bias towards home ownership rather than rental and policies focusing on supporting home ownership have spurred this growth in household debt. Additionally, car and vehicle loans also made up the next highest component of household debt. High car prices and an inefficient public transport system also exacerbate household debt levels.

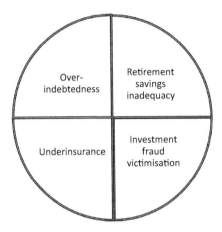

Figure 1.5 Consumer financial vulnerabilities.

Nonetheless, a high level of debt is not a problem as long as households can afford to service the loans without much difficulty. It is only when servicing monthly commitments take up a disproportionate amount of household income or when unexpected events lead to a disruption in the family budget, that the problem of over-indebtedness will arise.

However, for households in the lower income groups, the B40, and the lower M40, over-indebtedness can occur at a much lower threshold. Low and inse-cure incomes combined with rising costs of living creates an over-indebtedness problem even at lower levels of housing and car/vehicle loans. Reliance on con-sumer financing such as personal loans and credit card debts can quickly lead to spiralling indebtedness. Rising bankruptcies among the younger workforce is a worrying trend. Chapter 2 will further discuss the trends and factors related to over-indebtedness among consumers in Malaysia.

1.2.2.2 Retirement savings inadequacy

Malaysia is transitioning into an aged population. This phenomenon is a situ-ation in which the percentage of elderly population is increasing and will exceed those of the lowest age group. This evolution will result in a lower percentage of the labour force, thus will have significant consequences on the nation's social security and economic growth. Hence, Malaysians need to be adequately prepared for retirement and should not be heavily dependent on welfare and government social security if they wish to maintain their desired lifestyles during their golden years.

The Employees' Provident Fund (EPF) is the mandatory retirement plan subscribed by private-sector employees in Malaysia. Employees contribute 11% of their income, while employers contribute 12%–13% of income into the

EPF. Statistics show that the average savings in 2018 are RM209,861, which is estimated to last less than five years after retirement. Given the increasing life expectancy among Malaysians which is 73.9 for males and 78 for females, the estimated retirement savings is viewed as inadequate. Thus, it is essential that Malaysians adequately plan and prepare for their retirement, or they will remain financially vulnerable as they face numerous risks associated with ageing such as depletion in income and increasing health-care expenses.

The retirement planning process as described in personal finance textbooks are complex and requires one to have sufficient financial knowledge and skills. This complexity is one of the reasons identified that prevents Malaysians from properly planning for their retirement. There are also other behavioural and psychological reasons that influence successful retirement planning, such as financial literacy, time preference, financial planning, and goal clarity. These factors will be discussed in more detail in Chapter 3.

1.2.2.3 Financial fraud victimisation

Dynamic shifts or changes in financial frauds' techniques and strategies that come with different names and titles have made Malaysian consumers more vulnerable to financial frauds and scams. The criminals are getting smarter and have scrupulously used the advancement of technology for their benefit in order to deceive their victims. Therefore, it is imperative for Malaysian consumers to understand the different nature of financial frauds in order to prevent themselves from falling victims to them.

The Divisions of Commercial Crime Investigation Department, Royal Malaysian Police reported a total of 121,127 commercial fraud and scam cases with approximately RM7.54 billion value of losses between year 2010 and 2017. Previous studies show that many investors who participated in fraudulent schemes believe that they were investing with legal institutions or persons. Incidentally, their bad experience results in them having lower trust in financial systems and doubting the credibility of the government and financial regulators. It is believed that with good knowledge and awareness on financial fraud and scams, Malaysians will be able to make the distinction between legitimate products and fraudulent schemes and be aware of avenues to seek help when in doubt.

Many Malaysians struggle to build and safeguard their wealth, making them bearing more risks and responsibilities for their own financial decisions. Therefore, apart from having generic financial knowledge about frauds, consumers need to also understand the modus operandi and persuasion techniques used by fraudsters. The common modus operandi on how frauds usually happen will be discussed in more detail in Chapter 4.

1.2.2.4 Underinsurance

On average, Malaysia is enjoying an annual GDP growth rate of 4.77% which in turn should have a significant positive influence on the growth of insurance and takaful sector, yet the real premium growth rate for the insurance industry remained lowest (life 4.4%, non-life 1.4%) among ASEAN-5 countries between 2013 and 2018. During this period, the life insurance penetration rate in Malaysia hovered at approximately 56% while takaful stands at 15.2%, and only about 40% of Malaysians own a life insurance or family takaful policy. However, life insurance or the family takaful penetration rate among the B40 income group in Malaysia is much lower than the M40 and T20 income groups. Treating insurance as unimportant and putting it at the bottom of their priority list might make Malaysians underinsured and vulnerable against a rising number of health-related risks and other challenges.

Although insurance provides protection against various risks and serves as a tool to accumulate funds and preserve wealth, its importance in personal finance is largely overlooked by Malaysian households. Low-income or affordability issues may not be the single important factor that is preventing them from having adequate insurance protection, but rather, the lack of willingness to set aside a portion of income to prepare for low probability events and other psychological factors such as the lack of trust in insurers and agents. Hence, nationwide public awareness and education campaigns together with policy intervention might help to achieve the targeted penetration rate in Malaysia.

Given the fact that Malaysians' life expectancy and living expenses are increasing while savings in general are declining and retirement savings are inadequate, Malaysian households should purchase savings and investment-linked insurance or takaful policies to assist themselves in enjoying their anticipated living standards in old age. More information on the issue of underinsurance will be discussed in Chapter 5.

1.3 Malaysian National Strategy for Financial Literacy 2019–2023

Having discussed the consumer financial vulnerabilities in Malaysia, this section will review the Malaysian National Strategy for Financial Literacy (MNSFL) 2019–2023 that was launched on 23 July 2019 by the seventh Malaysian Prime Minister, Tun Dr. Mahathir Mohamad. The strategy envisages to improve the financial well-being of Malaysians. Its objective is to elevate the financial literacy of Malaysians and to promote responsible financial behaviour and rational attitudes. The strategy aims to empower Malaysians in three (3) main ways: (i) save, manage, and protect money; (ii) plan ahead and ensure a sustainable future; and (iii) protect oneself from fraud and financial scams. The MNSFL seeks to empower Malaysians of all life stages, starting from school children, youths, adults, and those approaching retirement as well as those already retired. An overview of the MNSFL is illustrated in Figure 1.6.

The four consumer financial vulnerabilities discussed in this book are depicted on the left side of Figure 1.7. This book addresses the issues of consumer over-indebtedness, insufficiency of retirement savings, being victimised in fraudulent investments, and being under-protected by insurance and takaful. On the right

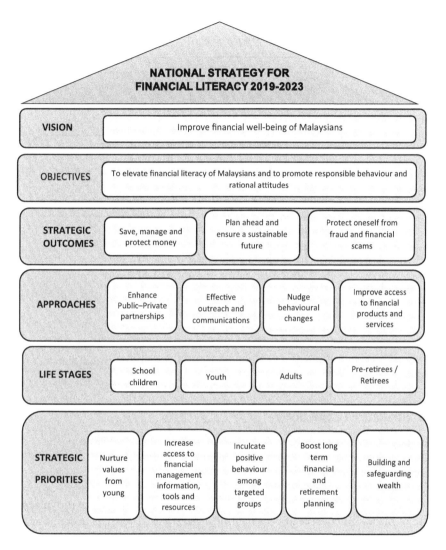

Figure 1.6 Malaysian National Strategy for Financial Literacy 2019–2023.
Source: Financial Education Network (2019).

side of Figure 1.7 are the three strategic outcomes outlined in the MNSFL. Clearly, the issues addressed in the book are considered timely and precisely address the issues of concern by the Malaysian government.

Finally, as can be noted in the most bottom panel of Figure 1.6, the MNSFL outlines five main strategic priorities that will be undertaken over a five-year period (i.e. from 2019 to 2023). These strategic priorities will act as a basis as to how recommendations will be developed in the conclusion chapter of this book.

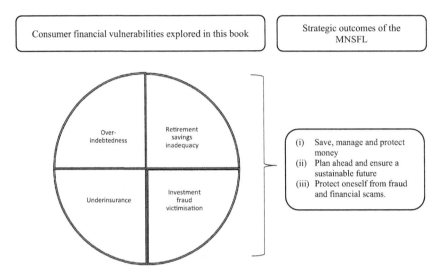

Figure 1.7 Consumer financial vulnerabilities and its relation to the strategic outcomes of the MNSFL.

The recommendations that will later be discussed in Chapter 6 will be aligned to the five strategic priorities developed by the Financial Education Network of Malaysia, as shown in Table 1.4.

1.4 Structure of the book

This book consists of six chapters, organised and explained as follows:

The present chapter, Chapter 1, is an introductory chapter that provides a background of the issues explored in the book. It provides an overall picture of the economic situation in Malaysia, followed by a general background of consumer finances in Malaysia. The chapter paints an overview picture of the current state of Malaysian households and their financial status. The chapter then briefly explains the four consumer financial vulnerabilities that will be addressed in subsequent chapters, namely, over-indebtedness, retirement savings inadequacy, financial fraud victimisation, and under-protection among Malaysians. The chapter also provides an overview of the Malaysian National Strategy of Financial Literacy 2019–2023, in which the book is very timely as it directly addresses the strategic outcomes of the MNSFL. The chapter also outlines the structure and contents of the other chapters in the book.

Chapter 2 discusses a major issue that plagues the finances of most Malaysian, specifically, consumer indebtedness. Taking on debt is often seen as a necessity among consumers, specifically to finance large ticket items, and the situation is not problematic as long as borrowers can pay off the debt within the stipulated contractual terms. However, problems may arise when consumers take up loans

Table 1.4 Strategic priorities of the MNSFL

SP1: Nurture values from young
- Expand financial education fundamentals into the curriculum for preschool, primary, and secondary schools
- Reinforce financial education through co-curriculum activities
- Introduce capacity development and support for teachers
- Encourage financial education advocates among students, parental groups, and the community

SP2: Increase access to financial management information, tools, and resources
- Make basic financial education information easily understood, available, and accessible to all
- Heighten awareness and intensify financial education initiatives through nationwide outreach campaigns

SP3: Inculcate positive behaviour among targeted groups
- Impart financial knowledge to promote positive financial behaviour among the youth
- Encourage financial education at the workplace to promote financial resilience, which will have a positive impact on employees' productivity
- Foster good money management practices through community-based financial education
- Equip the self-employed with financial knowledge to encourage self and business sustainability

SP4: Boost long-term financial and retirement planning
- Promote use of innovative guides and tools to improve long-term financial planning
- Create awareness and promote the benefits of seeking professional advice on financial planning
- Promote voluntary saving channels and platforms to encourage income diversification
- Educate Malaysians to make long-term financial plans for retirement

SP5: Building and safeguarding wealth
- Promote better understanding of risks and returns to build wealth
- Improve awareness on the innovation of financial products and services and its implications
- Raise awareness on financial scams and fraud
- Develop and publish materials relating to sophisticated financial products and services

---

Source: Financial Education Network (2019).

and credit from too many sources at the same time and become excessively burdened with debt repayment. The situation may aggravate into more serious problems such as delinquency and possibly even bankruptcy.

Hence, this chapter will provide statistical evidence of the state of indebtedness among Malaysian households and evaluate incidences of loan default and bankruptcy. The causes of over-indebtedness from the perspective of the consumers will be discussed, emphasising on behavioural factors as highlighted by past literature and empirical evidence. Among the factors highlighted by behavioural scholars to be the cause of over-indebtedness are the lack of self-control, materialism, social norms, and financial illiteracy. The discussions from the chapter will then be used to formulate recommendations on actions that policymakers can take to reduce the incidences of over-indebtedness among Malaysian consumers.

Chapter 3 will first describe the scenario of population ageing in Malaysia. It will discuss the retirement issues in the context of Malaysia, particularly regarding retirement saving schemes and Malaysia's overall savings. Data from the EPF savings will be extracted and presented to show some trends in retirement saving among Malaysians. The roles and policies in regards to mandatory retirement schemes and voluntary retirement schemes such as the Private Retirement Scheme (PRS) will be discussed.

Next, the chapter will deliberate on the retirement planning process and challenges in retirement planning. The chapter also provides a theoretical perspective on retirement saving and reviews the literature on behavioural factors influencing retirement planning and retirement saving behaviour. The behavioural and psychological factors that may be influencing Malaysians in planning for retirement are financial literacy, time preference, financial planning, and clarity of financial goals. Finally, the chapter ends with suggestions for policymakers, particularly the EPF, and other regulatory bodies such as Securities Commission (SC), Malaysian Financial Planning Council (MFPC), and the financial services industry, on ways to address the issue.

Chapter 4 assesses the issue of financial fraud victimisation among Malaysian consumers. The chapter begins by addressing some of the main arguments explaining why there are still Malaysians falling victim to fraud even though various information, as well as their modus operandi, have been disseminated. This chapter will then describe the different patterns of frauds and scams specific to consumers. The factors that influence Malaysian consumer behaviour to believe in frauds and scams, focusing on psychological and behavioural aspects, will also be discussed.

The chapter ends with suggestions and implications for the financial service sector and policymakers. The main argument of this chapter is profiling studies that analyse consumers by types of financial scams as well as psychological and behavioural aspects that will yield a clearer picture of scam-specific profiles. This will help to mobilise a better relationship between consumers and related agencies such as Bank Negara Malaysia (BNM), the SC Malaysia, Malaysia Deposit Insurance Corporation, and the Counselling Agency to coordinate in fighting the financial frauds and scams discussed earlier.

Chapter 5 analyses some of the pressing issues causing the low national insurance penetration rate in Malaysia. It aims to evaluate factors explaining why insurance and Shariah compliance insurance (takaful) are less attractive to many Malaysian consumers who have yet to own any form of protection policy despite having existing consumer education and awareness campaigns. The chapter will first provide an overview on the status of the insurance and takaful penetration rate in Malaysia by providing statistics from the BNM and other agency reports. The chapter then discusses the most common issues and challenges faced by insurance and takaful industries in Malaysia. It then presents various insurance and takaful schemes offered in Malaysia.

The chapter then proceeds by outlining the insurance planning process and discusses relevant theories justifying the low penetration rate in Malaysia. Next, relevant socio-demographic factors (e.g. life expectancy, marital status, age, education, dependency ratio, employment status, and income) and psychological factors such as risk perception, trust in agents, worry and fear, social norms, and others are discussed. The chapter ends by offering recommendations for the Malaysian government as well as the insurance and takaful industry. It is believed that the findings would be useful to insurance and takaful industries by developing their products and services to make them more attractive. A comprehensive analysis of factors causing the low penetration rate should help to speed up BNM's objective to achieve the targeted national insurance penetration rate.

Finally, Chapter 6 summarises the discussions from the previous chapters and discusses the factors influencing consumer financial vulnerability from the perspective of three psychological domains, namely cognition, motivation, and disposition. Lastly, the chapter offers overall suggestions for policymakers, financial institutions, and other players in the industry on ways to deal with these consumer financial vulnerabilities. It also offers advice for consumers on ways to deal with these financial vulnerabilities. The recommendations will be positioned according to the strategic priorities of the MNSFL by focusing on financial education, financial technology, financial planning, and the financial services industry.

References

Department of Statistics Malaysia (2016). *Key Statistics of Household Income and Expenditure 2016*. Retrieved 16 December 2019 from www.dosm.gov.my/v1/index.php?r=column/cone&menu_id=UllqdFZoVFJhMi9zekpWKzFaSTdvUT09

Department of Statistics Malaysia (2019). *Current Population Estimates, Malaysia, 2018–2019*. Retrieved 16 December 2019 from www.dosm.gov.my/v1/index.php?r=column/cthemeByCat&cat=155&bul_id=aWJZRkJ4UEdKcUZpT2tVT090Snpydz09&menu_id=L0pheU43NWJwRWVSZklWdzQ4TlhUUT09

Financial Education Network (2019). *Malaysian National Strategy of Financial Literacy 2019–2023*. Retrieved 1 February 2020 from www.fenetwork.my/wp-content/uploads/2019/07/National-Strategy-English.pdf

International Monetary Fund (2019). *GDP in Current Prices*. Retrieved 11 March 2020 from www.imf.org/external/datamapper/NGDPD@WEO/THA/MYS/SGP/PHL/IDN

World Economic Forum (2018). *The Global Competitiveness Index 4.0 2018 Rankings*. Retrieved 22 April 2020 from http://reports.weforum.org/global-competitiveness-report-2018/competitiveness-rankings/

2 Consumer debt: Friend or foe?
Exploring its causes and consequences

2.0 Introduction

This chapter discusses a major issue that plagues the finances of most Malaysians – consumer indebtedness. Indebtedness refers to borrowers' debt obligations. While being in debt is sometimes seen as a necessity among consumers, specifically to finance large ticket items, this situation is not problematic as long as borrowers can pay off their debts within the stipulated contractual terms. However, problems may arise when loans do not get repaid in a timely fashion or when loan repayments take up a disproportionate amount of household income. When consumers take up loans and credit from too many sources at the same time or become excessively burdened with debt repayment, the situation may aggravate into more serious problems such as delinquency and possibly even bankruptcy.

In this regard, this chapter will first provide statistical evidence on the state of indebtedness among Malaysian households and evaluate incidences of loan default and bankruptcy. The causes and consequences of being over-indebted from the perspective of the consumers will be discussed, emphasising on individual behavioural, socio-demographic, and economic factors as highlighted by past literature and empirical evidence. Among the factors highlighted by behavioural scholars to be the cause of over-indebtedness are the lack of self-control, overconfidence, materialism, following social norms, and financial illiteracy. Lack of self-control and materialism causes an individual to spend excessively, further leading to over-indebtedness and repayment obligations that are beyond one's capability. Socio-economic factors focus on the ease of consumer credit facilities, level of interest rates, credit bureau monitoring, and legal implications that have an effect on consumers' borrowing behaviours.

Our findings will be used to formulate recommendations on actions that policymakers can take to reduce the incidences of over-indebtedness among Malaysian consumers. Should the focus be on financial education and literacy, or should policy be geared towards tightening financing terms to mitigate excessive borrowing? The aim is to avoid policies that may backfire and shove consumers into the hands of loan sharks, exacerbating their debt problems further.

2.1 Definition of concepts

2.1.1 Definition of consumer debt

Consumer debt comprises of debts incurred due to obtaining goods that are consumable and/or do not appreciate. Consumer debt is synonymous with household debt as both are often connected with housing and vehicle loans, credit cards, as well as personal loans. Nonetheless, it can be argued that property or housing loans are personal investments as the asset tends to appreciate in value over time. In other words, consumer debt is different from other forms of debt due to the fact that consumer debt is usually to finance consumption purposes, and not for investment or to finance a business enterprise. This debt is also incurred by individuals, and not by businesses or the government.

The most common forms of consumer debt are in the form of unsecured loans including credit cards, personal loans, and student loans. These are usually at higher interest rates relative to those charged on long-term secured loans such as housing loans. Consumer loans are usually obtained from commercial banks. Other lenders include credit unions or co-operatives (also known as non-bank financial institutions [NBFI]) and the government (in the form of study loans by National Higher Education Fund Corporation, also known by its Malay acronym PTPTN). Informal finance providers such as moneylenders and pawn shops also provide consumer debt to borrowers who are perhaps unable to borrow from financial institutions and NBFI.

In Malaysia, Bank Negara Malaysia (BNM) uses the concept of *financial margin* (FM) and *debt service ratio* (DSR) to measure households' debt sustainability. The formulas for each concept are shown in Eqs. 2.1 and 2.2. FM assesses households' ability to withstand unforeseen circumstances such as income shocks, unexpected increase in cost of living and borrowing cost, as well as the effect vulnerable borrowers may have on financial intermediaries. If the FM is negative, it indicates that they are at a higher risk of defaulting their debt. DSR is the ratio of monthly debt obligations (from banks and non-banks) to monthly disposable income (net of statutory deductions such as Employees' Provident Fund [EPF], Social Security Organisation [SOCSO], etc.). BNM's (2016) study has found that consumers are more likely to have a negative FM if they earn less than RM3,000 per month and have a DSR level above 60%.

$$\text{FM} = \text{Disposable income} - \text{Debt repayment obligations} \\ - \text{Expenditure on basic necessities} + \text{Liquid financial assets} \qquad \text{(Eq. 2.1)}$$

$$\text{DSR} = \frac{\text{Debt repayment obligations}}{\text{Disposable income}} \qquad \text{(Eq. 2.2)}$$

Based on BNM's 2018 report, borrowers with negative FM make up about 6.5% of total borrowers and 12.8% of total household debt (totalling RM139 billion). Most of them have a DSR level above 60% and earn less than RM5,000. Borrowers in this income group have a larger exposure to motor vehicle loans (22%) and personal financing (30%) and are made up of those in the under-40 age bracket. They are also most likely to be affected by a fall in their total income.

Consumer debt is usually considered sub-optimal as most consumption goods do not have high levels of utility that would make incurring debt on them worthwhile. It is better to purchase consumer goods by cash. Additionally, consumer debt is often associated with predatory lending (loan sharks, payday lenders, etc.), which tend to charge higher interest rates and may employ hard-handed tactics to recover payments in the likely event that the borrower defaults. Predatory lenders target consumers with less access to and less understanding of more formal forms of financing from financial institutions.

2.1.2 *Definition of over-indebtedness*

There is little consensus in the literature and across countries on the definition of over-indebtedness. Over-indebtedness occurs either as a temporary or permanent disequilibrium in a household budget resulting from expected or unexpected increases in expenditure or decreases in household income. Over-indebtedness is a complex concept as defined by scholars and international organisations regarding the nature of its impacts and dimensions.

The accumulation of consumer debt in various forms and the extent that this leads to difficulties in servicing interest charges and principal repayment cause a problem of over-indebtedness. Consumers are considered over-indebted when they do not have the ability to meet all their financial commitments at the end of the month without lowering their standard of living below the acceptable minimum in the country they are living in (Anderloni & Vandone, 2008). Hence, a definition that encompasses all the situations where households are considered over-indebted should include if they are struggling or late with their household commitments inclusive of debt servicing (secured and unsecured debts), payment of rent, utility, insurance, taxes and duties, and other household bills.

There are various measures depending on how one defines over-indebtedness. A definition used by the German Federal Ministry describes it as a state where household income "in spite of a reduction of the living standard, is insufficient to discharge all payment obligations over a long period of time." In other words, it is the inability of the borrowers to repay all debt fully and on time (Haas, 2006). D'Alessio and Iezzi (2013) stated that in France, one is considered over-indebted when, although willing, one is unable to fulfil one's personal debt obligations. In the United Kingdom (UK), it is defined as a state "where households or individuals are in arrears on a structural basis, or at a significant risk of getting into arrears on a structural basis" (Oxera, 2004). Betti, Dourmashkin, Rossi, and Yin's (2007) cross-country study introduced a subjective definition, which focusses on individuals' own evaluation of their debt burden. However, this definition is difficult to measure accurately as some people may have an issue disclosing their debt problems, and the measure may also have problems due to different understanding on what repayment difficulties mean.

The European Commission has not officially defined over-indebtedness and has commissioned a study to find a common definition of over-indebtedness across the EU which reads as follows,

> An over-indebted household is, accordingly, defined as one whose existing and foreseeable resources are insufficient to meet its financial commitments without lowering its living standards, which has both social and policy implications if this means reducing them below what is regarded as the minimum acceptable in the country concerned.

Common features of over-indebtedness in all EU countries (European Commission, 2008) include:

1 Economic dimension – in terms of the amount of debt repayment.
2 Temporal dimension – payment period typically medium to long term.
3 Social dimension – basic expenses that need to be paid before repayment of debts.
4 Psychological dimension – stress of being in an over-indebted position.

A report by the Consultative Group to Assist the Poor (CGAP) stated six different approaches used to define over-indebtedness. These include negative impact, defaults and arrears, debt ratios, multiple borrowing, struggle and sacrifice of the borrowers, and composite indicators. According to the definition by the Center for Microfinance, University of Zurich, over-indebtedness is the ratio of a household's monthly repayments over monthly net income (gross income minus expenses).

From the above definitions, it can be summarised that over-indebtedness is a social issue that has both psychological and policy implications. Over-indebtedness is an unhealthy debt balance of an individual or a household, which is due to the inability of the borrower to service the debt repayment over a period that causes reduction in their living standards. As of late, the issue of over-indebtedness is a growing concern in Malaysia. The presence of many lenders (big, small, regulated, and unregulated) has led to an increase in household debt levels. However, Malaysia does not have an official definition or measurement of over-indebtedness. BNM calculations of DSR and FM mainly measure if borrowers are in financial distress and refer to the effects of borrowing to financial institutions, and not the effect it has on the borrower itself. As the issue of over-indebtedness can cause severe damage to social and economic stability, perhaps it is timely that Malaysian policymakers consider a working definition and measurement of over-indebtedness in order to better address this phenomenon.

2.2 Statistics on household debt and bankruptcy in Malaysia

Figure 2.1 compares the household debt-to-GDP ratios among Malaysia's neighbouring Association of Southeast Asian Nations (ASEAN) countries for the past ten years. Malaysia's household debt ratios remain the highest in the region at more than 80% of GDP for most of this period. Thailand and Singapore are the next highest, respectively, and both countries show a similar pattern to Malaysia although the ratios for both stayed well below Malaysia over this period. The ratios in the Philippines and Indonesia trail largely behind. Rising household debt seemed to be a feature among the more developed ASEAN nations, although it is clear that the household debt situation in Malaysia is the most worrying.

Comparing similar household debt ratios of developed nations, Figure 2.2 shows the pattern for G-5 countries. The United Kingdom showed a clear pattern of high household debt ratios, in excess of 90% of GDP throughout the past decade, although the ratio has moderated slightly in recent years. Most of the other developed nations have maintained household debt ratios at below 60% of GDP over the same period, with the exception of France which has ratios of around 70% of GDP. Hence, Malaysia's current household debt ratios are comparable only to the United Kingdom and are much higher than most other developed nations in the world.

2.2.1 Composition of household debt

Taking on debt fills the negative gap between income and expenditure. There are various types of debt that households are involved in. This section will

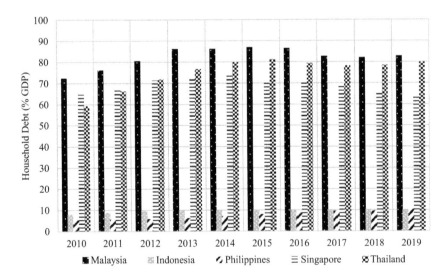

Figure 2.1 ASEAN-5 household debt-to-GDP.
Source: Census and Economic Information Center (CEIC) (*n.d.*).

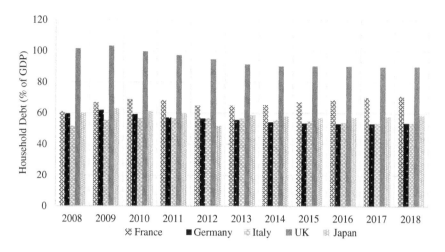

Figure 2.2 Developed nations' household debt-to-GDP.
Source: Census and Economic Information Center (CEIC) (*n.d.*).

first evaluate the trends in Malaysia for the different types of household credit instruments and the implications that this credit growth has on the financial well-being of households and the economy in general. Household debt represents liabilities that need to be repaid in the future and includes loans to purchase property and securities, as well as to finance consumption such as vehicle loans, personal loans, and credit card facilities.

As can be noted in Figure 2.3, Malaysian statistics show that total household debt-to-GDP ratio increased to 82.7% as of December 2019 compared to 82.0% in the previous year and is one of the highest in Asia. Figure 2.3 shows that Malaysian household debt-to-GDP has risen markedly after the 2008 global financial crisis. It reached a peak of 86.9% in December 2015, from its low of 60.4% in December 2008. However, based on the trendline, household debt-to-GDP has moderated since 2017, indicating that stricter lending policies have started to show some results.

Lombardi, Mohanty, and Shim's (2017) study noted that economic growth will be negatively affected if household debt-to-GDP ratio is above 80%. However, their data only includes total household debt to the banking system. Comparable data for Malaysia (excluding debt to non-banking financial institutions) was at 69.3% of GDP, which would make it below that threshold.

As of December 2019, the total household debt reached USD301.9 billion, up from USD294.3 billion in the previous year. Although the percentage of household debt-to-GDP has moderated somewhat since 2015, total household debt has continued to rise year-on-year and showed no signs of declining or tapering off (see Figure 2.4). In fact, in the past two years (2018 and 2019), the total household debt reached its highest levels of the decade. Can Malaysian households afford this level of debt? Is the economy growing fast

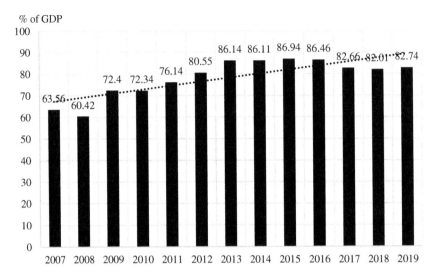

Figure 2.3 Malaysia's household debt-to-nominal GDP.
Source: Census and Economic Information Center (CEIC) (*n.d.*).

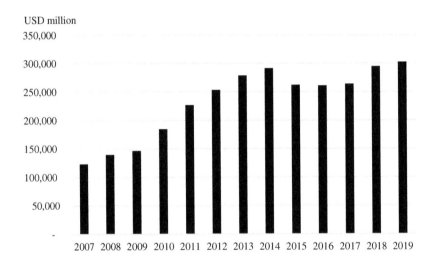

Figure 2.4 Malaysia's total household debt.
Source: Census and Economic Information Center (CEIC) (*n.d.*).

enough to justify this increase? Are wages growing fast enough to ensure households can afford to service their debts? Figure 2.5, which plots household debt growth relative to GDP, wage growth, and inflation rates, discusses these issues further.

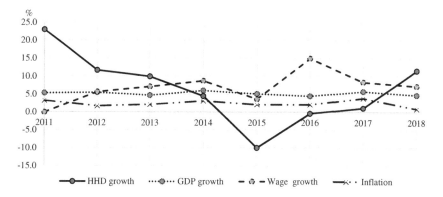

Figure 2.5 Malaysia's household debt, GDP and wage growth, and inflation rates.

Source: Census and Economic Information Center (CEIC) for household debt (HHD), World Development Indicators (WDI) for GDP, Trading Economics for wages and The World Bank for inflation.

Total household debt growth rate was on a declining trend in the earlier half of this decade but has been on an uptrend since 2015. Household debt growth has remained lower than GDP growth in the latter half of this decade, although this trend reversed in 2018. As GDP and wage growth have moderated in recent years, this recent surge in household debt growth is worrisome. Wage growth also remained higher than inflation, indicating that, in general, households are able to sustain the cost of living.

Malaysia's interest rates have consistently remained low in recent years, which would have contributed towards cheaper credit to consumers, and thus the rising trend in household debt levels. Figure 2.6 charts the overnight policy rate (OPR) from BNM, which is used by banks to compute their base lending rate (BLR).[1] Malaysia's short-term base interest rate has consistently hovered below 3.5% during the past few years. However, interest rates fell by 0.25% in mid-2016 and remained at that low level until end-2017.[2] Although interest rates increased again throughout 2018, rates have started falling in the second quarter of 2019. The low interest rate climate is a reflection of the challenging economic environment in recent years due to several factors such as the United States–China trade war. Being a small open economy highly reliant on international trade, Malaysia is significantly impacted by these events. An extended period of low interest rates that is a reflection of low economic growth hurts the poor and vulnerable the most, more so if they are already in debt, as wages stagnate due to a slowing economy.

Some of the factors that will affect the interest rates charged by lenders include:

1 Collateral – A secured loan is usually charged a lower interest rate.
2 Credit risk – Borrowers with weaker credit scores are perceived to have higher default (or credit) risk, and higher interest rates will be imposed.

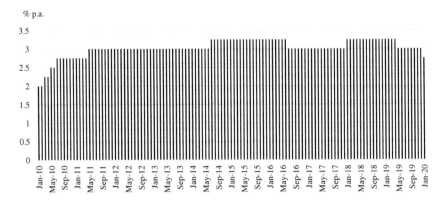

Figure 2.6 Malaysia's short-term interest rates (BNM overnight policy rate [OPR]).
Source: Bank Negara Malaysia (*n.d.*).

3   Debt-to-income ratio – Higher ratio indicates higher default risk and thus, higher interest rates will be charged.
4   Loan amount – The bigger the loan, the higher the interest rate charged to offset the increased risk that the lender faces.

BNM has set rules that govern charges that can be imposed by lenders in Malaysia. This includes a maximum interest rate of 12% per year for secured loans and 18% per year for unsecured loans. Lenders are also permitted to charge stamp duty, which are fees payable for legal documentation. From January 2010 to January 2020, Malaysia's short-term interest rates have typically ranged between 2% and 3.25%, as illustrated in Figure 2.6.

Household debt distribution across various income and asset groups is useful in evaluating households' debt burden. Income, age, and occupation are critical factors that affect debt levels among households. Whether the level of household debt is a burden or not is determined by the capacity of the borrower to service their debts.

As indicated in Figure 2.7, the largest component of household debt is for mortgages. The share of property loans has remained steady over the years at just under 40% of total household debt holdings. The second largest component of debt is for vehicle loans. Both of these debts are asset-backed and as such, should not exhibit increasing risk to the financial industry. However, it does indicate the problem of high cost of properties and an inadequate rental sector to support the housing needs of the population. Wider public transport coverage beyond just the city centres would also help to reduce dependence on private vehicle ownership that is currently taking up about 20% of the household debt burden. Consumption credit (comprising mainly of personal and credit card debt) also remained relatively constant at around 40% of household debt, with credit card loans contributing the largest portion. However, the proportion of personal loans-to-GDP increased up

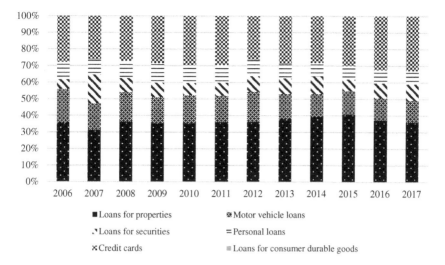

Figure 2.7 Composition of household debt in Malaysia.

Source: Malaysian Administrative Modernisation and Management Planning Unit (MAMPU) (*n.d.*).

until 2013 before showing a decreasing trend. Credit card debt, on the other hand, has continued to increase over time, indicating a preference of taking up credit card debt to cover short-term household budget imbalances. Borrowing on a credit card is perhaps more flexible, but it is the most costly form of short-term financing. Nonetheless, both these non-asset-backed loans are deemed riskier (compared to collateralised property and vehicle loans) and also point to the mismatch between households' expenditure and income levels.

This mismatch in household income and expenditure may be due to multiple factors. Some can be attributed to consumers' own behaviour, while others are due to socio-economic factors. It is easy to put the blame on consumers for spending beyond their means – the bane of consumerism and always wanting what their peers have. But "keeping up with the Joneses," or what is termed in psychology as following social norms, have always been a problem documented even during the early post-war period. Perhaps there are just more "Joneses" now, given how pervasive social media is as an avenue to see or "follow" celebrities or influencers, rather than just comparing oneself to the person next door. On the other hand, this shortfall in income relative to expenditure could be the result of either deteriorating real income or the rising cost of living. If so, these are institutional factors that may require some policy direction to mediate the situation from further deterioration. Waiting for such imbalances to correct themselves through the market (i.e. the market will always revert to equilibrium) may lead to periods where the problem overshoots before it corrects itself, and this can be destabilising for the economy and society.

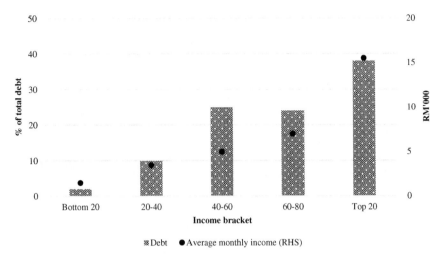

Figure 2.8 Malaysia's household income and distribution of debt by income.
Source: Bank Negara Malaysia (2016).

There is also the issue of over-lending by financial institutions driven by profit-oriented performance indicators. Increased competition among financial providers will lead to them offering easy credit facilities to certain segments of the population, especially those with steady income streams. Industry self-regulation to ensure that an individual borrower does not get over-indebted is one way of managing this issue. Credit report providers such as Credit Tip-Off Service (CTOS) and Central Credit Reference Information System (CCRIS)[3] can provide the necessary information to lenders before any loan applications are approved.

In order to avoid simple deductions, an evaluation of the distribution of income and debt between borrowers from different income groups will enable a better understanding on where the main problem lies. Who are these households that are indebted, and are these debts posing a problem for them?

Figure 2.8 shows that debt levels increase with households' income levels. The top 20% income households (T20) are the most indebted, holding around 40% of total household debt. The average monthly income for T20 households is RM16,088. Debt levels for the upper and lower middle income (M40) households are similar at around 25% of total household debt, respectively. However, as average monthly income of the upper M40 household is higher at around RM7,000 compared to the lower M40 at RM5,000, the upper M40 household is better able to service their debts. As for the bottom 40% (B40) households with average monthly income of under RM3,000, their debt levels are also the lowest at around 10% of total household debt. However, it should be noted that these debt figures only include those from formal finance providers – it is likely that the

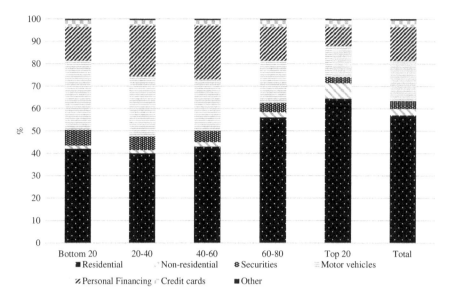

Figure 2.9 Debt by loan purpose and by income groups.
Source: Bank Negara Malaysia (2016).

B40 households are also borrowing via informal finance providers, and as such, their household debt levels are probably under-reported.

Are these debt levels something to be worried about? If households earn enough to service their debts, then this should not be a problem. However, even if the household debt level is low, but income is barely sufficient to service the loans, this will trigger defaults should any untoward events occur that will negatively affect the household's ability to service their loans. Households with low and irregular incomes are vulnerable to income shocks due to unemployment, health emergencies, and natural disasters.

As Figure 2.9 illustrates, debt for higher income households (T20) is mainly made up of mortgages – residential and non-residential (totalling almost 80%) – which is a symptom of high property prices. Nonetheless, asset-backed obligations pose much lower risk in the event of a default. However, this is perhaps true for financial institutions as the collateral can be sold to pay off any outstanding debt owed. But for the borrower, they are now left without a home and are also likely to still owe the lender for any shortfalls between the liquidated price of the property and the outstanding loan amount. A fire sale of a distressed property is unlikely to fetch its desired value.

As compared to T20 households, a higher portion of the middle income households' (M40) debt are to finance consumption (personal financing and motor vehicles); this is especially so for the lower middle income group. In fact, a big chunk of debt for the lower income groups (B40 and lower M40) are to finance consumption – there is a big reliance on personal loans and motor vehicle financing.[4] Policies to reduce vehicle prices or investment to expand public transport coverage are matters that can be taken into consideration. Increasing real income levels, especially for the lower income group, by introducing minimum wage legislation, are long overdue. The recent rise in the minimum wage (RM1,200 for workers in the cities and RM1,100 elsewhere) has tried to tackle this issue, although it was delayed for many years due to lobbying by business associations. The lower income groups are basically forced to take up the debt to cover shortfalls in income and finance their transportation needs to get to their workplaces. According to the Employees' Providence Fund's (EPF) reference budget, *Belanjawanku*, a single person living in the city who uses public transport needs a budget of RM1,870 monthly.[5]

2.2.2 Bankruptcy statistics

Is this debt composition a cause for concern? Is the inability to service loans leading to rising cases of bankruptcies? And if so, who are the most vulnerable groups facing this issue? The figures below further discuss these issues.

Figure 2.10 shows the trend in bankruptcies in recent years. The numbers are worrying, with an average of around 1,500 bankruptcies registered monthly. However, on a slightly positive note, these bankruptcies show a declining trend from 2016 onwards. Perhaps, efforts to restructure these delinquent debts by the debt counselling agency AKPK[6] have been successful in bringing down these numbers.

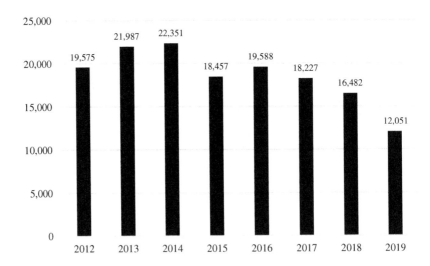

Figure 2.10 Number of bankruptcies in Malaysia.

Source: Malaysian Administrative Modernisation and Management Planning Unit (MAMPU) (*n.d.*).

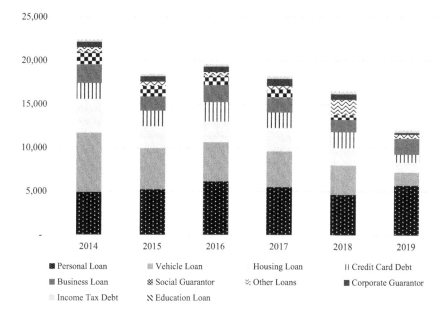

Figure 2.11 Malaysia's bankruptcies by type of debt.
Source: Malaysian Department of Insolvency (*n.d.*).

The most common types of debt that lead to bankruptcies are personal loans and vehicle loans (see Figure 2.11). Nonetheless, as the trend in bankruptcies is falling, so do the numbers of bankruptcy cases caused by these consumption loans. Mortgages, on the other hand, poses less risk of delinquencies, and the percentage of bankruptcy cases due to mortgage default has remained steady over the recent years. As mortgages are asset-backed loans, most default cases can be dealt with by disposal of the said property. Furthermore, a higher percentage of mortgages are held by the high-income households who are more likely to be able to service their debt. Cases due to credit card and business loans also remained proportionately steady over the years. As we discussed in the earlier section, credit card debt has remained a stable portion of total household debt. An interesting fact to note is the number of bankruptcies caused by being a guarantor to a loan, either corporate or social/personal.

Are these bankruptcies destabilising to the financial sector? Table 2.1 shows the trend in impaired and delinquent household debt, which show an overall declining trend from 2016 to 2018. A loan is impaired when it is likely that the lending bank will not be able to receive all payments due (interest and principal) based on the loan agreement terms. On the other hand, a delinquent or non-performing loan is when the borrower has defaulted and has not paid any principal or interest payments for some time (usually if the borrower is 90 days past due). Overall, the ratio of both impaired and delinquent loans remains low at

Table 2.1 Household sector: Gross impaired and delinquent loans in the banking system and non-bank financial institutions

	Gross impaired loans						Gross delinquent loans					
	Ratio (%)			Annual change (%)			Ratio (%)			Annual change (%)		
	2016	2017	2018	2016	2017	2018	2016	2017	2018	2016	2017	2018
Overall	1.5	1.4	1.2	5.7	2.9	-10.1	1.5	1.4	1.2	3.1	-0.5	-12.9
Residential Properties	1.5	1.4	1.3	4.9	3.4	0.7	1.4	1.3	1.1	4.5	-1.3	-4.9
Non-residential Properties	0.8	0.9	1.0	10.9	14.4	9.4	0.9	1.1	1.0	26.8	20.0	-9.2
Motor Vehicles	1.4	1.4	1.2	-0.6	-0.7	-18.5	2.8	2.7	2.1	-3.0	-2.1	-25.2
Personal Financing	2.0	2.2	1.5	15.3	7.8	-26.6	0.8	0.9	0.8	12.2	13.3	-9.4
Credit Cards	1.9	1.6	1.3	5.7	-11.9	-14.4	1.2	1.1	1.0	0.6	-10.3	-3.2

Source: https://bnm.gov.my/files/publication/fsps/en/2017/annex.pdf

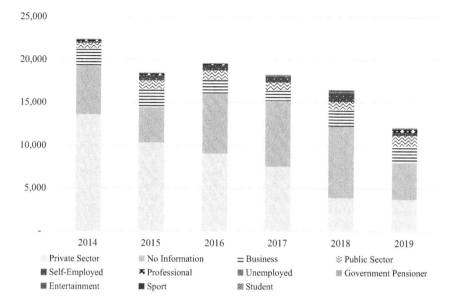

Figure 2.12 Malaysia's bankruptcies by type of employment.
Source: Malaysian Department of Insolvency (*n.d.*).

1.5% or lower, apart from motor vehicle and personal loans which has a default/ delinquent rate of over 2%. Hence, most of the problems for lenders stem from these consumption debt but given the low levels, it is unlikely to negatively affect the performance of the lenders that much.

Figure 2.12 shows the bankruptcy composition by sector of employment. The biggest segment to go bankrupt is from the private sector, although there is a significant decrease from 60% in 2014 to just above 20% in 2019. As the portion designated as "no info" remains large, we can only assume that most of the cases in this segment are also likely employed in the private sector or are self-employed. Public sector employees that go bankrupt, on the other hand, remain much smaller (and steady) at around 5% of total bankruptcies perhaps due to the nature of consumer borrowing practiced within the civil service. Most consumer borrowing by public sector employees tend to deduct the monthly payments at source (via salary deductions), and hence there is less likelihood that they will default.

It is worrying that the highest incidences of bankruptcies affect those within the ages of 35–44 (refer to Figure 2.13), which is just about double the cases in the 25–34 age group. Bankruptcies are also lower for the older age groups (45 and above). Males make up a significantly larger proportion of bankruptcy cases, reflecting their role as the main borrower in the household (see Figure 2.14). As they are also likely to be the main breadwinner, this factor will definitely affect the household's well-being negatively.

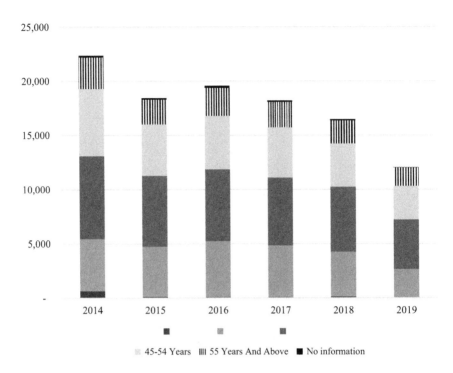

Figure 2.13 Malaysia's bankruptcies by age groups.
Source: Malaysian Department of Insolvency (*n.d.*).

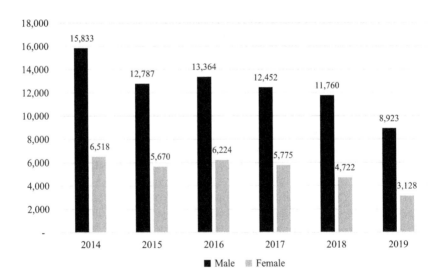

Figure 2.14 Malaysia's bankruptcy cases by gender.
Source: Malaysian Department of Insolvency (*n.d.*).

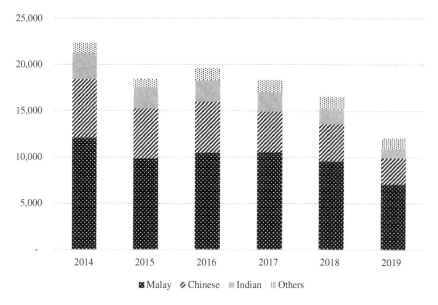

Figure 2.15 Malaysia's bankruptcies by ethnic groups.
Source: Malaysian Department of Insolvency (*n.d.*).

In terms of racial composition, bankruptcy cases roughly reflect the race composition of the nation (see Figure 2.15). Malays make up almost half of all bankruptcy cases, followed by the Chinese and Indians, respectively. This composition may have other social and political consequences in Malaysia, where ethnic discontent has a tendency to spill over on the political front. As such, policymakers should monitor and institute policies to better manage the causes of bankruptcies with targeted policies for different age and ethnic groups, where possible.

One point to note, however, is that in Malaysia, under the Insolvency Act 1967, there is no time limit to being declared bankrupt[7] – a person can be bankrupt for life, unless he pays off all the outstanding amount to his lenders. This is not the case for most developed nations. In the United Kingdom, legislations have been put in place since 2004 (under the Enterprise Act 2002) to allow personal bankruptcies to last no longer than 12 months or less (but if the bankrupt is considered culpable for his insolvency, then his bankrupt status can be extended up to 15 years). In the United States under Chapter 7, lenders will only receive proceeds from the sale of non-exempt property of the borrower (here the borrower is allowed to keep essential property such as his main home) or the applicable collateral asset, and the bankruptcy remains on his credit report only for 10 years.

There are many restrictions imposed on bankrupt individuals such as restrictions on travelling overseas, acting as a director for a firm, carrying out a business, and the need to pay to the bankruptcy estate on a regular basis for the lender's benefit. The bankrupt is also required to hand over other personal assets including their house and vehicles. As such, bankruptcy rules in Malaysia are harsh and make it hard for the bankrupt individuals to move out of that position as their ability to earn a living is severely impaired. Perhaps it is timely for policymakers to consider reviewing this (outdated) legislation and be fairer to the borrowers, and not just for the benefit of the lenders.

2.3 Types of household debt and providers of consumer financing

2.3.1 Types of consumer debt

1   Property or housing loans (mortgages)

Mortgages are home or housing loans to pay for purchase of residential and non-residential/commercial properties. There are several types of home loans offered in Malaysia. This includes term loans, fixed rate loans, overdraft, flexi loans, Islamic financing, refinancing, and government housing loans. Brief descriptions of each type are provided below to give an understanding on their differences within this category of consumer debt.

Term loans are the most common type and has a maximum tenure of 35 years where the instalment and interest charges are bundled together in the monthly payment. Interest rate charge in these loans is usually floating based on the lender's BLR. There are penalties involved in early repayment or if the borrower wants to settle their loans earlier than their agreed tenure. This early repayment penalty is in the range of 3% if they want to settle payment within the first 3 to 5 years. This is the period where the lenders earn the most in interest payments; thus, they will discourage early payments.

Fixed rate loans are also a relatively common type of property loan where the interest rate charges are fixed for the entire tenure. This type of loan is preferred by borrowers who do not want to face uncertainties due to fluctuating or increasing interest rates charged by the lenders.

Property can also be financed using an overdraft or a flexi loan. An overdraft is harder to obtain as the lender will need to verify the borrower's repayment ability (this can take the form of some financial collateral). However, on the upside, there is no fixed tenure, and the borrower is only required to pay the interest rate on the loan (which is automatically deducted monthly from their current account) and can settle all payments at any point. On the downside, the interest rate charged for overdraft facilities tends to be higher than term or fixed rate loans but still lower than personal loans.

A flexi loan is a combination of term loan and overdraft loan. The interest rate charged on the loan varies when the borrower adds (interest rate reduces) or withdraws (rate increases) funds from his current account that is linked to the flexi loan.

Islamic home financing consists of several types of Syariah-compliant contracts such as commodity home financing (*Murabahah*), deferred payment sales (*Al-bai' bithaman ajil*) and diminishing partnership (*Musharakah Mutanaqisah*).

The government housing loan is only offered to civil servants under the *Bahagian Pinjaman Perumahan*, if the borrower complies with the strict criteria for eligibility. The monthly repayments will be deducted directly from their salaries. As such, these loans are unlikely to be delinquent, but if the borrower is no longer a government employee, they would have to settle off this loan through any of the above methods.

Refinancing refers to taking another loan for a property that already has a loan attached to it. This is usually popular with borrowers whose property values have appreciated as they are able to cash out some of the equity out of their home. This is a cheaper way of borrowing extra cash compared to taking out a personal loan as this debt has a collateral backing it.

2   Vehicle or auto loans (hire purchase)

Hire purchase (HP) is also known as car loans as it is meant to finance the purchase of motor vehicles. The Higher Purchase Act 1967 (HPA Act 212) governs these transactions in Malaysia. The typical contract requires the car buyer or "hirer" (who becomes the borrower) to pay a minimum deposit of around 10% of the car value to the car dealer. The lender will pay the 90% balance in order to "purchase" the car (and now becomes the owner). Once all payments are settled, ownership of the car is transferred to the buyer. Two types of HP contracts are available in Malaysia, which are conventional and Islamic HPs.

3   Personal loans

Typically, a personal loan is borrowed from a lender for a fixed period of time. This loan must be repaid in fixed monthly instalments until the end of the agreed tenure. If it is a short-term loan, then the monthly instalments are higher (but the interest is lower), while if it is a long-term loan, the monthly repayments are lower (but the interest charged is higher). If the borrower is late with the repayments, the lender will impose a penalty fee on the overdue amount. In the event of a default (non-payment for over three months), the lender will impose a higher finance charge or take legal action – both of which will affect the borrower's credit score and stay in the CCRIS database for up to 12 months (which means they will have difficulty in securing other loans in the future).

There are several types of personal loans available in Malaysia. This includes secured (with collateral and guarantor) and unsecured (no collateral and may or may not need guarantor) loans, conventional loan and Islamic financing, and these loans/financing can come with or without insurance or takaful (the coverage adds to the borrower's cost but provides the security that all unpaid balances will be settled in the event of death or total permanent disability of the borrower).

Personal loans are mainly used to finance several purposes including education, investment, emergency cash, business ventures, buying assets, and debt consolidation,[8] among others.

4 Credit cards

A credit card is a payment mechanism used to pay for purchases instead of using cash. That amount is owed to the lender (typically a bank) and needs to be repaid. Compared to other types of loans, credit cards are fast loans in which you do not have to wait for approval each time you make payments (as long as they are within your credit limit). If you are able to repay the full amount charged each month, the lender will not charge you interest, but if you are only paying the minimum amount, then the lender will charge interest (known as a finance charge) on the outstanding balance after the due date (the interest-free period is usually within 20 days). The finance charge is typically higher than other types of consumer loans. The credit card issuer also charges an annual fee to cardmembers to cover for benefits that come with the card (such as reward points, cashbacks, merchant promotions, and discounts, as well as air miles), but there are cards without annual fees and also those that allow for a fee waiver subject to meeting certain conditions.

The main requirement to be eligible for a credit card for first time applicants is to be at least 21 years of age and have an annual income of RM24,000 as per BNM guidelines.[9] However, each credit card issuing bank can set different minimum monthly salary requirements. BNM guidelines also state that if you earn RM36,000 or less annually, you can hold credit cards from a maximum of two different issuers with a credit limit capped at double your monthly salary. Those with incomes of RM36,000 or above annually can obtain as many credit cards as they want from multiple issuers. At the time of writing, there are 19 banks in Malaysia that offer credit card facilities. There are also four card networks in Malaysia: Visa, MasterCard, American Express and UnionPay. These card networks partner with Malaysian banks to issue credit cards to consumers.

5 Loans to purchase securities

Also known as share margin financing, it is a revolving credit facility to finance investor's share purchases and investment activities. In other words, this loan allows you to buy shares using borrowed money secured by your collateral of choice. In Malaysia, this type of loan is offered by banks or brokerages. As loan facilities offered by banks are governed by BNM and those offered by brokerage firms are regulated by the SC, the terms and conditions of their loans can differ. Acceptable forms of collateral include cash, unit trust, fixed deposits, and listed securities on Bursa Malaysia.

6 Others

Includes education loans to pay for own or children's education fees and other related costs. Also includes loans for weddings and home renovations.

2.3.2 *Types of lenders that provide loans to households*

1 Commercial banks
   Offers both conventional loans and Islamic financing. Includes domestic as well as international/foreign banks.[10]

2 Insurance companies
   There are currently 14 life insurance and 11 family takaful companies operating in Malaysia. They are all regulated under BNM. At the time of writing, only American International Assurance Company, Limited (AIA) offers housing loans directly to consumers.[11]

3 Credit co-operatives
   Co-operatives can offer credit facilities by using funds from members or borrowed from other sources. Co-operatives are registered under the Co-operative Commission of Malaysia (or its Malay acronym: SKM).[12] The Co-operative Society Act of 1993 regulates the activities of these co-operative societies. They are part of what is known as the shadow banking system in Malaysia. Credit co-operatives do not require a borrower's credit score to approve credit facilities as repayment is done at source. However, there are criticisms that credit co-operative loans are more expensive than those offered by banks. Although this charge may be true in the past, increased competition among co-operatives has resulted in interest charges declining, and most co-operative loans are now comparable to bank loans.
   Both insurance companies and credit co-operatives are categorised as NBFI.

4 Informal finance providers
   There is a growing marketplace for informal finance providers in Malaysia. Although most people associate informal finance with loan sharking activities, there are several different types of legal and regulated informal finance entities operating in the country. Borrowing from these regulated avenues are safer than from loan sharks, which are illegal. Terms of borrowing are also easier than banks, but the rates charged are typically higher to account for the higher risk taken by these lenders. Borrowers who are unable to get financing via banks and NBFI are the main customers in this segment. Household debt data generally do not capture lending done in this segment, so may underestimate borrowing for the lower income households. Nonetheless, informal financing promotes financial inclusion for these under-banked consumer segments.

   i   The oldest type of informal finance providers is the moneylenders (in the olden days, they were known as *chettiars*), which have existed in Malaysia even prior to Independence. Moneylenders are licensed by the Ministry of Housing and Local Government under the Money Lending Act 1951. They tend to charge higher interest rates on their loans compared to other formal finance lenders with a maximum rate of 18% per year. These loans can be collateralised or non-collateralised loans. They are also sometimes confused with loan sharks that are completely unlicensed and unregulated and is an illegal activity that charges exorbitant interest rates and use of threats to force repayments. The moneylending industry exists in almost all countries around the world with some forming networks across national boundaries. Moneylenders can give quick and hassle-free lending compared to financial institutions. Unlike banks, moneylenders cannot take deposits and thus lend money out of their own capital, and the interest rate they charge is capped by the Moneylenders Act. As such, moneylenders face full credit risk on their capital contributions unlike bank shareholders.

ii   Pawn shops have existed in Malaysia since 1871, and currently their operations are governed under the Pawnbrokers Act 1972 by the Ministry of Housing and Local Government. An Islamic alternative, *Ar Rahnu*, has existed since 1992, but they are governed under different regulations than conventional pawnbrokers, depending on the registration of the institution that offers the service.[13] A pawn loan is an easy and fast way of obtaining quick cash compared to arranging for a bank loan. All it takes is a quick assessment of one's item to be pawned, and there is no credit check required. If the borrower defaults, then the pawn shop will just auction off the pawned item (any excess amount will be returned to the borrower). Pawn loans are usually short term in nature (6 months but can be extended prior to expiry), and the maximum interest rate that can be charged is 2% per month (or 24% per year).

iii Payday lenders offer small loans in the form of unsecured lending that requires no collateral. It is meant to help the borrower get through an inconvenient or unexpected expenditure that requires immediate payment, such as a car breakdown or a medical emergency, before his or her next payday. When payday arrives, the idea is that the borrower then pays off the loan in one lump sum together with the interest charged. Payday loans are easier and faster to arrange compared to credit cards or personal loans. Due to the short duration and uncollateralised nature of payday loans, these lenders tend to charge interest rates equivalent to credit card rates (i.e. a maximum of 18% per year). So the best strategy is to borrow on the shortest tenure that you can to minimise interest charges. However, if you are unable to pay the full sum owed at the end of the agreed tenure or delay your payments, additional fees are charged which can be really expensive. For example, Credit Express charges a minimum of RM300 for late payments, and these late charges can vary for larger amounts. On the other hand, Doctor Ringgit does not charge late fees but will charge the borrower debt collecting fees in order to recover the debt.

iv   Microfinance institutions are seen as providing financial inclusion for the unbanked sector to finance small-scale enterprises. However, loans from microfinance institutions can be diverted towards the household's other more pressing consumption needs, which may exacerbate their indebtedness position as consumption spending does not generate the returns required to service the loans.

v   Peer-to-peer (P2P) lenders are relatively new lending providers that only began their operations in Malaysia since 2017. P2P financing platforms link investors who want to lend money directly to borrowers (either individual or businesses). These loans are easier to arrange as they do not have the strict requirements of bank loans. However, the interest rate charged is higher than banks (between 10% and 18% per year) and will depend on the risk profile of each borrower. P2P lending is regulated and licensed by the SC. At the time of writing, there are currently nine P2P lending platforms in Malaysia.

vi Loan sharks, or more commonly known in Malaysia as *ah longs*, are unlicensed moneylenders. They are illegal moneylenders that impose repayment at an interest rate higher than the maximum limit allowable under the law and will use intimidation or force in order to ensure repayment. Newspapers often report stories of loan shark intimidation tactics such as red paint being thrown on someone's porch, harassment of the borrower's family members, and even violence.

2.4 A theoretical perspective on over-indebtedness

In this section, we discuss several consumer behaviour models that can be applied to analyse the issue of consumer indebtedness. Although some of these theories were developed to explain savings and consumption behaviour, we can extrapolate their implications for the embedded borrowing behaviour within them.

2.4.1 Consumption theories

In the main consumption theory, the life-cycle hypothesis (LCH), debt is a means of smoothing out consumption over one's lifetime (Modigliani & Brumberg, 1954; 1990). As Figure 2.16 shows, LCH argues that consumption level is smoothed over time; when one's income is lower in the early and later parts of life, people take on debt or liquidate their assets, and when income is high during their middle prime earning years, people will save or pay off their debts. Thus, LCH suggests that consumers borrow when they are young, build up wealth when they are middle aged, and run down their wealth upon retirement. However, in reality, it is common to instead observe that a person continues to borrow throughout their lifetime. Although LCH is primarily a theory to explain consumption and savings behaviour, it is also useful in understanding the consequences of debt accumulation over one's lifetime. As such, LCH would hypothesise that the household debt level is determined by socio-demographic and economic factors including income expectations, age, and number of dependents in the household.

Life-cycle theory states that households borrow from the credit markets to enable them to have a stable standard of living over time. Generally, income rises

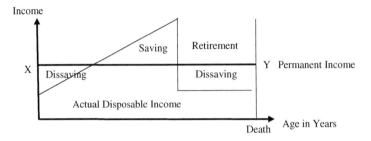

Figure 2.16 The 'hump-shaped' pattern of the life-cycle hypothesis.
Source: Adapted from Modigliani (1986).

from the start of an adult's life and decreases upon retirement, and as such, debt is used to smooth out expenditure and consumption in one's life. For households, this means that young families that expect their future income to grow will spend more than what they currently earn, adding on debts that they plan to pay back as their family matures.

LCH assumes that people are rational and plan for their future. However, behavioural economics have suggested that many people do not plan for all sorts of reasons. People may lack the self-control required to reduce spending and save for the future. They prefer instant gratification and as such, they will borrow even when they cannot afford it and do not save for the future. Additionally, those on low incomes may have little disposable income left to save and may even rack up high levels of debt to cover spending shortfalls. There are also people who, as their incomes rise, value leisure more and cut down on their working hours and may continue to work part-time in retirement.

Behavioural life-cycle hypothesis (BLCH) takes this human cognitive and emotional errors into account when people try to balance between their desire to borrow and spend now, and their desire to pay off debt and save for tomorrow. Shefrin and Thaler (1988) argued that a savings model that omits temptation is mis-specified, and willpower is the psychological cost of exercising self-control in order to delay immediate pleasure and attain long-term savings targets. Their proposed BCLH states that in order to reconcile these conflicting wants, personal and institutional mechanisms can play a decisive role. Personal control mechanisms such as framing and self-control rules can prohibit irrational or impulsive decisions. Institutional (or public) policies include government nudges such as enrolment in financial literacy programmes for schools and colleges, and shoves such as mandatory limits on one's borrowing capacity. Thaler and Sunstein's (2008) nudge theory points this out as an influencing behaviour without coercion, in that, it alters consumer behaviour without sacrificing their choices.

Thaler's (1985) idea of mental accounting further accentuates the fact that when people mentally categorise their budgets into different categories (which seems like a rational thing to do), these mental accounts can influence their spending and saving decisions in unexpected ways that deviate from standard rational consumer behaviour. For example, when you receive an unexpected cash inflow such as a tax refund, birthday money, or a bonus, you have the tendency to spend that on unplanned items rather than to pay off an outstanding loan. Loewenstein and Prelec (1992) also showed that people apply differing discount rates at different times, whereby people apply a higher discount on utility in the present, but a lower one in the future; this is called hyperbolic discounting. This can explain why people borrow to buy something now rather than save up to buy it later.

Friedman's (1957) permanent income hypothesis argues that one's consumption at any time is determined not only by their income at that time but also by their expected income in future years, or in other words, their permanent income. Similar to LCH, it is a theory that is based on the economic rationality whereby individuals who want to maintain their living standards at a certain level will smooth consumption over time via saving and borrowing.

There are other consumption theories that argue that consumption decisions are determined by external factors including other people's consumption patterns, as well as our own personality traits. One of the earliest theories to point this out is Veblen's (1899) conspicuous consumption theory, which highlights that when one makes a consumption decision, one takes into consideration one's relative position within the society. The effect is an act of buying and using some types of goods and services, not for survival per se, but in order to identify with other wealthier people and those of higher social standing. Consumption decision is, thus, based on a "want" rather than a "need." This pressure can lead some consumers to borrow to "keep up with the Joneses" rather than setting a limit to spending based on their own income level – a phenomenon we now call consumerism.

Duesenberry's (1949) relative income hypothesis reinforces this idea of social comparison in consumption decision. Consumption is not dependent on one's own income but instead on a "reference" income that results from the social influence of consumption by others. In other words, consumption standard is determined by the consumption of those earning the average (or relative) income in that society. Households earning below that average income will try hard to achieve that consumption standard by borrowing to cover the extra expenditure required for that "acceptable" level of consumption. Additionally, Duesenberry also hypothesises that current consumption is not just influenced by current levels of absolute and relative income but also by levels of consumption they were used to in a previous period. As such, it will be hard for households to reduce the level of consumption they have once attained, and they will resort to borrowing to maintain this standard.

2.4.2 *Rational choice theory*

Rational choice theory (RCT) is the bedrock that underpins conventional economic theories. The substance of this theory is that individuals use rational calculations to make rational choices, among the multiple choices facing them, which have outcomes that maximise their own personal objectives. Adam Smith's (1776) "invisible hand" is built on the actions of self-interest together with rational choice, which lead to the notion that rational actors acting on their own self-interests can actually create benefits for the economy. RCT can be accommodated to include individuals who are not rational actors, but the consensus decision at market level will still be rational. Nonetheless, RCT is not without its criticisms and limitations, and it is often found that individuals do not always make rational, utility maximising decisions.

In most instances, rationality of individuals can be "bounded," in which individuals often have to make decisions based on the information available to them as they may not have all the relevant information at the time the decision is made. Simon's (1956) bounded rationality concept postulates that due to this limit to thinking capacity, available information and time, consumers make less than optimal decisions. There is also the concept of anchoring, or habit, that suggests individuals rely on choices they are accustomed to in order to avoid the mental effort and risk of picking alternatives. These ideas can explain certain behaviours in credit markets, such as borrowing from a lender that gives you the easiest credit even if it is ultimately more costly.

Additionally, RCT states that the discount rate is an increasing function, that is, more current events have a lower discount rate compared to future events. However, in reality, individuals making intertemporal choices use a much higher discount rate for shorter time horizons and a lower rate for events further in the future (or hyperbolic discount rates). This essentially means that they tend to systematically overestimate immediate costs and benefits and underestimate those in the future. As such, individuals give more importance to present events over those that will occur in the future (Kilborn, 2005). When this concept is applied to the debt market, the hyperbolic discount factor leads individuals deciding whether to purchase on credit terms or not to buy immediately. This explains the "buy now, pay later" decision that brings immediate pleasure at a future cost, and as such, this short-sighted behaviour makes them unable to be fully aware of the consequences that their spending decision will have on the sustainability of their debt situation (Meier & Sprenger, 2007).

The field of neuroeconomics have tried to link biological reactions to decision-making abilities. For example, Hartley and Phelps' (2012) study showed that when individuals are anxious, they fail to make rational decisions. Stressors that lead to anxiety have been shown to suppress parts of the brain that support rational decision-making. Low-income households are more likely to borrow to cover immediate needs even if they know they are incapable of servicing the loan. This borrowing will, ultimately, have a knock-on effect of increasing the household's stress level as their debt keeps increasing.

2.4.3 Prospect theory

Kahneman and Tversky's (1979) prospect theory (PT) assumes that losses and gains are valued differently; thus, when faced with gains, one prefers certain

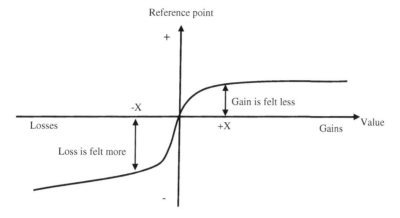

Figure 2.17 Value function in prospect theory.
Source: Adapted from Kahneman & Tversky (1979).

instead of perceived gains, but when faced with losses, will choose perceived instead of certain losses. In other words, PT argues that if given the option, individuals prefer a sure gain rather than the prospect of larger gains but with more risk (or a loss aversion). This choice is reversed when faced with a loss, as they would opt for a higher potential loss that is uncertain rather than accept a lower loss that is certain. Figure 2.17 depicts this risk-aversion behaviour when faced with gains with a concave function and the risk-seeking behaviour when faced with losses with a convex function.

Debt can be analysed as a choice, in which a person deciding to take a loan to purchase a house is choosing between several alternatives that they can take. These alternatives can be renting, or postponing the house purchase until the time one has saved up the required amount needed, or foregoing the current consumption of other goods and services and using that savings to pay for the house. For example, a person is more willing to borrow in order to buy a house or a car for the certainty over its use rather than face the potential uncertainty of renting or using public transportation (loss aversion), even though the probability of those risks is tiny.

There is also the "disposition effect," which is usually used to explain the behaviour of disposing off winning stocks too soon and holding on to losing stocks too long in order to avoid realising those losses (Barberis, 2013; Frazzini, 2006; Odean, 1998). The same argument can be used to explain one's borrowing behaviour to purchase an asset. For example, an asset (or a house) owner have a greater tendency to sell assets that have risen in value since purchase rather than assets that have fallen in value. This reluctance to sell assets at a loss follows the proposition of PT, from the convexity of the value function in the region of losses (see Figure 2.15), implying a risk-seeking attitude. The intuition is that if the asset performs poorly then its owner will be in the loss region of the value function. Because of the convexity, the owner becomes risk-seeking, which means that the owner might hold on to the asset to avoid realising the losses and hope that prices might go up later. So, although a homeowner may be suffering from negative equity on his/her house, the owner will be reluctant to sell the house to pay off the loan. He/she is willing to continue to service the loan in the hopes that the house price will eventually increase. This behaviour is likely to make his/her indebtedness situation worse as the asset is now unable to cover for the value of the debt taken to purchase it.

The disposition effect is also a consequence of "realisation utility" – that individuals find satisfaction from selling an asset at a gain relative to purchase price and dissatisfaction from selling at a loss. This is driven by them thinking that selling assets at a gain relative to purchase price leads to an increase in wealth accumulation (and vice versa when selling below purchase price) (Barberis & Xiong, 2012). All these reasons are rooted in PT in which it relies on the owner deriving utility from gains and losses rather than from wealth levels in absolute terms. This can perhaps explain why homeowners are willing to borrow to buy a property that has the potential to increase in value (appreciate in price) and take large debts to cover the purchase.

2.5 Empirical studies on consumer indebtedness

As can be seen from the statistics in Section 2.2, high levels of debt in itself may not be a problem for as long as the debt can be serviced without putting too much burden on households. Asset-backed debt, such as to finance properties, are also a safer form of debt burden. In the event of a default, these assets can be liquidated to repay the outstanding loans. However, this position is mainly true perhaps only for households within the higher income tiers (the T20 and the upper M40). For those in the middle and lower income groups, although their debt levels are lower, they face an over-indebtedness problem as it is evident that servicing this debt with their income would be difficult given the mismatch in income relative to debt.

2.5.1 *Research themes on over-indebtedness*

Over-indebtedness is a multi-faceted issue with social, economic, legal, and political aspects. Depending on the different aspects, the definition of over-indebtedness may differ. A broad definition would consider people are over-indebted if they have difficulties meeting or are late in their payment obligations or household commitments. What is clear from that definition is that those who borrow a lot may not have over-borrowed or be over-indebted if they are able to service their debt payments without difficulties. There are many factors that could influence an individual to be in a situation of over-indebtedness, which includes *psychological* and *demographic* causes. The implications of these factors have clear repercussions to an *individual's psychological welfare* and *the socio-economic foundation of the country*. Figure 2.18 demonstrates these themes.

Literature on household debt behaviour mainly focus on developed nations, although findings still varies. As such, while rising household debt is a universal

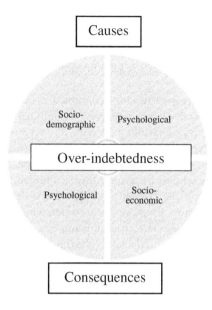

Figure 2.18 Research themes on over-indebtedness.

trend, the explanation in terms of psychological, socio-demographic, and socio-economic is unique to each society.

2.5.2 Causes of over-indebtedness: Psychological factors

Vitt (2004) and Eberhardt, de Bruin, and Strough's (2019) findings show that consumers' financial decisions may be a reflection of their psychological and social values. The psychological factors influencing consumer debt behaviour can be categorised into cognitive, motivational, and dispositional dimensions. The cognitive dimension includes *financial literacy*, which is the ability of the individual to comprehend and effectively apply different types of financial skills in managing their household finances. The motivational dimensions relevant to indebtedness behaviour are *attitudes* and *social norms*, which applies to informal understandings that govern the behaviour of the members of a society. Dispositional or personal dimension of indebtedness includes *overconfidence, materialism,* and *self-control*.

2.5.2.1 Financial literacy

Among the behavioural determinants, financial literacy, which aims to improve the individual's ability to comprehend financial issues, has a more positive impact on financial decisions in the long-run (Azma, Rahman, Adeyemi, & Rahman, 2019). Ward and Lynch Jr. (2019) also found that financial literacy can assist individuals to make smart financial decisions and manage their income appropriately.

Lusardi, Michaud, and Mitchell (2013) and Munoz-Murillo, Alvarez-Franco, and Restrepo-Tobon (2020) found that financial literacy is crucial for individuals when they first start their career. From young, children see how their parents manage money and learn from those behaviours (Kalwij, Alessie, Dinkova, Schonewille, van der Schors, & van der Werf, 2019; Okech, Mimura, Mauldin, & Kim, 2013).

A widely accepted definition by the Organisation for Economic Co-operation and Development (OECD) characterises financial literacy as "a combination of awareness, knowledge, skill, attitude and behaviour necessary to make sound financial decisions and ultimately achieve individual financial wellbeing" (OECD INFE, 2011). There are some studies that describe a household to be over-indebted due to financial illiteracy. Households with lower financial literacy tend to borrow at higher interest rates (Stango & Zinman, 2009), are less likely to save (Smith, McArdle, & Willis, 2010), and are more likely to default on their mortgages (Gerardi, Goette, & Meier, 2013). Therefore, it is important to alleviate financial vulnerability by increasing households' level of financial literacy.

Lusardi and Mitchell's (2014) findings show that individuals, in general, lack the required financial knowledge to make essential financial decisions. Inability to properly understand interest rate calculations has been found to correlate with higher indebtedness, paying more fees in debt contracts, loan defaults, and delinquencies (Disney & Gathergood, 2011; Gerardi et al., 2013). Much of the literature suggest that financial literacy is positively correlated with good financial behaviour. Financial numeracy and knowledge of basic financial concepts are strongly negatively correlated with undertaking overly expensive debt, even after controlling for age, income, education, and other variables that can proxy for financial vulnerability and suffering income shocks (Lusardi & de Bassa Scheresberg, 2013).

A common finding is that incurring higher debt levels can be partly due to weak money-management skills (Elliot & Lindblom, 2019). Financial literacy programmes are most effective when they target a specific audience and/or area of financial activity rather than a generic, one-size-fits-all programme (Lusardi & Mitchell, 2014). It is widely acknowledged in the area of investment that financial literacy is related to better investing decisions (Lusardi & Mitchell, 2007; van Rooij, Lusardi, & Alessie, 2011), higher stock market participation (van Rooij et al., 2011), and better portfolio diversification (Guiso & Jappelli, 2008). The literature on financial literacy has also extended its focus on credit-related issues such as credit conditions, and specifically, prohibitively costly credit (Disney & Gathergood, 2013), usage behaviour of credit cards and over-indebtedness (Lusardi, Schneider, & Tufano, 2011), general debt delinquency (Disney & Gathergood, 2013), and subprime mortgages (Gerardi et al., 2013).

2.5.2.2 *Attitudes*

Psychologically, society's attitude towards debt has changed in terms of the role that debt plays in household finances. It is no longer taboo to discuss taking up debt, and more debt may actually signal one's higher social status given that financial institutions will have higher requirement for increased borrowing. Thus, attitude is expected to be a major factor explaining the increase in household indebtedness. In other words, given a similar economic status, one who is more positive about debt will have a higher probability to borrow, as opposed to one that is more negative towards debt. However, empirical findings regarding the role of attitude on household debt decisions are mixed. Cosma and Pattarin (2010); Davies and Lea (1995); and Lea, Webley, and Levine (1993) suggest that being more tolerable towards debt increases the probability of taking on more debt. This finding is also supported by Zainudin, Mahdzan, and Yeap (2019) who found a significant positive relationship between credit card attitudes and credit card misuse. On the other hand, Zhu and Meeks (1994) and Lea, Webley, and Walker (1995) found that attitude is insignificant in explaining household debt behaviour. Hayhoe, Leach, and Turner (1999) and Xiao, Noring, and Anderson (1995) found that although an individual's overall attitude towards debt is positive, their behavioural aspect such as intention to use credit cards may not be as positive. Wang, Wei, and Jiang's (2011) study in Shanghai, China found that behavioural and affective components of attitude increase the usage of credit, but the cognitive aspect (such as knowledge of the credit process and interest calculation) can act to deter the use of credit.

2.5.2.3 Social norms

Social norms are the accepted standard of behaviour in a particular social group or culture (McLeod, 2008). There is strong pressure to conform to these social norms, and it is common to compare ourselves to our neighbours as a benchmark for social class; hence, the popular saying "keeping up with the Joneses" aptly describes this behaviour.

Social comparison and aspirations are indeed relevant to debt-taking behaviour. Over-indebted individuals do feel that they are inferior, feel poorer than their friends, relatives, colleagues, and even people they see on television. However, this becomes insignificant when other factors are controlled for (Lea et al., 1995). Other findings show that indebted individuals like to express their identity by consumption (Bernthal, Crockett, & Rose, 2005). A study of Gen Y's credit card misuse in Malaysia reveals a significant positive relationship between the influence of peers and credit card misuse (Zainudin et al., 2019). Livingstone and Lunt (1992), on the other hand, did not find similar support in their findings, concluding that it is very likely that those taking up debt did not disclose that they borrowed to keep up with the Joneses.

2.5.2.4 Overconfidence

Overconfidence is the situation whereby one's confidence in their judgement and knowledge is more than the accuracy of these judgements. Overconfidence occurs either due to a bias in processing information or due to an error in judgement. Kilborn (2005) found that over-borrowing may stem from the psychological biases and mental shortcuts that influence an individual's decision and prediction about borrowing (or an overconfidence bias), which is the tendency to underestimate the probability of suffering an adverse event. Borrowers have been found to show a tendency of underestimating how much their interest rate could change with their adjustable-rate mortgages due to unexpected events (Bucks & Pence, 2008).

Grohmann, Menkhoff, Merkle, and Schmacker (2019) analysed the effect of overconfident income expectations on borrowing behaviour using an experimental study to generate biased income expectations, and they showed that participants that expect their income to be higher end up borrowing more. In another study, Hyytinen and Putkuri (2018) analysed a survey in which respondents were asked to predict their financial situations over the next one year and compared these predictions with their actual situation. They found that respondents that make optimistic forecast errors tend to have higher debt-to-income ratios. Souleles' (2004) study also found that households that underestimate economic shocks and those that exhibit more positive sentiment exhibit higher consumption. As such, the literature seems to show that individuals who are overconfident with their income expectations will be particularly affected when a negative shock occurs either to the economy or individually, as they have already incurred higher consumption levels to begin with.

2.5.2.5 *Materialism*

An additional determinant of indebtedness is materialism – the idea that goods and wealth are the most important things in life – which is due to consumption (Mishra & Mishra, 2016; Richins & Dawson, 1992). Individuals who are highly materialistic are known as spenders, while those less materialistic are savers as they will invest in stocks, bonds, and mutual funds (Chatterjee, Kumar, & Dayma, 2019; Watson, 2003). dos Santos and Fernandes' (2011) study also noted that people relate excessive materialism with a search for status. Additionally, when the motivation to spend is based on collective values within that society, materialism is regarded positively (Flores & Vieira, 2014).

Zakaria, Jaafar, and Ishak's (2016) study in Malaysia found that household debt is not a poverty-related issue as the determinants are more "wants" rather than "needs" with factors such as attitude and social comparison explaining a borrower's propensity to use credit. Needs indicators including income, number of children, and employment status are insignificant. As such, they conclude that the high levels of indebtedness within urban households in Malaysia are not an indication of economic sufferings, but rather due to choice. Rahman, Azma, Masud, and Ismail's (2020) recent study in Malaysia found that risk perception and indebtedness are related to behavioural factors such as materialism and emotion. However, they found that socio-demographic factors such as gender, marital status, age, and income do affect indebtedness in terms of the usage of credit cards and other debts. Zainudin et al. (2019) discovered that Gen

Y's in Malaysia with higher sense of materialism had a higher tendency of misusing their credit card. Endut and Toh (2009); Abdul Ghani (2010); and Mann, Chidambarathanu, Caparusso, and Chandra (2013) found that many Malaysians reported suffering from financial problems and feel ashamed by their indebtedness issues. Azma et al. (2019) found that both low- and high-income consumers get into debt for different reasons. For the low-income earners, they are indebted as they are unable to pay for essential expenses, but for the high-income earners, their indebtedness is due to their strong desire to spend. Similar findings were found by Flores and Vieira (2014); Darriet, Guille, Vergnaud, and Shimizu (2020); and Katona (1975), with an overall finding that both income groups lack a desire to save.

2.5.2.6 *Self-control*

Self-control is the ability to control one's own behaviours and emotions when faced with temptation and immediate gratification in order to achieve long-term goals. This ability to plan, evaluate alternate action, and avoid actions that one will regret later rather than immediately act to every impulse as it arises is what separates humans from other mammals. Lack of self-control has been shown to be related to sub-optimal borrowing behaviour and over-indebtedness (Gathergood, 2012).

Cobb-Clark, Kassenboehmer, and Sinning (2016) found a positive link between an individual's locus of control and their savings behaviour. An individual who has an external locus of control believes that life's outcome is due to external factors, while those with an internal locus of control believe that life's outcome is a product of their own actions. As one's belief that their actions will lead to the desired outcome is the key driver of self-control and motivation (Bandura, 1989; Rosenbaum, 1980), it is important to understand an individual's perception of control. In their study, Cobb-Clark et al. (2016) also found that households in which the reference person has an external locus of control tend to save less and allocate less wealth to their pensions compared to households with internal locus of control, after controlling for the household's education and income levels. Additionally, Perry and Morris (2005) found that a person with an internal locus of control believe they are better able to manage their finances as they are more capable of controlling their spending, paying their bills on time, plan for their future, and manage their savings.

Nonetheless, Mastrobuoni and Weinberg's (2009) study noted that an individual's struggle with self-control is not all equal in real life. In other words, economic conditions can affect self-control. Poverty can weaken self-control as willpower is more difficult to exercise when consumption is low (Shefrin & Thaler, 1988); imperfect credit markets can constrain the usefulness of having self-control (Bernheim, Ray, & Yeltekin, 2013); or the marginal propensity to spend on temptation goods fall as consumption rises (Banerjee & Mullainathan, 2010).

Tekçe (2013) attributed over-indebtedness to individuals that make sub-optimal decisions when they are irrational and are guided by feelings, heuristics, or mental shortcuts. To describe the habit of the persons, Schicks (2010) also added that some people find it hard to change their habits (habit persistence), while others tend to focus exclusively on the short term (who constantly live in a precarious situation).

2.5.3 Causes of over-indebtedness: Socio-demographic factors

The socio-demographic and economic characteristics of borrowers also contribute towards over-indebtedness. Demographic factors including age, education, and income levels were found to have lower explanatory power to explain household debt relative to psychological factors (Cosma & Pattarin, 2010; Livingstone & Lunt, 1992; Wang et al., 2011). Stearns (1991) describes some factors that increases the input prices, for example, natural disasters and changes in the government's tax policy, which could be attributed to increases in over-indebtedness. These events or shocks to income can be viewed as passive factors, which are beyond the control of the household. Other factors include economic and political crises, and fluctuations in the foreign currency markets, low income, low wealth, income instability, and low return on investment on which the loan is used (Anderloni & Vandone, 2008; Del-Rio & Young, 2005; Disney, Bridges, & Gathergood, 2008; Gonzalez, 2008; Webley & Nyhus, 2001).

For socio-demographic factors, research based on various countries, time periods and target groups often show differing findings. Age and income are the most common variables that are measured in previous studies. The highest risk groups are those in their 30s, followed by the age groups before or after them (Anderloni & Vandone, 2008). However, the chances of being in financial difficulty tend to exist for younger property holders, while young people living in their parent's home are less likely to face this issue. As age increases from 40 and above, over-indebtedness decreases either due to having sufficient incomes to cover household expenditure or due to more conservative behaviour towards being in debt. Although the life-cycle theory postulates that debt should decrease with age, empirical results are mixed. While Lea et al. (1993) and Livingstone and Lunt (1992) support this claim, Davies and Lea (1995) found the opposite, in which older people are more likely to be heavily indebted. Daud, Marzuki, Ahmad, and Kefeli (2019) and Keese (2012) found that younger people perceive their indebtedness as significantly lower, while those over 45 have a tendency to have more debt. Keese (2012) also found that young people under 30 take a lighter view of their debt burden compared to the heads of families aged over 45. This indicates that the heads of families take the debt burden seriously in order for other family members to be less affected by it. On the other hand, Flores and Vieira (2014) and Sevim, Temizel, and Sayilir (2012) found that people aged below 30 have higher levels of debt, while Ponchio (2006) found that older people are less likely to be indebted.

While it is logical to expect debt to be negatively related to income, research has instead found that debt varies positively with income. Debt has evolved from being a signal of poverty to a signal of prosperity (Katona, 1975). It is also true that as one's income increases, the probability of default decreases; thus, they are able to borrow larger amounts. Those who are employed and with higher incomes are more likely to borrow as they have wider opportunities to obtain credit and can benefit from better economic and financial terms such as the rate they can borrow and length of loan contracts. They are also better equipped to face challenging life events. However, those who are less creditworthy often have to access more expensive credit conditions. Sudden unemployment is a common reason one falls into over-indebtedness. Generally, most households that are inactive economically due to retirement or long-term unemployment resort to less borrowing. In other words, empirical evidence shows that over-indebted people are usually employed rather than self-employed or retired (Anderloni & Vandone, 2008).

According to the CGAP (2011), debt-to-income ratios are very intuitive. It is mentioned that wealthier families can easily tolerate debt, but it is devastating for low-income families. Measuring default is also not perfect, as default does not directly measure over-indebtedness, and can also be difficult to distinguish "accidental" defaults produced by external unexpected shocks from people who choose not to pay their debts on purpose. Schicks (2013) pointed out that lenders should not over-lend; otherwise, these loans will be at risk of late or missed instalment payments. Some other costs will increase the risk of creditworthiness assessment as higher interest rates and fees will specifically create "bad borrowers."

Other socio-demographic factors that may have an influence on indebtedness include the number of dependents, gender, and unexpected life changes. Life changes can lead to financial difficulties. These refer to increasing number of dependents, health shocks, family breakdowns such as separation or divorce, death, or disability of either spouses in the household. Although it is generally assumed that households with more children or dependents are more indebted to cover their cost of living, some studies have found that households with more children tend to have lower debt (Livingstone & Lunt, 1992). Fletschner and Mesbah (2011) and Farrar, Moizer, Lean, and Hyde (2019) found gender and financial literacy to be significantly related, in which women are less financially informed compared to men, although this is significantly improved with better education, wealth, and spousal encouragement. Hsu (2016) also found that women increase their financial literacy when their spouses begin losing cognitive skills. However, Ponchio (2006) and Lin, Revindo, Gan, and Cohen (2019) found that men are not more favourable to debt compared to women, while Flores and Vieira (2014) found that women are less favourable to debt than men.

2.5.4 Consequences of over-indebtedness on psychological welfare

Over-indebtedness may affect an individual or household's health due to several reasons. Debt troubles are linked to lower self-esteem, more negative view on life, and mental health issues due to depression, severe anxiety, and hostility (Bridges & Disney, 2010; Fitch, Chaplin, Trend, & Collard, 2007). Financial hardship constraints rational behaviour and can lead to unhealthy behaviours including too much drinking, smoking, and high calorie intake (Averett & Smith, 2014; Wardle, Chida, Gibson, Whitaker & Steptoe, 2012).

The issue of over-indebtedness basically creates hopelessness, with a relationship between financial stress and suicide. Brown and Taylor's (2008) findings from the British Household Panel Survey showed that debt has important costs on the head of household's psychological well-being. Similarly, Bridges and Disney (2010) found that financial problems cause more suicide attempts than other psychological conditions, with the exception of depression. Since 2008, suicide rates have been rising in the EU when the eurozone went into a recession, mainly in countries where the financial crisis is most severe (Gili, Roca, Basu, McKee, & Stuckler, 2012).

However, Gathergood (2012) found that individuals experiencing indebtedness problems living in areas where bankruptcy rates are more common suffer less problems with their mental well-being. In other words, the psychological effect of their debt problem is less severe for people who live in areas in which over-indebtedness is more prevalent. Perhaps this could be due to "herd mentality," whereby people are content with their situation, even if it is bad, when others around them are in a similar position.

2.5.5 Consequences of over-indebtedness on socio-economic welfare

Increases in consumer indebtedness cause concerns from an economic and social perspective. Over-indebtedness is a problem for people as they are in economic distress that they are unable to escape from. It is first a social issue that can be measured by the number of individuals affected and the degree of their difficulty. Additionally, it is also an economic issue as it affects financial intermediaries and, thus, the stability of the wider financial system – which can be measured by the quantity of debt and the size of collateral backing those loans (D'Alessio & Iezzi, 2013). Authorities focus on over-indebtedness as the sustainability of households' indebtedness will affect financial system stability. In terms of the social impact, excessive debt accumulation causes households' liquidity constraints which then leads to a decline in households' social and economic well-being. Over time, this may lead to social exclusion and poverty.

According to Schicks (2013), the drivers of over-indebtedness can be external and are either lender-related or borrower-related. Negative shocks to income or expenses are one of the external factors that can make one's debt situation spin out of control. Additionally, institutional and legal frameworks can be used to control lenders and borrower's behaviour and can lower the risk of over-indebtedness. In many countries, there is no provision to protect borrowers from the issue of over-indebtedness due to the weak institutional protection measures, and lenders are made responsible for this issue. Elevated levels of competition among financial institutions are also responsible for this increase in over-indebtedness. On the other hand, the presence of credit bureaus would reduce this risk to some extent. Anderloni and Vandone (2008) and Vandone (2009) suggested that free flow of market information, an efficient judicial system, and the availability of affordable credit alternatives are vital in alleviating the phenomenon.

Therefore, from the above literature, it is understandable that over-indebtedness is a very critical issue that demands further understanding. Many scholars argue that this is a complex social issue, which is linked to many social phenomena of an individual or household. This has a very unusual effect on the borrower's life and their well-being. The above-mentioned literature attribute individuals or household behaviour to being over-indebted through consumer loans and the depression that arises from such situation may even lead one to commit suicide.

2.6 Policy recommendations

Over-indebtedness is a complex phenomenon and structural in nature. Over-indebtedness is also a social issue. As such, it is important for policymakers to study and understand the main reasons why households live in a situation of being disadvantaged. Although over-indebtedness is usually viewed as an issue at an individual or household level, it could eventually lead to economic instability. The role of over-indebtedness on economic growth, financial crises, and unemployment has therefore received increased policy attention (IMF, 2012; 2017).

The policy response to tackle the issue of over-indebtedness should be focused on two main aspects:

1   To prevent over-indebtedness
2   To alleviate over-indebtedness

As the popular saying goes, prevention is better than cure; so more effort should be expanded on prevention measures. Policies to prevent over-indebtedness should include responsible lending, responsible borrowing, and smart money management. Responsible lending legislation and regulation are already implemented by financial institutions regulated by BNM. However, informal finance providers should be brought more in-line with these responsible lending practices. Perhaps information from credit reporting agencies can be made available to them to prevent over-lending from occurring. Part of responsible lending should also include ensuring lenders have policies in place to work out suitable payment schedules for those in payment arrears. There should be some level of protection of dignity and minimum living standards for the borrowers. Other policy responses that can be considered to encourage responsible lending include ensuring that credit is affordable and more effort is being put into policing illegal lending/loan sharks.

Non-bank lenders (including money lenders and credit co-operatives) have contributed around 20% of total household debt and was the main driver for the increasing level of household debt. The main form of debt from these lenders are in the form of unsecured financing. They also typically target borrowers from the lower income group or those with weaker credit ratings that may have difficulties getting loans from a bank. Hence, more oversight is needed in this NBFI segment to safeguard borrowers' well-being.

The largest component of household debt is made up of residential mortgages. There is an increasing discrepancy between new home prices and borrowers' actual affordability (BNM, 2017). In the worst affected parts of Malaysia, the median house price is more than five times the annual median household income. This imbalance has led to increasing levels of borrowings by households to purchase a home. Apart from policy efforts to expand affordable housing projects, renting should also be promoted as a viable alternative for households.[14]

Financial literacy programmes can inculcate responsible borrowing and smart money management skills. Better understanding of financial numeracy should start from young. School activities can incorporate different money management skills tailored to various age groups. Of course, financial literacy programmes should also be offered to the general public and especially to those in lower income households. Opportunities to harness financial technologies (fintech) to broaden the reach of financial literacy, as well as affordable and accessible alternative credit facilities, should be explored.

Policymakers and researchers have recognised that one of the main determinants of consumers' financial vulnerabilities is financial illiteracy. According to the S&P Global Financial Literacy Survey,[15] Malaysians have low financial literacy, at only 36%. Credit products, many of which carry high interest rates and complex terms, are becoming more readily available. However, many borrowers do not fully understand how fast interest compounding can increase the total amount owed, and this puts them at risk of over-indebtedness, loan defaults, or bankruptcies. The survey found these risks are even higher for women, the poor, and the less educated as they suffer from lower levels of financial literacy. As such, it is imperative that policymakers build strong consumer protection regimes to safeguard households from financial abuse and ensure lenders behave fairly and responsibly towards their customers. As such, although financial literacy programmes can be costly, the consequences of illiteracy more than outweigh it.

However, once someone is already deep in debt, curative measures are required instead, and policies to alleviate over-indebtedness should be made available to help them get out of that situation so that they can continue to be productive members of the society. Debt counselling services should be expanded and be made available at a minimal cost or better still, free of charge, as over-indebted borrowers are unlikely to have excess financial means to pay for these services. To this end, AKPK has been providing free one-on-one counselling service on budgeting, money management, and credit-related issues to provide guidance to those facing financial constraints on how to handle their debts responsibly. AKPK's Debt Management Programme (DMP) aims to work out a personalised debt repayment plan, and those enrolled in the programme are protected from legal action and harassment from debt collecting agencies. However, AKPK's DMP only covers debt services provided by financial institutions governed by BNM who are not yet declared bankrupt. Perhaps such arrangements can be extended to those indebted to informal lenders too in the future.

Additionally, bankruptcy procedures can also be reviewed to be brought more in-line with the current best practices around the world. There should be a balance between protecting the interests of lenders and safeguarding the future of borrowers. Current bankruptcy rules in Malaysia seem to be lopsided to be in favour of the lenders. Perhaps some form of non-judicial process can also be put in place to complement bankruptcy proceedings.

Notes

1 Commercial banks charge their customers lending rates relative to their BLR (which could be some percentage higher or lower than the BLR). A bank's BLR differs from other banks depending on their cost of funds.
2 BNM cut interest rates by 25 basis points to 3% to spur economic growth as inflation declines and risk from financial imbalances subsides (*Financial Times*, 13 July 2016) www.ft.com/content/22ea1100-f423-335b-9a10-cf42aa4f2086
3 CTOS is Malaysia's leading credit reporting agency regulated under the Credit Reporting Agencies Act 2010. The CCRIS report is generated by the Credit Bureau, which is an agency set up by BNM.
4 Findings from AKPK through its Debt Management Programme show a rising trend for borrowers in this income group to default due to weak financial management and planning (BNM, 2018).
5 www.kwsp.gov.my/documents/20126/131635/Panduan_Belanjawanku.pdf/
6 The Credit Counselling and Debt Management Agency (also known as Agensi Kaunseling dan Pengurusan Kredit, AKPK) is an agency set up by BNM in April 2006 to assist individuals in managing their debt positions.
7 A debtor can be declared a bankrupt by the High Court (subject to an Adjudication Order Section 3(3) of the Insolvency Act 1967) if he is unable to settle debts of at least RM50,000 within six months prior of the creditor's petition. A debtor can also submit a petition to make himself bankrupt to protect himself from his creditors' claim that he cannot settle. In this case, no minimum amount of debt owed is required before a debtor's petition can be submitted.
8 A debt consolidation is meant to simplify multiple debts by pooling them into a single facility. The borrower can then repay them at a lower interest rate and longer tenure and thereby save on monthly instalments.
9 www.bnm.gov.my/index.php?ch=57&pg=144&ac=811&bb=file
10 The list of approved licensed financial institutions operating in Malaysia can be obtained from BNM website at www.bnm.gov.my
11 More details on AIA's fixed rate home loans can be found at www.aia.com.my/en/our-products/home-protection/home-loans.html
12 For a list of licensed co-operatives, visit SKM website at www.skm.gov.my
13 The first Islamic pawnbroking entity was *Muasasah Gadaian Islam Terengganu (MGIT)*, followed by *Koperasi Permodalan Kelantan (now Permodalan Kelantan Berhad, PKB)*. Both began their operations in 1992. At present, Ar Rahnu operators include banks and NBFIs, state-linked companies such as MGIT and PKB, and cooperatives such as Yayasan Pembangunan Ekonomi Islam Malaysia (YAPEIM).
14 Residential Rental Act together with the Tenancy Tribunal was formulated by the government under Budget 2018 to provide better safeguards to renters. To spur the rental market, a 50% tax exemption from residential property rental income up to RM2,000 from 2018 to 2020 was also introduced.
15 https://gflec.org/wp-content/uploads/2015/11/3313-Finlit_Report_FINAL-5.11.16.pdf?x47626

References

Abdul Ghani, N. (2010). Household indebtedness and its implications for financial stability in Malaysia. In Chapter 3, *Household Indebtedness and Its Implications for Financial Stability*. The South East Asian Central Banks (SEACEN), Research and Training Centre, Kuala Lumpur.

Anderloni, L. & Vandone, D. (2008). *Households Over-Indebtedness in the Economic Literature*. Working Paper n2008-46, Dipartimento di Scienze Economiche Aziendali e Statistiche, Universiti Degli Studi di Milano.

Averett, S.L. & Smith, J.K. (2014). Financial hardship and obesity. *Economics and Human Biology, 15*, 201–212.

Azma, N., Rahman, M., Adeyemi, A.A., & Rahman, M.K. (2019). Propensity toward indebtedness: Evidence from Malaysia. *Review of Behavioral Finance, 11*, 188–200.

Bandura, A. (1989). Human agency in social cognitive theory. *American Psychologist, 44*(9), 1175–1184.

Banerjee, A. & Mullainathan, S. (2010). The shape of temptation: Implications for the economic lives of the poor. *NBER Working Paper Series*, No. 15973, National Bureau of Economic Research (NBER), Cambridge, MA.

Bank Negara Malaysia (BNM). (2016). Looking Beyond Headline Household Debt Statistics, in Financial Stability and Payment Systems Report, *Risk Developments and Assessment of Financial Stability in 2016*, BNM.

Bank Negara Malaysia (BNM). (2017). Imbalances in the Property Market, 3rd Quarter 2017, *Quarterly Bulletin*, 26–32.

Bank Negara Malaysia (BNM). (2018). *Indebted to Debt: An Assessment of Debt Levels and Financial Buffers of Households*, March, BNM.

Bank Negara Malaysia (*n.d.*). Malaysia's short-term interest rates (Overnight Policy Rate). Retrieved on 26 April 2020 from www.bnm.gov.my

Barberis, N.C. (2013). Thirty years of prospect theory in economics: A review and assessment. *Journal of Economic Perspectives, 27*(1), 173–196.

Barberis. N. & Xiong, W. (2012). Realization utility. *Journal of Financial Economics. 104*(2), 251–271.

Bernheim, B.D., Ray, D., & Yeltekin, S. (2013). Poverty and self-control. *NBER Working Paper Series*, No. 18742, National Bureau of Economic Research (NBER), Cambridge, MA.

Bernthal, M.J., Crockett, D., & Rose, R. (2005). Credit cards as lifestyle facilitators. *Journal of Consumer Research, 32*(1), 130–145.

Betti, G., Dourmashkin, N., Rossi, M., & Yin, Y.P. (2007). Consumer overindebtedness in the EU: Measurement and characteristics. *Journal of Economics Studies, 34*(2), 136–156.

Bridges, S. & Disney, R. (2010). Debt and depression. *Journal of Health Economics, 29*(3), 388–403.

Brown, S. & Taylor, K. (2008). Household debt and financial assets: Evidence from Germany, Great Britain and the United States. *Journal of the Royal Statistical Society, 171*(3), 615–643.

Bucks, B. & Pence, K. (2008). Do borrowers know their mortgage terms? *Journal of Urban Economics*, Elsevier Inc., *64*(2), 218–233.

Census and Economic Information Center (CEIC). (*n.d.*). Household Debt-to-GDP, Malaysia's Household Debt-to-Nominal GDP, Malaysia's Total Household Debt. Retrieved on 14 March 2020 from www.ceicdata.com

Chatterjee, D., Kumar, M., & Dayma, K.K. (2019). Income security, social comparisons and materialism. *International Journal of Bank Marketing, 37*, 1041–1061.

Cobb-Clark, D.A., Kassenboehmer, S.C., & Sinning, M.G. (2016). Locus of control and savings. *Journal of Banking and Finance*, doi:10.1016/j.jbankfin.2016.06.013

Consultative Group to Assist the Poor (CGAP). (2011). *Too Much Microcredit? A Survey on the Evidence of Over-Indebtedness*, Occasional Paper No. 19. Retrieved on 15 March 2020 from: www.cgap.org/sites/default/files/CGAP-Occasional-PaperToo-Much-Microcredit-A-Survey-of-the-Evidence-on-Overindebtedness-Sep-2011.pdf

Cosma, S. & Pattarin, F. (2010). Attitudes, personality factors and household debt decisions: A study of consumer credit. Retrieved on 16 March 2020 from http://dx.doi.org/10.2139/ssrn.1685765

D'Alessio, G. & Iezzi, S. (2013). Households over-indebtedness: Definition and measurement with Italian data. *Bank of Italy Occasional Paper*, no. 149, Rome.

Darriet, E., Guille, M., Vergnaud, J.-C., & Shimizu, M. (2020). Money illusion, financial literacy and numeracy: Experimental evidence. *Journal of Economic Psychology*, *76*, 102–211.

Daud, S.N.M., Marzuki, A., Ahmad, N., & Kefeli, Z. (2019). Financial vulnerability and its determinants: Survey evidence from Malaysian households. *Emerging Markets Finance and Trade*, *55*, 1991–2003.

Davies, E. & Lea, S.E.G. (1995). Student attitudes to student debt. *Journal of Economic Psychology*, *16*(4), 663–679.

Del-Rio, A. & Young, G. (2005). The impact of unsecured debt on financial distress among British households. *Bank of England Working Paper*, No. 262, London: Bank of England.

Disney, R. & Gathergood, J. (2011). Financial literacy and indebtedness: New evidence from UK consumers. *EconPapers*. Retrieved from: http://econpapers.repec,org/paper/notnotcfc/11_2f05

Disney, R., & Gathergood, J. (2013). Financial literacy and consumer credit portfolios. *Journal of Banking & Finance*, *37*(7), 2246–2254.

Disney, R., Bridges, S., & Gathergood, J. (2008). Drivers of over-indebtedness, *Report to the Department of Business, Enterprise and Regulatory Reform*, Center for Policy Evaluation, University of Nottingham.

dos Santos, C.P. & Fernandes, D.V.D.H. (2011). A Socializacao de Consumo e a Formacao do Materialismo Entre os Adolescents. RAM, *Revista de Administracao Mackenzie*, *12*, 169–203.

Duesenberry, J.S. (1949). *Income, Saving and the Theory of Consumer Behavior*. Cambridge, MA: Harvard University Press.

Eberhardt, W., de Bruin, W.B., & Strough, J. (2019). Age differences in financial decision making: The benefits of more experience and less negative emotions. *Journal of Behavioral Decision Making*, *32*(1), 79–93.

Elliot, V. & Lindblom, T. (2019). Indebtedness, over-indebtedness and wellbeing. In *Indebtedness in Early Adulthood: Causes and Remedies*, Chapter 2, 21–48, Springer, doi:10.1007/978-3-030-13996-4_2

Endut, N. & Toh, G.H. (2009). Household debt in Malaysia. *BIS Papers*, *46*, 67–86, May.

European Commission. (2008). *Towards a Common Operational European Definition of Over-Indebtedness*. EU.

Farrar, S., Moizer, J., Lean, J., & Hyde, M. (2019). Gender, financial literacy, and preretirement planning in the UK. *Journal of Women and Aging*, *31*, 319–339.

Fitch, C., Chaplin R., Trend, C., & Collard, S. (2007), Debt and mental health: The role of psychiatrists. *Advances in Psychiatric Treatment*, *13*, 194–202.

Fletschner, D. & Mesbah, D. (2011). Gender disparity in access to information: Do spouses share what they know? *World Development, 39*, 1422–1433.

Flores, S.A.M. & Vieira, K.M. (2014). Propensity toward indebtedness: An analysis using behavioral factors. *Journal of Behavioral and Experimental Finance, 3*, 1–10.

Frazzini, A. (2006). The disposition effect and underreaction to news. *Journal of Finance, 61*(4), 2017–2046.

Friedman, M. (1957). The permanent income hypothesis: Comment. *American Economic Review, 48*, 990–991.

Gathergood, J. (2012). Self-control, financial literacy and consumer over-indebtedness. *Journal of Economic Psychology, 33*(3), 590–602.

Gerardi, K., Goette, L., & Meier, S. (2013). Numerical ability predicts mortgage default. *Proceedings of the National Academy of Sciences, 110*, 11267–11271.

Gili, M., Roca, M., Basu, S., McKee, M., & Stuckler, D. (2012). The mental health risks of economic crisis in spain: Evidence from primary care centres 2006 and 2010. *The European Journal of Public Health, 23*(10), 103–108.

Gonzalez, A. (2008). *Microfinance, Incentives to Repay and Overindebtedness: Evidence from a Household Survey in Bolivia*, PhD Dissertation, Ohio State University, Columbus.

Grohmann, A., Menkhoff, L., Merkle, C., & Schmacker, R. (2019). Earn more tomorrow: Overconfident income expectations and consumer indebtedness. *Rationality & Competition* CRC TRR 190, Discussion Paper No. 152.

Guiso, L. & Jappelli, T. (2008). Financial literacy and portfolio diversification. CSEF Working Papers 212, *Centre for Studies in Economics and Finance (CSEF)*, University of Naples, Italy.

Haas, O.J. (2006). Over-indebtedness in Germany, employment section. *Social Finance Program Working Paper*, No.44, International Labour Office (ILO), Geneva.

Hartley, C.A. & Phelps, E.A. (2012). Anxiety and decision-making. *Biological Psychiatry, 72*(2), 113–118.

Hayhoe, C.R., Leach, L., & Turner, P. (1999). Discriminating the number of credit cards held by college students using credit and money attitudes. *Journal of Economic Psychology, 20*(6), 643–656.

Hsu, J.W. (2016). Aging and strategic learning: The impact of spousal incentives on financial literacy. *Journal of Human Resources, 51*(4), 1036–1067.

Hyytinen, A. & Putkuri, H. (2018). Household optimism and overborrowing. *Journal of Money, Credit and Banking, 50*(1), 55–76.

International Monetary Fund (IMF). (2012). Dealing with household debt. In *World Economic Outlook: Growth Resuming, Dangers Remain*. Chapter 3, 89–124. IMF.

International Monetary Fund (IMF). (2017). Household debt and financial stability. In *Global Financial Stability Report: Is Growth at Risk?* Chapter 2, 53–89. IMF.

Kahneman, D. & Tversky, A. (1979). Prospect theory: An analysis of decision under risk. *Econometrica, 47*(2), 263–291.

Kalwij, A., Alessie, R., Dinkova, M., Schonewille, G., Van der Schors, A., & Van der Werf, M. (2019). The effects of financial education on financial literacy and savings behavior: Evidence from a controlled field experiment in dutch primary schools. *Journal of Consumer Affairs, 53*, 699–730.

Katona, G. (1975). *Psychological Economics*. New York: Elsevier.

Keese, M. (2012). Who feels constrained by high debt burdens? Subjective vs. objective measures of household debt. *Journal of Economic Psychology, 33*, 125–141.

Kilborn, J.J. (2005). Behavioural economics, overindebtedness and comparative consumer bankruptcy: Searching for causes and evaluating solutions. *Emory Bankruptcy Developments Journal, 22*, 13–45.

Lea, S.E.G, Webley, P., & Walker, C.M. (1995). Psychological factors in consumer debt: Money management, economic socialization and credit. *Journal of Economic Psychology*, *16*(4), 681–701.

Lea, S.E.G., Webley, P., & Levine, R.M. (1993). The economic psychology of consumer debt. *Journal of Economic Psychology*, *14*(1), 85–119.

Lin, L., Revindo, M.D., Gan, C., & Cohen, D.A. (2019). Determinants of credit card spending and debt of chinese customers. *International Journal of Bank Marketing*, *37*, 545–564.

Livingstone, S.M., & Lunt, P.K. (1992). Predicting personal debt and debt repayment: Psychological, social and economic determinants. *Journal of Economic Psychology*, *13*(1), 111–134.

Loewenstein, G. & Prelec, D. (1992). Anomalies in intertemporal choice: Evidence and an interpretation. *Quarterly Journal of Economics*, *107*(2), 573–597.

Lombardi, M. Mohanty, M., & Shim, I. (2017). The real effects of household debt in the short and long run, *Bank for International Settlements (BIS) Working Paper*, No. 607, January.

Lusardi, A. & de Bassa Scheresberg, C. (2013). Financial literacy and high-cost borrowing in the United States, *NBER Working Paper Series*, No. 18969, doi:10.1017/CBO9781107415324.004.

Lusardi, A. & Mitchell, O.S. (2007). Baby boomer retirement security: The roles of planning, financial literacy and housing wealth. *Journal of Monetary Economics*, *54*(1), 205–224.

Lusardi, A. & Mitchell, O.S. (2014). The economic importance of financial literacy: Theory and evidence. *Journal of Economic Literature*, *52*(1), 5–44.

Lusardi, A., Michaud, P.C., & Mitchell, O.S. (2013). Optimal financial knowledge and wealth inequality, *NBER Working Papers Series*, No. 18669, National Bureau of Economic Research (NBER), Cambridge, MA.

Lusardi, A., Schneider, D.J., & Tufano, P. (2011). Financially fragile households: Evidence and implications. *Brookings Papers on Economic Activity*, Spring, 83–134.

Malaysian Administrative Modernisation and Management Planning Unit (MAMPU) (*n.d.*). Number of Bankruptcies in Malaysia. Retrieved on 25 April 2020 from www.data.gov.my

Malaysian Department of Insolvency (*n.d.*). Malaysian Bankruptcy by Type of Debt, Type of Employment, Age Group, Gender and Ethnic Groups. Retrieved on 25 April 2020 from www.mdi.gov.my

Mann, D., Chidambarathanu, N., Caparusso, J., & Chandra, P. (2013). *Asia Leverage Uncovered*. London: Standard Chartered.

Mastrobuoni, G. & Weinberg, M. (2009). Heterogeneity in intra-monthly consumption patterns, self-control, and savings at retirement. *American Economic Journal: Economic Policy*, *1*(2), 163–89.

McLeod, S.A. (2008). *Social Roles, Simply Psychology*. Retrieved on 25 April 2020 from: www.simplypsychology.org/social-roles.html

Meier, S. & Sprenger, C. (2007). Impatience and credit behavior: Evidence from a field experiment. *Centre for Behavioral Economics and Decision Making, Federal Reserve Bank of Boston*, Working Paper No. 07-3.

Mishra, M. & Mishra, S. (2016). Financial risk tolerance among Indian investors: A multiple discriminant modeling of determinants. *Strategic Change*, *25*, 485–500.

Modigliani, F. & Brumberg, R.H. (1954). Utility analysis and the consumption function: An interpretation of cross-section data, in Kurihara, K.K. ed, *Post-Keynesian Economics*, New Brunswick, NJ, Rutgers University Press, 388–436.

Modigliani, F. & Brumberg, R.H. (1990). Utility analysis and aggregate consumption functions: An attempt at integration, in Abel, A. ed, *The Collected Papers of Franco Modigliani: Volume 2, The Life Cycle Hypothesis of Saving*, Cambridge, MA: MIT Press, 128–197.

Modigliani, F. (1986). Life cycle, individual thrift, and the wealth of nations. *The American Economic Review, 76*(3), 297–313.

Munoz-Murillo, M., Alvarez-Franco, P.B., & Restrepo-Tobon, D.A. (2020). The role of cognitive abilities on financial literacy: New experimental evidence. *Journal of Behavioral and Experimental Economics, 84,* 101–482.

Odean, T. (1998). Are investors reluctant to realize their losses? *Journal of Finance. 53*(5), 1775–1798.

OECD International Network of Financial Education (OECD INFE) (2011). *Measuring Financial Literacy: Questionnaire and Guidance Notes for Conducting an Internationally Comparable Survey of Financial Literacy.* Paris: OECD.

Okech, D., Mimura, Y., Mauldin, T., & Kim, J. (2013). The influence of financial factors on motivation to save among poor individuals. *Journal of Policy Practice, 12,* 107–124.

Oxera. (2004). *Are UK Households Over-Indebted?* Commissioned by the Association for Payment Clearing Services, British Bankers Association, Consumer Credit Association and the Finance and Leasing Association.

Perry, V. & Morris, M. (2005). Who is in control? The role of self-perception, knowledge and income in explaining consumer financial behavior. *Journal of Consumer Affairs, 39,* 299–313.

Ponchio, M.C. (2006). *The Influence of Materialism on Consumption Indebtedness in the Context of Low Income Consumers from the City of Sao Paulo.* PhD Thesis, Escola de Administracao de Empresas de Sao Paulo, Bela Vista, Brazil.

Rahman, M., Azma, N., Masud, M.A.K., & Ismail, Y. (2020). Determinant of indebtedness: Influence of behavioral and demographic factors. *International Journal of Financial Studies, 8*(8), 1–13.

Richins, M.L. & Dawson, S. (1992). Consumer values orientation for materialism and its measurement: Scale development and validation. *The Journal of Consumer Research, 19,* 303–316.

Rosenbaum, M. (1980). A schedule for assessing self-control behaviors: Preliminary findings. *Behavior Therapy, 11*(1), 109–121.

Schicks, J. (2010). Microfinance over-indebtedness: Understanding its drivers and challenging the common myths. *Centre Emile Bernheim (CEB) Working Paper, 10,* 047.

Schicks, J. (2013). The definition and causes of microfinance over-indebtedness: A customer protection point of view. *Oxford Development Studies, 41*(1), 95–116.

Sevim, N., Temizel, F., & Sayilir, O. (2012). The effects of financial literacy on the borrowing behavior of turkish financial consumers. *International Journal of Consumer Studies, 35,* 573–579.

Shefrin, H.M. & Thaler, R.H. (1988). The behavioral life-cycle hypothesis. *Economic Inquiry, 26*(4), 609–643.

Simon, H. (1956). Rational choice and the structure of the environment. *Psychological Review, 63,* 129–138.

Smith, A. (1776). *An Inquiry into the Nature and Causes of the Wealth of Nations.* Petersfield, Hampshire: Harriman House Ltd.

Smith, J.P., McArdle, J.J., & Willis, R. (2010). Financial decision making and cognition in a family context. *Economic Journal, 120,* F363-F380.

Souleles, N.S. (2004). Expectations, heterogenous forecast errors, and consumption: Micro evidence from the michigan consumer sentiment surveys. *Journal of Money, Credit and Banking*, *36*(1), 39–72.

Stango, V. & Zinman, J. (2009). Exponential growth bias and household finance. *The Journal of Finance*, *64*(6), 2807–2849.

Stearns, K. (1991). The Hidden Beast: Delinquency in Microenterprise Credit Programs. *Discussion Paper Series* 5, Washington, DC: ACCION International.

Tekçe, B. (2013). What Factors Affect Behavioral Biases? Evidence from Turkish Individual Stock Investors. Retrieved on 16 March 2020 from www.unicreditanduniversities.eu/uploads/assets/UniCRedit_BPA_4th_ed/WhatFactorsAffect BehavioralBiasesEvidencefromTurkishIndividualStockInvestors_Bulent_Tekce.pdf

Thaler, R.H. & Sunstein, C.R. (2008). *Nudge: Improving Decisions about Health, Wealth and Happiness*. New Haven, CT: Yale University Press.

Thaler, R.H. (1985). Mental accounting and consumer choice. *Marketing Science*, *4*(3), 199–214.

The World Bank (*n.d.*). Inflation. Retrieved on 25 April 2020 from https://data.world bank.org

Trading Economics (*n.d.*). Wages. Retrieved on 25 April 2020 from https://tradinge conomics.com

van Rooij, M., Lusardi, A., & Alessie, R. (2011). Financial literacy and stock market participation. *Journal of Financial Economics*, *101*(2), 449–472.

Vandone, D. (2009). *Consumer Credit in Europe: Risks and Opportunities of a Dynamic Industry*. Berlin: Springer-Verlag.

Veblen, T.B. (1899). *The Theory of the Leisure Class: An Economic Study in the Evolution of Institutions*. Macmillan.

Vitt, L.A. (2004). Consumers' financial decisions and the psychology of values. *Journal of Financial Service Professionals*, *58*, 68–77.

Wang, L., Wei, L., & Jiang, L. (2011). The Impact of attitude variables on the credit card behavior. *Nankai Business Review International*, *2*(2), 120–139.

Ward, A.F. & Lynch Jr., J.G. (2019). On the need-to-know basis: How the distribution of responsibility between couples shapes financial literacy and financial outcomes. *Journal of Consumer Research*, *45*, 1013–1036.

Wardle, J., Chida, Y., Gibson, E.L., Whitaker, K.L., & Steptoe, A. (2012). Stress and adiposity: A meta-analysis of longitudinal studies. *Obesity*, *19*(4), 771–778.

Watson, J. (2003). The relationship of materialism to spending tendencies, saving and debt. *Journal of Economic Psychology*, *24*, 723–739.

Webley, P. & Nyhus, E.K. (2001). Life-cycle and disproportionate routes into problem debt. *British Journal of Psychology*, *92*, 423–446.

World Development Indicators (WDI) (*n.d.*). Gross Domestic Product. Retrieved 25 April 2020 from https://data.worldbank.org/wdi

Xiao, J.J., Noring, F.E. & Anderson, J.G. (1995). College students' attitudes towards credit cards. *Journal of Consumer Studies and Home Economics*, *19*(2), 155–174.

Zainudin, R., Mahdzan, N.S., & Yeap, M.Y. (2019). Determinants of credit card misuse among gen y consumers in Urban Malaysia. *International Journal of Bank Marketing*, *37*(5), 1350–1370.

Zakaria, R.H., Jaafar, N.I.M., & Ishak, N.A. (2016). Household debt decision: Poverty or psychology? *International Journal of Business and Society*, *18*(3), 515–532.

Zhu, L.Y. & Meeks, C.B. (1994) Effects of low income families' ability and willingness to use consumer credit on subsequent outstanding credit balances. *Journal of Consumer Affairs*, *28*(2), https://doi.org/10.1111/j.1745-6606.1994.tb00859.x

3 Will Malaysians retire in contentment or misery?

Financial behaviour issues approaching old age

3.0 Introduction

The second issue on consumer financial vulnerability explored in this book is the issue of retirement savings inadequacy. This is an issue that has long been debated globally as well as domestically in Malaysia. Reports by the Employees' Provident Fund (EPF, 2015) suggested that most Malaysians are not saving enough, hence, are at risk of having insufficient retirement savings and possibly falling below the poverty line (*The Edge*, 2015). These financial impacts are severe and need to be addressed urgently as Malaysia experiences a demographic shift and moves towards becoming an aged population.

Following this introductory section, the second section in the chapter will begin by describing the scenario of demographic shifts in Malaysia, by drawing on data from the Department of Statistics Malaysia (DOSM). It will present the population pyramids in Malaysia from 2010 to 2040 and will also discuss the economic consequences of an ageing population. The third section of the chapter will deliberate on the retirement saving schemes in Malaysia, particularly the defined benefit (DB) and defined contribution (DC) plans. Under the DC plans, discussions about the EPF and Private Retirement Scheme (PRS) will be given. The fourth section of the chapter will present statistics on the declining trend of the national savings rate and also the perturbing facts on the average savings of EPF contributors. Concerns about low savings among Malaysians will also be discussed.

Consequently, the fifth section of the chapter will review the retirement planning process. The purpose of the section is to demonstrate the complexities involved in each stage of the process. Thereafter, the sixth section of this chapter will review the theoretical perspectives on retirement saving. Two theories will be discussed, which are the life-cycle theory and the behavioural life-cycle hypothesis. The seventh section will deliberate on empirical studies that have examined the issues of retirement saving and retirement planning. Finally, the chapter ends with implications for policymakers, particularly the EPF and other regulatory bodies such as the Securities Commission (SC), Malaysian Financial Planning Council (MFPC), and the financial service industries in general, on ways to address the issues of retirement preparedness and retirement savings inadequacy in Malaysia.

3.1 Retirement issues – the Malaysian scenario

3.1.1 Population ageing

Malaysia is currently experiencing a shift in its demography in which the number of its elderly population will gradually increase year by year. In the year 2020, the proportion of elderly persons aged 65 and above is estimated to reach 7.2%, and by year 2040, the percentage will double to 14.5% (Department of Statistics Malaysia, 2016a). This phenomenon is referred to as population ageing, and such situation occurs as a result of declining birth rates and increasing life expectancy – a trend which is also occurring globally. The World Health Organization (2011) suggested that an ageing population reflects a situation where the number of older adults aged 65 and above will outnumber children aged five and below. This trend has also been observed in Malaysia whereby in 2015, the Department of Statistics of Malaysia reported that the percentage of those aged 60 and above was 9.1% compared to those aged five years and below which was 8.5% (Khazanah Research Institute, 2015). Figures 3.1 through 3.3 show that between years 2014 and 2016, the population composition by age group in Malaysia has shifted towards a smaller percentage of individuals in the lower age group and a larger percentage of individuals in the higher age group. Between year 2014 and 2016, the percentage of the Malaysian population falling between ages 0 and 14 declined from 25.3% to 24.5%; the proportion of population between ages 15 and 64 slightly increased from 69% to 69.4%; and the percentage of population aged 65 and above increased from 5.6% to 6% (Department of Statistics Malaysia, 2016b). Although these changes seem marginal, the continuous downward trend could result in significant structural changes in the population over the long run. This trend is depicted in Figures 3.1 through 3.3.

Meanwhile, the median age of the Malaysian population increased from 27.4 years to 28 years between 2014 and 2016, as illustrated in Figure 3.4. An increase in the median age is also expected to persist following the shift towards an ageing population. By 2040, the median age group is expected to be 38.3 years, which is an increase of 12 years over a period of three decades (Department of Statistics, 2016).

The phenomenon of population ageing in Malaysia is depicted in the following population pyramids for the years 2010–2040 (Figures 3.5 through 3.8). The population pyramids show an increasing proportion of the elderly (aged 60 and above) and a declining portion of those aged 14 years and below.

The life expectancy of Malaysians is also on an increasing trend, as depicted in Table 3.1. The life expectancy in 1990 was 69.02 for males and 72.86 for females, and in 2017, it was 73.90 for males and 78.01 for females. While the higher life expectancy suggests improvements in medical and healthcare, it also implies higher longevity risks for the Malaysian population, hence emphasising the importance of retirement planning among Malaysians.

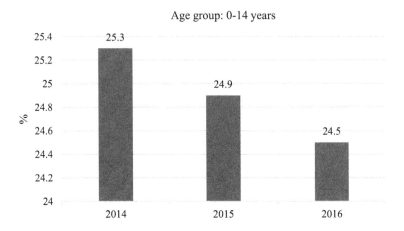

Figure 3.1 The Malaysian population composition for the age group of 0–14 years (2014–2016).

Source: Department of Statistics Malaysia (2016b).

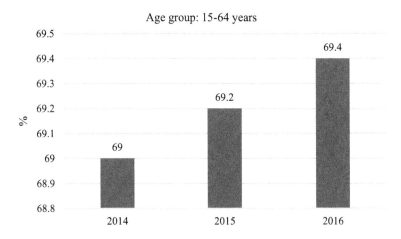

Figure 3.2 The Malaysian population composition for the age group of 15–64 years (2014–2016).

Source: Department of Statistics Malaysia (2016b).

3.1.2 Economic consequences of population ageing

The global shifts in population ageing are viewed as a historically unprecedented occurrence. Increased life expectancy implies that the need for health and long-term care for the elderly is becoming more crucial in the Malaysian scenario – and

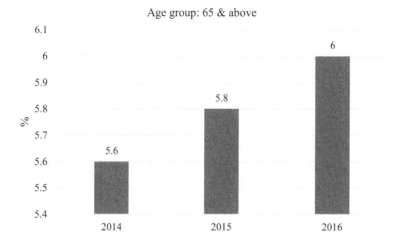

Figure 3.3 The Malaysian population composition for the age group of 65 & above (2014–2016).
Source: Department of Statistics Malaysia (2016b).

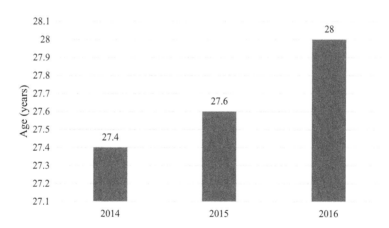

Figure 3.4 Median age of the Malaysian population (2014–2016).
Source: Department of Statistics Malaysia (2016b).

the heightened expenditures to cater for the needs of the elderly will pose a more significant burden on a smaller proportion of the population (Bloom et al., 2015).

In this vein, Malaysia's evolvement into an ageing population will have significant consequences on the nation's economy and social security system. First, an aged population means that the portion of the working-age population will decrease as the elderly will be less likely to participate in the labour force. It

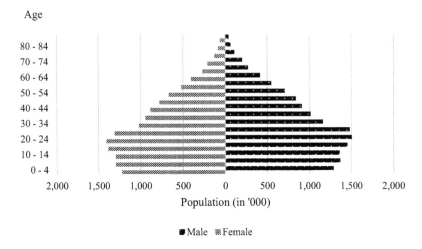

Figure 3.5 Malaysia's population pyramid for the year 2010.
Source: Department of Statistics Malaysia (*n.d.*).

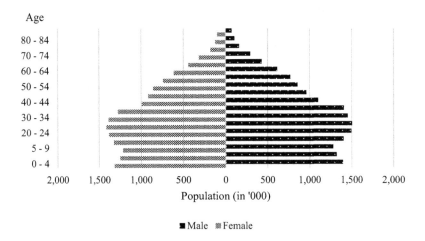

Figure 3.6 Malaysia's population pyramid for the year 2020.
Source: Department of Statistics Malaysia (*n.d.*).

can be seen from the population pyramids shown in Figures 3.5 through 3.8 that Malaysia's ageing population is expected to grow from 2010 to 2040. The lower proportion of the working-age population (those aged between 16 and 65) suggests lower productivity and economic growth for the nation (KRI, 2015). However, Bloom et al. (2015) stressed that appropriate and early strategies by

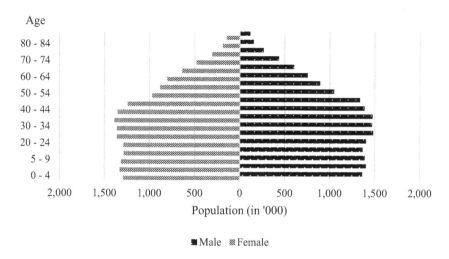

Figure 3.7 Malaysia's population pyramid for the year 2030.
Source: Department of Statistics Malaysia (*n.d.*).

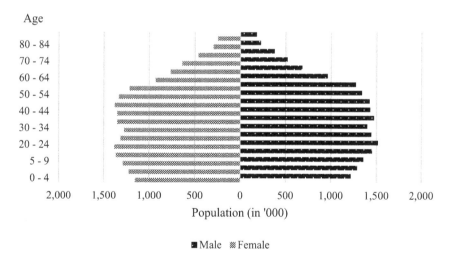

Figure 3.8 Malaysia's population pyramid for the year 2040.
Source: Department of Statistics Malaysia (*n.d.*).

governments could mitigate the effects of lower productivity and economic deceleration. For example, higher life expectancy may suggest that there may be a need to extend the retirement age as the people are healthier and are able to continue working.

Table 3.1 Life expectancy at birth for male, female, and total population in Malaysia
(1990–2017)

Year	Male	Female	Total	Year	Male	Female	Total	Year	Male	Female	Total
1990	69.02	72.86	70.87	2000	70.60	74.79	72.59	2010	72.50	76.73	74.49
1991	69.27	73.09	71.11	2001	70.77	75.00	72.78	2011	72.70	76.92	74.68
1992	69.49	73.31	71.33	2002	70.94	75.22	72.98	2012	72.90	77.11	74.88
1993	69.68	73.51	71.52	2003	71.12	75.43	73.17	2013	73.11	77.29	75.07
1994	69.84	73.69	71.69	2004	71.31	75.63	73.36	2014	73.32	77.48	75.27
1995	69.98	73.86	71.83	2005	71.51	75.82	73.56	2015	73.52	77.66	75.46
1996	70.10	74.02	71.97	2006	71.70	76.01	73.74	2016	73.72	77.84	75.65
1997	70.21	74.20	72.11	2007	71.90	76.19	73.93	2017	73.90	78.01	75.83
1998	70.33	74.38	72.26	2008	72.10	76.37	74.12				
1999	70.46	74.58	72.42	2009	72.30	76.55	74.31				

Source: World Bank (*n.d.*).

Another effect of population ageing is increased pressure on the nation's health, pension, and social protection systems. There will be a strain on public funds as more allocations will be needed to fund social protection of the elderly, while taxes collected from the working population decrease (KRI, 2015). As life expectancy expands, there will be more reliance on public funds for pensions. Increasing urbanisation will also have implications on post retirement funding. Finally, an aged population implies that the importance of the nation's health system will increase. Health deteriorations that come with ageing suggest that there will be more dependency on healthcare systems, especially for critical illnesses and life-threatening diseases. Hence, there will also be financial pressures on Malaysia's health system whereby public healthcare organisations will require more funding to support the ageing population. According to the Malaysian Department of Statistics (2016a), the dependency ratio will increase from 47.8 in 2010 to 49.5 in 2040. These statistics show that almost 50 individuals will be dependent on every 100 individuals of the working age. The issue of providing long-term healthcare systems for the elderly is a concern that the younger generation will have to deal with in their families, as they will have to care for the older generation in their family. Nonetheless, these longevity risks can be mitigated through early preparations such as adequate retirement savings and long-term insurance plans that can be implemented ahead of time.

3.2 Retirement savings schemes in Malaysia

Many countries worldwide practice dual retirement plan systems for employees – the DB plans and DC plans. According to the Malaysian Accounting Standards Board (MASB), *DB* plans are retirement plans "under which amounts to be paid as retirement benefits are determined by reference to a formula usually based on employees' earnings and/or years of service." Meanwhile, *DC* plans "are retirement benefit plans under which amounts to be paid as retirement benefits are determined by contributions to a fund together with investment earnings thereon." These plans in the context of Malaysia will be explained in the forthcoming sections.

3.2.1 Defined benefit plans

3.2.1.1 Public-sector employees

Malaysian public-sector employees with permanent employment status generally participate in the DB plan and thus are entitled to pensionable funds upon retirement. However, they are also given the option to participate in the Employees' Provident Fund (EPF) if they choose to (Public Service Department, *n.d.*). The entities responsible in managing the pension are the Public Service Department (PSD) and the Retirement Fund (Incorporated) (also known as *Kumpulan Wang Persaraan*, KWAP). The retirement age for Malaysian public sector employees is either 55, 56, 58, or 60, depending on the employee's date of appointment. Table 3.2 shows the chronology of changes in the retirement age of Malaysian civil servants, as published by the PSD.

The funds are paid out upon retirement and are in the form of a lifetime annuity payment (Rahim, Yusof, & Ismail, 2011). The monthly retirement benefits are computed based on the employees' last drawn earnings and years in service. As described by Chee (1997), these benefits include:

i   retirement benefits (monthly pensions, gratuity, and cash award in lieu of unclaimed accumulated leave),
ii survivors' benefits (payable to the deceased's surviving dependent [spouse or minor children] – derivative of pension and gratuity, as well as the dependent's pension), and
iii disability pension – paid out in the event of retirement due to disability.

The maximum pension payable is three fifth (3/5) of the last drawn pay, which is achieved upon 30 years or 360 months of service (Public Service Department, *n.d.*)

3.2.1.2 Armed forces

The retirement scheme for the Malaysian Armed Forces are separate from the public sector employees' pension funds and are managed by the Armed Forces

Table 3.2 Changes in mandatory retirement age of public sector employees

Date	Changes in mandatory retirement age
1/10/2001	From 55 to 56
1/7/2008	From 56 to 58
1/1/2012	From 58 to 60

Source: Public Service Department (*n.d.*).

Fund Board. The Armed Forces Fund Board (or more commonly known in the local language as *Lembaga Tabung Angkatan Tentera*, LTAT) was established in 1972 to manage the retirement funds of the armed forces. Contributions into the LTAT are compulsory for the "other ranks" in the Armed Forces, who are required to contribute 10% of their monthly salary, while the government (as the employer) will contribute 15%. Meanwhile, voluntary contributions can be made by the officers in the Armed Forces, including commissioned officers and mobilised forces (volunteer forces). However, there will be no contributions from the government as the officers will generally receive pension funds similar to public-sector servants. The DB programmes for members of the armed forces covers old-age benefits, disability, and survivorship benefits. The withdrawal of contributions from the LTAT is in lump-sum, rather than annuities, and will be paid out upon discharge or retirement from service, or when they have reached the age of 50 years.

3.2.2 Defined contribution plans

3.2.2.1 Private-sector employees

The private sector and non-pensionable public sector employees' retirement benefits are under DC plans of which contributions are made obligatory for employees as well as employers. These private-sector retirement funds are placed under the national retirement scheme, i.e. the EPF. At age 55, the contributions will be consolidated into an account called *Akaun 55* and can be withdrawn. Nonetheless, for those who opt to retire at age 60, further contributions will be allocated into a separate account called *Akaun Emas*.

The EPF is a social security institution under the purview of the Ministry of Finance, Malaysia. Through the enactment of the Employees' Provident Fund Act 1991 (Act 452), the EPF manages the retirement savings of its members. As of December 2018, the total number of EPF members stood at 14.190 million members, out of which 7.36 million members are active contributing members. This data suggests that there are only approximately 50% of members with positive balance in their accounts, while the remaining accounts have zero balance. A total of 507,080 employer companies and organisations are registered members of the EPF (EPF, 2018).

Contributions into the EPF retirement funds are mandatory for private-sector employees and employers. Since 2012, the new EPF guidelines stipulate that for employees with a monthly salary of RM5,000 and below, employees and employers are mandated to contribute 11% and 13% of monthly salary into EPF, respectively. For employees with monthly salaries above RM5,000, the employees' contribution remains at 11%, while the employers' contribution is 12%. The total amount of contributions are channelled into two accounts, called Account 1 and Account 2 for each EPF contributor. 70% of contributions are allocated into Account 1, and 30% of contributions are allocated into Account 2. The difference between the two accounts lie in their withdrawal options,

Table 3.3 EPF contribution rates by employee and employer (1952–present)

	Employee	Employer	Total
1952 – Jun 1975	5	5	10
Jul 1975 – Nov 1980	6	7	13
Dec 1980 – Dec 1992	9	11	20
Jan 1993 – Dec 1995	10	12	22
Jan 1996 – Mar 2001	11	12	23
Apr 2001 – Mar 2002	9	12	21
Apr 2002 – May 2003	11	12	23
Jun 2003 – May 2004	9	12	21
Jun 2004 – May 2005	11	12	23
Jun 2005 – Dec 2008	11	12	23
Jan 2009 – Dec 2010	8	12	20
Jan 2011 – Dec 2011	11	12	23
Jan 2012 – 2019			
• Income ≤ RM5,000	11	13	24
• Income ≥ RM5,000	11	12	23

Source: EPF annual reports.

which will later be discussed. For the year of assessment 2019, contributions to EPF are tax exempted up to a maximum of RM4,000 (Inland Revenue Board of Malaysia, 2019).

Table 3.3 depicts the EPF contribution rates by employee and employer since the first inception of EPF in 1952 to the current year.

The EPF generally invests in an array of investments such as government securities, equity, and bond markets, property, and other money market instruments. Contributing members of the EPF can opt to invest their funds into either the conventional or Shariah savings fund. Conventional savings fund comprises both non-Shariah and Shariah-compliant investments and guarantees a minimum of 2.5% dividend annually. The Shariah savings fund was introduced in August 2016 to give members the option of Shariah-compliant investment funds. There is no minimum guaranteed dividend rate as dividends depend on the actual performance of Shariah-compliant investment funds.

Figure 3.9 shows the dividend rates paid out by EPF since 1952. In 2018, 6.15% of dividends was paid out under the conventional EPF fund, while 5.9% was paid out under the Shariah EPF fund. Over the past 10 years (2008–2017), the dividend rates for the conventional fund have averaged at 6.02%. This rate is quite reasonable given the economic challenges globally and domestically over the past years.

Contributors of the EPF are generally allowed to withdraw their entire savings (from both Account 1 and Account 2) upon reaching the age of 55. However, there are also possibilities of early withdrawals before age 55. Funds from Account 2 can be withdrawn prior to age 55 to purchase or build a home, to fund medical expenses, to pay for Hajj pilgrimage, or for education

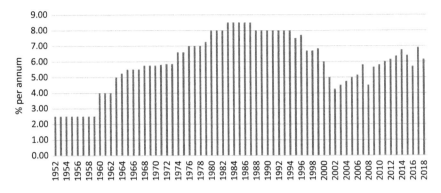

Figure 3.9 EPF dividend rates (% per annum) (1952–2018).
Source: EPF annual reports.

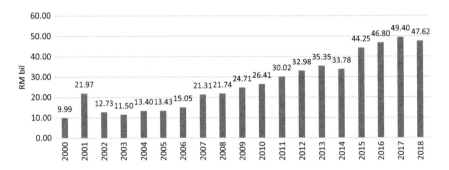

Figure 3.10 Total EPF withdrawals (RM bil).
Source: EPF annual reports.

purposes. Contributors who have reached the age of 50 can also withdraw from Account 2, either fully or partially, as pre-retirement preparation (EPF, *n.d.*). Figure 3.10 shows an increasing trend in the total withdrawals from EPF from 2006 to 2017. In 2018, the total of withdrawals were RM47.62 billion (EPF, 2018).

3.2.2.2 Private Retirement Scheme

The PRS is a DC plan that allows contributors to voluntarily contribute into an investment scheme as part of their retirement savings, on top of the EPF. The PRS, which was first launched in 2012, can be viewed as a supplementary plan that will give individuals a broader option to plan for their retirement. The PRS is an essential component in the Malaysian private pension industry and is provided by a number of private mutual fund companies. All employed and self-employed individuals can participate in this plan and have the freedom to contribute any amount they wish. All activities under the PRS are administered by the Public Pension Administrator (PPA) Malaysia and are regulated under the purview of the SC of Malaysia.

Under the PRS, individuals can select from a variety of funds that typically give investors the option of conservative, moderate, or growth funds. One crucial aspect that investors need to be aware of is the risk of investments. As with any mutual funds, returns are not guaranteed, and fluctuations in the market will also affect the unit price of investments in these schemes. Therefore, individuals should select the plan that is most suited to their retirement goals and risk tolerance levels. As with the EPF, withdrawals from PRS are allowed only at age 55. To discourage contributors from withdrawing early, a penalty of 8% is charged on the amounts of withdrawals before age 55. One of the benefits of the PRS is that amounts allocated to the PRS are tax exempted up to RM3,000 yearly.

Since the PRS is voluntary and gives contributors a more extensive range of fund options to choose from, individuals should take responsibility for their investments and equip themselves with adequate financial knowledge to make the decisions on their own. Investors should be aware of the risks involved and should always bear in mind that the PRS acts as a long-term investment similar to the EPF. Hence, to stay on track to meet one's retirement goals, early withdrawals should be avoided. Early withdrawals also have negative implications of penalty, which would adversely affect the investment net returns.

There is, however, evidence suggesting that Malaysians are still not aware of the existence of the PRS. Zabri, Ahmad, and Lian (2016) conducted a survey on 155 respondents from five private companies in Malacca and found that only 45% of the respondents were aware about the PRS, while the remaining 55% were not aware of its existence. However, over the years, the SC of Malaysia and industry players have widened their efforts in promoting awareness of the PRS. As a result of these endeavours, the SC recorded a significant 38% growth in the total number of PRS participants, from 301,279 in 2017 to 416,913 in 2018. Meanwhile, the total net asset value (NAV) recorded a 20% growth within the same period, to RM2.66 billion in 2018. Almost 40% of the PRS members are reported to be aged 30 years and below (Focus Malaysia, 2019). These statistics imply that the concerted efforts undertaken by SC and industry players have been fruitful and their positive effects prospering.

3.3 Malaysia's savings

The objective of this section is to provide an overview of Malaysia's national savings rate. The purpose is to show the trends in household savings rate at the macro level. Section 3.3.1 will discuss the definition of savings, before presenting data on household savings rate in Malaysia (Section 3.3.2). This section will thereafter discuss the EPF savings rate (Section 3.3.3), and finally, concerns about low retirement savings in Malaysia are discussed (Section 3.3.4).

3.3.1 Definition of savings

The definitions of savings observed from the literature are mixed and inconsistent. Typically, two broad definitions of savings are used in scholarly research and national statistics. The first definition of savings is the excess of income over expenditure for a given period (Keynes, 1936), and the second is "the difference in net worth at the end of a period and net worth at the beginning of a period" (Wärneryd, 1999, p. 47). The difference in the two definitions is that the former denotes that savings is a *flow of funds*, but the latter implies that savings is an amount of *reserves* or *stock* of wealth for a certain time period.

The inconsistencies in these definitions suggest that there may also be variances in measurement. The first measurement of savings is the difference between personal expenditures and disposable personal income, and second, as the household sector's net assets (including housing) minus total liabilities (Browning & Lusardi, 1996). The difficulties in measuring household savings are attributed to the inconsistencies in definition, measurement, and data employed (Browning & Lusardi, 1996). However, according to the Organisation for Economic Co-operation and Development (OECD), national savings rate at the macroeconomic level are typically computed as the percentage of national income that is not consumed and is available to purchase financial and non-financial assets (OECD, *n.d*). Hence, these rates are usually used to compare relative economic positions across nations and is viewed as an appropriate assessment of household savings.

3.3.2 Malaysia's national saving rates

The chart in Figure 3.11 depicts Malaysia's gross national savings rate, which is defined as the difference between gross national income and public and private consumption, plus net current transfers. While these statistics show savings at the macro level, they are a worthy representation of the amount of household savings held on an aggregate basis. Figure 3.11 illustrates Malaysia's Gross National Savings as a percentage of GDP for the year 1990 to 2018. The dotted line shows a declining trend in the savings rate during the period. Notable downward trends are seen after the year 1997 (signifying the effects of the Asian Financial Crisis) and after the year 2008 (signifying the effects of the Global Financial Crisis). After a slight increase in 2017 to 32.5%, the rate dropped again in 2018 to 30.73%.

The downward trend of Malaysia's gross savings (% of GDP) appears to be similar to the downward movement of Philippines' rate, although the gross savings rates for other ASEAN countries seem to be increasing (e.g. Singapore, Thailand, and Indonesia). Singapore appears to have the highest gross savings rate of over 50% compared to Malaysia's gross savings rate, which averages around 30% (Figure 3.12).

Figure 3.13 shows Malaysian's household consumption expenditure as a percentage of GDP. In comparison to savings, the trend line shows a slight upward

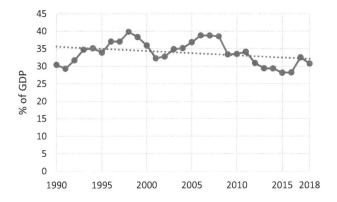

Figure 3.11 Malaysia's gross savings (% of GDP) (1990–2018).
Source: Index Mundi (*n.d.*).

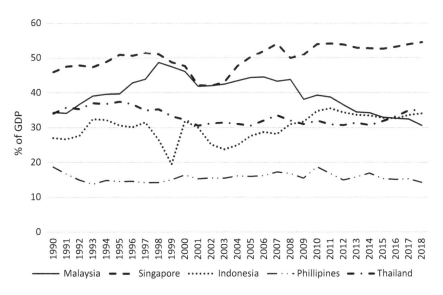

Figure 3.12 Gross savings (% of GDP) of ASEAN-5 countries (1990–2018).
Source: Index Mundi (*n.d.*).

movement in the expenditure rates from 1990 to 2016. The consumption expenditure showed a decline from 1991 to 1998; however, it regained from 1999 onwards. This suggests a quick rebound after the Asian Financial Crisis in 1997. The Global Financial Crisis in 2008 seems to have no effect on the Malaysian households' consumption expenditures, with the expenditure trends slowly on the upward move.

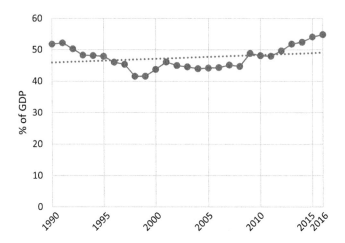

Figure 3.13 Malaysia's household final consumption expenditure (% of GDP) (1990–2016).
Source: Index Mundi (*n.d.*).

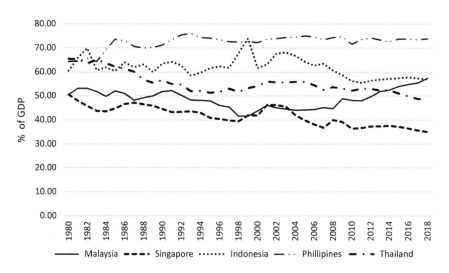

Figure 3.14 Household final consumption expenditure (% of GDP) of ASEAN-5 countries
(1990–2018).
Source: Index Mundi (*n.d.*).

As can be seen in Figure 3.14, Malaysia's household final consumption expenditure as a percentage of GDP in 2018 almost matched that of Indonesia, around
57%. In the same year, Philippines had the highest rate at 74%, while Singapore
had the lowest rate at 35%.

3.3.3 *Retirement savings in EPF*

Having depicted the gross national savings rate as per Figure 3.11, this section provides an overview of the retirement savings in EPF. The average savings (in RM) appears to be increasing from 2002 to 2017. However, the general observation that appears to be quite worrying is the low amount of average savings among retirees at age 55. Statistics from the EPF annual reports indicate that the average savings of EPF members at age 54 in 2018 is only RM232,738 for males and RM177,462 for females, or an average of RM209,861 (see Table 3.4). Ideally, the amount should last the entire remaining lifetime of retirees. Based on the assumption of an average living expense of RM3,090[1] monthly, the funds would last for approximately only 68 months or less than six years. Given the life expectancy rate in Malaysia of 72.7 years for males and 77.6 for females, these implications are indeed worrisome and involves concerted efforts by all stakeholders in ensuring that future retirees will have sufficient means to support their living at old age.

3.3.4 *The concern about low savings*

Savings are a fundamental component in an economy's financial system and are central in maintaining the economic stability of the nation. Savings, which is the portion of income not used for expenditure, are usually held in financial

Table 3.4 EPF members' average savings at age 54

	Average savings (RM)	*Average savings (RM)*	*Average savings (RM)*
	Male	*Female*	*Overall*
2002	101,608.58	56,216.93	88,429.31
2003	105,620.67	62,033.62	92,406.15
2004	112,789.15	67,686.13	99,047.76
2005	122,143.02	73,968.74	107,534.00
2006	129,563.19	81,482.54	114,402.92
2007	138,895.48	84,955.62	121,163.53
2008	150,280.40	96,856.03	132,539.78
2009	159,252.85	101,694.63	139,816.38
2010	163,977.05	111,497.63	145,733.52
2011	166,417.00	118,436.00	149,216.76
2012	175,377.00	128,682.00	158,302.09
2013	183,997.00	137,612.00	166,650.20
2014	199,128.00	149,616.00	180,152.70
2015	214,911.00	162,296.00	194,438.37
2016	223,030.00	174,974.00	204,288.24
2017	233,861.00	182,765.00	213,852.23
2018	232,738.00	177,462.00	209,861.71

Source: EPF annual reports.

institutions which are then channelled back into the economy as loans that will then finance investments by businesses. Investments by firms are crucial to the economy as they fuel productivity and propel economic growth. Furthermore, savings act as a cushion against macroeconomic fluctuations and financial crisis. The effects of economic slowdowns are less severe when there are higher savings because lower consumption rates are affected in such events. Therefore, savings are imperative to economic growth and the sustainability of a nation.

At the microeconomic level, household savings have short-term as well as long-term benefits. In the short run, savings act as a precautionary measure to absorb shocks in income that occur due to unexpected events such as loss of job, health conditions, and other contingencies. Savings also allow individuals to fund planned life-cycle events such as weddings, furthering education, vacations, building a family, and so on. In the long run, savings act as a supplement of income that can be used to maintain people's standard of living during retirement.

In view of the importance of savings from a macro- and micro-perspective, declining savings rates within a nation are perturbing due to their implications for financing national investments. Such situation may increase dependency on foreign individuals and firms, which will be reflected as current account deficits. Furthermore, Peach and Steindel (2000) assert that low household savings are worrisome as they indicate a "spendthrift nation" and signals a population that is not forward-looking and unprepared for the future. Low savings will lead to diminishing wealth levels, suggesting that future standards of living among societies may be compromised. Therefore, the significance of savings to the economy as a whole, and to households in particular, cannot be undermined.

Meanwhile, the implications of low retirement savings are greater dependency on the working age population and on social security benefits provided by the government. The situation is aggravated by the situation of higher longevity, increased urbanisation, increased divorce rates, and other social factors that would affect the elderly (Holzmann, 2015). Hence, it is the aim of this chapter to discuss the factors that cause low retirement saving, from a behavioural and psychological perspective. However, before discussing these factors, the following section will discuss the retirement planning process that should ideally be practiced by individuals to ensure a comfortable future retirement.

3.4 Retirement planning

3.4.1 The retirement planning process

In view of increased life expectancy among Malaysians, early planning is imperative so that individuals are prepared to face the risks during retirement. Longevity risks include the risk of loss of employment income and health risks. Therefore, the need for retirement planning is augmented as one gradually approaches retirement age.

Retirement planning is one of the key aspects of an individual's personal financial planning. According to the Malaysian Financial Planning Council (MFPC, *n.d.*), retirement planning is defined as:

> the process of determining retirement income goals and the actions and decisions necessary to achieve those goals. Retirement planning includes identifying sources of income, estimating expenses, implementing a savings programme, and managing assets. Future cash flows are estimated to determine if the retirement income goal will be achieved.

As noted from above, retirement planning is a process that involves various steps to achieve one's financial goals at old age. It is essential to understand the entire process to evaluate if any one of them are overlooked at any stage. The process can be illustrated in Figure 3.15.

The *first step* in the retirement planning process is *setting retirement goals* and prioritising the goals. An individual will need to think about when he wishes to retire (retirement age), how he will retire (the kind of lifestyle he wants to live during retirement), who will be there to support and care for him during

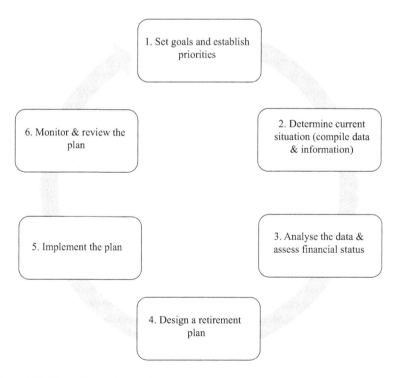

Figure 3.15 The retirement planning process.

retirement, how he will fund his retirement needs, and so on. After listing down the goals, one would need to prioritise them. Setting goals is the first necessary step towards achieving one's desired retirement goal.

The *second step* in the retirement planning process is to *determine one's current situation*. This process will require compiling all relevant financial and personal data and information. A list of assets and liabilities, a personal budget, and personal family data would be relevant at this stage. One's family and health situation are also important considerations.

The *third step* is to *analyse the data* and assess one's financial status based on the information obtained in Step 2. One would need to assess if there are any problems faced in terms of finances, family, or health situations. This information is crucial so that an appropriate solution can be developed in order to meet one's retirement goals. According to MFPC, there are four stages under Step 3 of the retirement planning process:

i   To determine the retirement income needed during the first year of retirement. There are two ways to determine this, either by (a) *Income replacement ratio* or (b) *Expense method*. In the two assessments, one would need to think about either the proportion of last earned income wished to be replaced during retirement or to determine how much expenses are required during retirement. For the first method (income replacement ratio), financial planners usually require a 70%–80% replacement ratio.

ii   To compute the lump-sum capital needed at retirement. There are two methods used to compute the capital required: (a) capital liquidation – where it is assumed that the capital lump-sum is drawn down gradually and completely till the end of life or (b) capital conservation method – where it is assumed that the capital lump-sum is preserved, and only the returns from that investment are used to fund monthly retirement needs.

iii   To determine current and future resources. One will need to evaluate all types of assets and liabilities and to recognise the income-generating potential of different assets held in one's financial portfolio.

iv   To determine future value of assets. In this stage, the value of current assets is converted to a future value at retirement. There will be many factors to be taken into consideration in determining this future value, such as the inflation rate, salary growth rate, growth rate of assets, and risks involved. In addition, the replacement ratio will also need to be considered to calculate the lump sum of capital required at retirement.

The *fourth step* in the retirement planning process is to *design a retirement plan*. If the help of a financial planner is sought, then the financial planner or advisor will recommend a retirement plan for the client. If one is planning for oneself, then he would need to know the available financial products and services that are available in the market in order to design a plan that is tailored to one's goals.

The *fifth step* in the retirement planning process is the *implementation of the retirement plan*. Based on the retirement plan designed in the fourth step, one would assess if the products and services available in the financial market correspond to one's retirement goals and aspirations. Implementing the plan at an early stage in life will ensure that the goal is attainable, since there is more time to realise the goal. The longer one procrastinates on planning for retirement, the less time there will be to realise those goals. Early planning would always be advantageous in order to invest in investments that match the risk tolerance and planning time horizons.

The *sixth step* in the process is *monitoring and reviewing the retirement plan periodically*. At times, there will be changes in one's life that were not initially accounted for. Thus, these changes need to be factored in so that the retirement goals can be achieved. Sometimes, the goals will also change based on changes in family life and the existence of offspring and hence, the number of dependents. Therefore, the retirement planning process is a continuous cycle that needs to be re-evaluated from time to time.

3.4.2 Challenges in retirement planning

In regards to the above process, there are several factors that may obstruct people from conducting proper retirement planning. These challenges are conceptualised in five dimensions. *First*, as can be noted from the explanation in the preceding section, the **complexities** of the retirement planning process can be overwhelming for the ordinary person. Some of the steps in the retirement planning process require technical skills such as the ability to use time value of money to compute future value of retirement needs. It would be advantageous to take efforts to increase one's own financial literacy or to seek the help of a financial advisor or financial planner to assist in the planning process. A financial planner would have the expertise and skills to evaluate the needs of the client and to recommend suitable financial products that are tailored to the client's needs. However, not everyone may have access to, nor have the confidence and trust in financial planners. This is the *second* factor that may obstruct one from successfully planning for retirement – the (lack of) **confidence** in financial planners. Customers sometimes have lack of access to financial planners and do not fully trust the motivations of a financial planner, and furthermore, engaging in the services of a financial planner could be costly. Therefore, it is imperative for players in the financial planning industry to consider appropriate ways on how to reach out to the public and to develop strategies to gain trust from the people.

Third, apart from retirement, there are many other **competing** financial objectives that one may have that may impede one's retirement plans. For example, one may have the desire to purchase a better home, upgrade their car, upgrade or maintain their home, fund their children's education, go for a vacation, and so on. All these may hinder one's desire to allocate more for their retirement, especially when the time horizon of those financial goals is shorter than that of retirement goals.

Fourth, **calamities** or unforeseen events may occur in one's life. Unexpected life-changing events such as the demise of a loved one, sudden health deterioration,

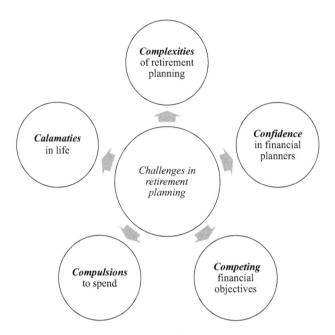

Figure 3.16 Conceptualisation of the challenges in retirement planning.

loss of a job, separation with spouse, loss of property, and other precipitous events may suddenly occur and disrupt any savings plan that was earlier implemented. In view of these uncertainties, one may need to have other contingency plans to deal with these events.

Compulsions to spend is the *fifth* factor that may impede or divert one from his or her original savings plan. As normal human beings, we are prone to be lured into purchases of things we do not really need, therefore leading us to over-spend. One way to go about this issue is to set aside savings first before spending. We should be motivated by the growth in our savings rather than the material things that are usually short-lived. We should always live within our means and avoid taking up unnecessary debt to satisfy short-term wants. The challenges in retirement planning are conceptualised in Figure 3.16.

The following section will discuss the theories on savings and empirical evidence on the factors influencing retirement saving behaviour and retirement planning. The focus of the discussion will be on psychological and behavioural factors in planning for retirement.

3.5 A theoretical perspective on retirement saving

In this section, the theories of saving are first discussed. Two main theories are explained – the life-cycle hypothesis and the behavioural life-cycle hypothesis.

3.5.1 Theories of saving

3.5.1.1 Life-cycle hypothesis

The main theories of saving are grounded in the economics literature, developed mainly by prominent economic scholars such as Keynes (1936) and Modigliani and Brumberg (1954). Keynes (1936) suggests that there are eight motives for people to save; among others, the *precautionary motive*, *life-cycle motive*, *intertemporal substitution motive*, and *the bequest motive*. Specifically, under the life-cycle motive, Keynes suggests that people would save "to provide for an anticipated future relationship between the income and needs of the individual," which Browning and Lusardi (1996) interpret as the life-cycle motive. This motive is an outcome of transient disparities between income and expenditures that arise throughout the life cycle. Income will likely increase with career progression, and at the same time, life-cycle expenditures will also evolve according to life cycle needs such as purchasing non-durable goods, marriage, children's education, purchasing a car or a home, and other expenses. Hence, saving for life-cycle motives means that people would save to cater for future life-cycle expenditures that may arise throughout their lifetime.

Modigliani and Brumberg's (1954) life-cycle hypothesis (LCH) is one of the established theories conceptualising saving behaviour, which have some similarities to the notions of Keynes (1936). The theory conceptualises the idea that individuals "smooth out" their life-cycle spending patterns by dividing lifetime resources by the number of years they anticipate to continue living. Such smoothing out patterns would keep the real consumption levels constant over the lifetime. During the early stages of life, when income is relatively low, individuals will need to borrow or dissave to support the expenditures required during this stage, such as to purchase a car or a home. However, there will come a stage in the life cycle in which earnings ability will increase; hence, savings will also gradually rise. Simultaneously, this will be the stage in which individuals will pay off their earlier borrowings, thus further increasing the ability to accumulate wealth. During this period, individuals increase their savings with the intention of preparing for episodes of declining income in the future, particularly retirement. The pattern of increasing income and saving during the mid-cycle of the lifespan and the decrease in income and saving at retirement produces a hump-shaped pattern of accumulated wealth (Jappelli & Modigliani, 1998), as earlier depicted in Chapter 2 (Figure 2.16).

As a theory that is grounded in the economics paradigm, one of the basic premises of the LCH is that consumers are rational and continuously seek to maximise their utility, and they would allocate their resources optimally to consumption during their lifetime (Fisher & Montalto, 2010; Modigliani, 1986). Despite the stylised notions of the LCH, there is empirical evidence showing stark discrepancies with its propositions. The first evidence is that elderly consumers are not dissaving as proposed by the theory but are, in fact, continuing to save during retirement (Baranzini, 2005). The second evidence is that individuals are not saving adequately for retirement (Ghilarducci, Papadopoulos, & Webb, 2017; Pang & Warshawsky, 2014).

The above evidence that contradicts the tenets of the LCH has led to several criticisms of the theory. One of the criticisms is that economic agents are not always "rational" as the theory assumes, but instead, are largely influenced by emotions. Rationality in the economic sense suggests that agents would efficiently revise their beliefs upon the acceptance of new information. Simon (1955) presented the idea of "*bounded rationality*" in which agents are not irrational but fail in making important decisions due to limitations in human cognition and emotions.

Proponents of behavioural economics argue that the rational-agent model is too idealistic as humans are prone to errors and biases and make decisions based on simplistic methods. Stemming from the psychology discipline, humans are argued to make their judgements based on two types of cognitive processes, *intuition* and *reasoning* (Kahneman, 2003). *Intuitive* decisions are made on a more casual and quicker basis and are made without much effort. Decisions based on intuition can be influenced by emotions and can be associated with inferior outcomes. However, continuous practice using intuition (e.g. strategies taken in a game of chess) can lead to high skills and positive outcomes. *Reasoning*, on the other hand, is made in a deliberate, controlled, and effortful manner and is guided by rules (Kahneman, 2003). An example of reasoning is a decision made in solving a mathematical problem in which solving the complexity of the problem requires using the certain mathematical rules and are done within a controlled situational context.

3.5.1.2 Behavioural life-cycle hypothesis

The behavioural life-cycle hypothesis (BLCH) by Shefrin and Thaler (1988) is an attempt to make the traditional life-cycle theory more pragmatic from a behavioural perspective. Three types of behaviour are incorporated into the model: (i) *self-control*, (ii) rules, (iii) *mental accounting*, and (iv) *framing*. Each of these will be elaborated as follows.

SELF-CONTROL

Retirement saving is a form of long-term planning that involves foresight of what may happen in the future. Saving for retirement requires self-control because consuming in the present moment yields immediate satisfaction than consuming at a later date. Therefore, setting aside a portion of income that can only be used in decades ahead requires considerable amount of discipline and willpower to restrain oneself from instant temptations. An individual may be aware of the importance of saving for retirement and understands the consequences of retirement saving inadequacy, but lack of self-control will result in failure to meet targeted financial retirement goals. The lack of self-control thus may lead to deviations in the saving pattern in the manner suggested by the LCH. Hence, efforts in dealing with the mental difficulties associated with these temptations must be enforced to deal and overcome the lack of self-control. Fostering good habits is one of the mechanisms that may help in tackling the problems of self-control.

Shefrin and Thaler (1988) argue that there are two types of conflicting "personalities" within oneself; a *planner*, who is concerned with long run benefits, and a *doer*, who is myopic and prefers short-run immediate gratification. The doer attempts to maximise utility which is the sum of the pleasure and pain associated with the consumption choice made. The willpower to resist current consumption pleasure is viewed as painful and costly and reduces the utility of the doer. To mitigate willpower cost, the planner may exercise methods to achieve self-control. Some of the measures are discussed in the following.

RULES

Among these measures to mitigate willpower cost is to place income in a fund that imposes certain rules and constraints that could change consumption patterns. Shefrin and Thaler (1988) gave an example of placing savings in a pension fund that restricts withdrawals and successfully alleviate the willpower effort. Such enforcement mechanisms are *external rules* since they are implemented by external authorities. *Internal rules* are self-imposed and therefore require more willpower strength, for example, restraining oneself from using credit to pay for current consumption.

MENTAL ACCOUNTING

Mental accounting refers to the propensity of grouping wealth into several "mental accounts" and use cognitive procedures to manage, assess, and monitor financial activities (Shefrin & Thaler, 1988; Thaler, 1999). As opposed to traditional LCH that assumes wealth is fungible, the BLCH postulates that wealth can be divided into three basic categories: current spendable income (I), current assets (A), and future income (F). Each category could further constitute various types of wealth; for example, wealth placed in savings account, stocks, and bonds may form a "current assets" category; while a checking account or cash may form a "current income" category, which can be used on a daily basis to fund consumption. Retirement savings refer to a "future income" category that is associated with funds earned in the future from retirement savings. Having different mental accounts imply that people may have different risk attitudes for the different mental accounts.

FRAMING

Framing effect is a cognitive illusion that may influence the process of decision-making. Mental frames, as earlier proposed by Tversky and Kahneman (1979), postulate that decisions are made in two stages. The first stage involves "framing and editing" in which people will first evaluate the problem, and in the second stage, people will assess the framed prospect and select the prospect with the highest outcome. Mental frames are illusionary states of mind that may influence perceptions and decisions. Shefrin (2002) states that a frame is "the form used to describe a decision problem."

Having discussed the two main theories of saving, the next section will discuss the empirical evidence specifically focusing on retirement saving, as gathered from the literature.

3.6 Empirical studies on retirement saving and planning

3.6.1 Research themes on retirement saving

The topic of retirement saving behaviour has been the interest of scholars from many fields, including economics, financial planning, psychology, and social welfare. The issues on retirement being focused on from the financial perspective include *retirement preparedness, retirement saving and accumulation, retirement planning, retirement outcomes, adjustment and well-being, retirement saving behaviour, and retirement savings adequacy.* Figure 3.17 illustrates these themes.

Following the themes identified from the literature, the concepts examined and their definitions and measurement are outlined in Table 3.5.

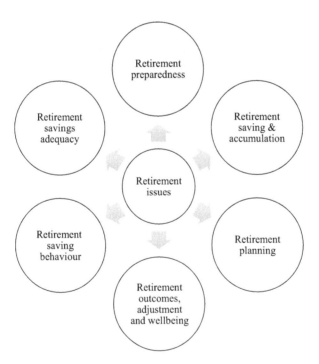

Figure 3.17 Research themes on retirement.

Table 3.5 Retirement concepts being studied and their definitions and measurements

Concept examined	Definition/measurement of concept	Author
Retirement planning	A series of activities involved in the accumulation of wealth to cover needs in the post-retirement stage of life.	Kumar, Tomar, & Verma (2019); Topa, Lunceford, & Boyatzis (2018)
	The extent to which the person has thought about retirement.	Lusardi & Mitchell (2017); Mahdzan, Mohd-Any, & Chan (2017)
	Whether an individual has any savings or investments set aside for the future (including retirement/pension funds).	Boisclair, Lusardi, & Michaud (2017)
	Retirement planning activities such as information seeking, plan initiation, instrumental activities, asset accumulation, and advice seeking.	Folk (2019); Hershey, Jaabocs-Lawson, McArdle, & Hamagami (2007); Stawski, Hershey, & Jacobs-Lawson (2007); Petkoska & Earl (2009)
Retirement preparedness	Knowledge and understanding of how much money would be needed to adequately meet retirement expenses and whether the appropriate computations had been made to ensure one would be financially solvent during the postemployment period.	Hershey & Mowen (2000); Lusardi & Mitchell (2017); Kasper, Mathur, Ong, Shannon, & Yingwattanakul (2019); Kim & Hanna (2015)
Retirement saving and accumulation	The change in accumulated retirement wealth within a certain period.	Hanna, Kim, & Chen (2016); Martin, Guillemette, & Browning (2016); Motika (2019)
	Voluntary contribution to a retirement savings plan within the past 12 months.	Hershey et al. (2007)
Retirement saving behaviour	Type of retirement plan implemented, annual contribution, and allocation of funds.	Benartzi & Thaler (2007); Clark & d'Ambrosio (2003); Hastings & Mitchell (2020); McKenzie & Liersch (2011); Thaler & Benartzi (2004, 2007)
	A conscious effort to save for retirement.	Jacobs-Lawson & Hershey (2005)
Retirement savings adequacy	Having resources that are sufficient to smooth the marginal utility of their consumption over time and finance the desired retirement consumption.	Burnett, Davis, Murawski, Wilkins, & Wilkinson (2018); Engen, Gale, & Uccello (1999); Kim & Hanna (2015); Knoef, Been, Alessie, Caminada, Goudswaard, & Kalwij (2016)

(*continued*)

Table 3.5 Cont.

Concept examined	Definition/measurement of concept	Author
Retirement outcomes, adjustment, and well-being	Perceived planning effort invested across three domains – public protection, self-insurance, and self-protection.	Earl, Bednall, & Moratore (2015); Muratore & Earl (2015)
	Positive/negative affect, self-image, self-esteem, self-efficacy, optimism, life satisfaction, and marital cohesion.	De Vaus, Well, Kendig, and Quine (2007)
	Retirees' satisfaction, depression, and loss of resources	Topa & Valero (2017)

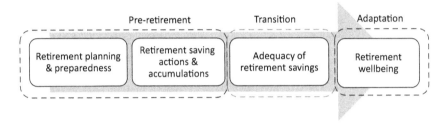

Figure 3.18 Typology of research on retirement planning.

It can be observed in Table 3.5 that some of the retirement concepts studies were from the preparatory perspective (e.g. planning for retirement), and some from the outcome perspective (e.g. retirement adjustment and well-being). Muratore and Earl (2015) suggested that there are three phases of retirement:

i   Pre-retirement: The phase when one would start to think about, plan, and form intentions on how to retire. This phase would relate to the planning, preparing, accumulation, and retirement saving behaviour.
ii Transition: The phase when one actually retires – the length of time would vary among individuals. This phase relates to retirement saving adequacy.
iii Adaptation: The phase when individuals have to adjust to retirement. This would involve stabilisation and adjustment.
    The phases of retirement are illustrated in the form of a typology in Figure 3.18.

3.6.2 Factors influencing retirement planning and retirement saving behaviour

The antecedents of the retirement issues outlined in the preceding section have been explored from various perspectives. Among the issues influencing individual's retirement planning and saving behaviour are cognitive factors such as *financial knowledge* and *financial literacy* (Boisclair et al., 2017; Lusardi & Mitchell, 2017; Mahdzan et al. 2017), *time preference* and *time perspective* (Earl et al., 2015; Hershey & Mowen, 2000; Hersey et al., 2007; Martin et al., 2016), and other *psychological factors* (Hershey & Mowen, 2000). Table 3.6 summarises the dimensions and factors adopted by different researchers. Although there

Table 3.6 Factors influencing retirement planning and saving

Dimensions		Specific factors	Author
Psychological factors	Disposition	• Time perspective • Financial risk tolerance • Conscientiousness • Emotional stability • Five-factor model (extraversion, agreeableness, conscientiousness, neuroticism, openness)	Bernheim et al. (2001); Hastings & Mitchell (2011); Hershey & Mowen (2000); Hershey (2004); Hershey et al. (2007); Jacobs-Lawson & Hershey (2005); Martin et al. (2016); Motika (2019); Robinson, Demetre, & Corney (2010)
	Cognition	• Financial knowledge/ literacy • Perceived task relevance • Feasibility and complexity • Financial self-efficacy • Belief in systems • Metacognitions and worries	Boisclair et al. (2017); Clark & d'Ambrosio (2003); Hastings & Mitchell (2011); Hastings & Mitchell (2020); Hershey (2004); Hershey et al. (2007); Jacobs-Lawson & Hershey (2005); Kasper et al. (2019); Lusardi & Mitchell (2017); Mahdzan & Tabiani (2013); Mustafa, Yusof, Silim, Adiman, & Hassan (2017); Topa et al. (2018)
	Motivation	• Retirement goal clarity • Financial goal strength • Personal values & self-beliefs • Retirement fear/ anxiety • Financial planning • Hope • Job/life satisfaction	Hershey (2004); Hershey et al. (2013); Hershey et al. (2007); Kim & Hanna (2015); Martin et al. (2016); Neukam & Hershey (2003); Neukam (2002); Stawski & Hershey (2001); Stawski et al. (2007); Topa & Valero (2017); Topa et al. (2018)
Social factors/cultural ethos		• Family • Societal • Peer norms • Early learning	Hershey (2004); Kasper et al. (2019); Kumar et al. (2018); Motika (2019).

(continued)

Table 3.6 Cont.

Dimensions	Specific factors	Author

	• Spousal support
	• Friends/
	  colleagues
		Mustafa et al. (2017); Reitzes &
		  Mutran (2004)

Financial & economic
  factors/Opportunity
	• Income base
	• Financial &
	  economic support
	• General economic
	  conditions
	• Employment
	  opportunity
	• Social support
	• Ageing
	  stereotypes
	• Organisational
	  climate for ageing
	• Social
	  security system
	• Cost of living
	• Education
	• Use of financial
	  planner
		Hershey (2004); Hershey et al.
		  (2007); Kim & Hanna (2015);
		  Kumar, Tomar, & Verma (2019);
		  Topa et al. (2018)

Circumstantial factors	• Loss of job
	• Spousal death
	• Divorce/
	  remarriage
	• Health issues
	• Sudden
	  inheritance
		Kumar et al. (2019)

appears to be many factors influencing retirement planning and saving, four factors will be selected for further deliberation, *financial literacy* and *financial planning* (from the psychological dimension of *cognition*), *time preference* (from the psychological dimension of *disposition*), and *goal clarity* (from the psychological dimension of *motivation*). Each of these factors will be explained in the following sections.

3.6.2.1 Financial literacy (Cognition)

Financial literacy is defined as "a combination of awareness, knowledge, skill, attitude and behaviour necessary to make sound financial decisions and ultimately achieve individual financial wellbeing" (Atkinson & Messy, 2012). From this working definition used by the OECD to study financial literacy of individuals all over the world, it can be conjectured that financial literacy is a comprehensive concept that includes all of these five basic elements. Hence, knowledge alone will not necessarily translate into positive actions that will lead to better financial decision making, it is the unification of all concepts that is necessary to produce positive financial outcomes. From the perspective of psychology, financial literacy falls under the broad domain of *cognition* since it requires processing financial knowledge into decisions and actions.

In the studies of retirement planning, financial literacy has been found to be a strong predictor leading to positive retirement saving behaviour. This is not surprising, given that the concept has also been found to have strong relationships with other financial behaviours such as investment behaviour and stock market participation (Almenberg & Dreber, 2015; Al-Tamimi & Kalli, 2009; Mahdzan et al., 2017; Van Rooij, Lusardi, & Alessie, 2011), savings behaviour (Jappelli & Padula, 2013; Mahdzan & Tabiani, 2013), and borrowing behaviour (Disney & Gathergood, 2013; Lusardi & Tufano, 2015; Sevim, Temizel, & Sayılır, 2012). The empirical evidence suggests that higher financial literacy would lead individuals to have more diversified portfolios, higher tendency to participate in stock markets, higher savings, and better borrowing behaviour.

In regards to retirement planning, Lusardi and Mitchell (2017) found that individuals in the United States who had a higher subjective and objective financial literacy would have a higher tendency to think about their retirement. These results were supported in another experimental study conducted in Chile (Hastings & Mitchell, 2020) and Canada (Boisclair et al., 2017). Individuals who planned about their retirement were defined as those who had any type of voluntary savings. In the context of Malaysia, Mahdzan and Tabiani (2013) employed a comprehensive measure of financial literacy by Lusardi (2008) and found that individuals who are more likely to have positive savings are those who are more financially literate. Hastings and Mitchell (2011) suggested that financial literacy is prevalent due to the lack of understanding regarding simple economic concepts and the inability to perform time value of money calculations as required in retirement planning – hence, causing individuals to make inferior financial evaluations.

Studies have also found that financial education could positively alter attitudes towards retirement saving and retirement saving behaviour. Clark and d'Ambrosio (2003) conducted a study, which revealed that employees who had attended financial education programmes would re-evaluate their retirement plans including savings and consumption practices. After attending the programme, attendees would increase their voluntary retirement savings, engage with a financial planner, or purchase long-term care insurance.

Indeed, retirement planning is not an easy task for the average person. There are many issues to consider when planning for retirement and many uncertainties to account for – e.g. the kind of lifestyle one wishes to have, when to retire, what the family structure will be like in the future, and whether there would be unexpected events in life (such as deteriorations in health, loss of job, loss of a spouse). As discussed in Section 3.5, to plan for retirement, one needs to know the various alternatives of saving instruments; evaluate future income needs; assess current savings and shortfall in savings; estimate inflation rate, factor in a growth rate factor for investments; and finally, to consider life expectancy. The ordinary person would certainly find all these issues an overwhelming task.

3.6.2.2 Time preference (Disposition)

Martin, Guillemette, and Browning (2016) referred to *time preference* as "the relative value placed on consumption at different points in time." It is closely connected to the concept of *intertemporal choice* and *personal discount rate*, in which one must choose between alternatives that take place at different time periods (Soman et al., 2005). An example of intertemporal choice or time preference is in deciding whether to receive RM100 today or to receive RM110 at the end of a year. One who has a higher personal discount rate would tend to favour present consumption compared to future consumption, or, would need to be compensated with a higher rate of return in order to defer consumption to a future time period (Martin et al., 2016). Kim and Zauberman (2009) highlighted that studies examining intertemporal decisions reveal that people tend to be biased towards outcomes at the present time rather than those in the future (O'Donoghue, & Rabin, 1999; Thaler, 1981; Zauberman, 2003).

Since time preference is characterised by patience and planning time horizon (Jacobs-Lawson & Hershey, 2005), it can be viewed that it falls under the psychological domain of *disposition* or personality. A study by Hastings and Mitchell (2011) indicated that individuals preferred instant gratification as opposed to larger payoffs at a future point in time. However, such preference and short-sightedness tended to impair their retirement planning and investment decisions. In their experimental study, Hastings and Mitchell (2011) classified respondents into three groups: the impatient ones who opted to receive a reward instantly, the "efficacious deferrers" who chose to receive the reward at a later date but at a higher value, and the "inefficacious deferrers" who chose to receive the higher reward but failed to follow through with the plan to receive the rewards, hence, ultimately leading them into receiving no reward at all. Findings of the study revealed that more than half of the respondents chose to receive the reward immediately, and that those who chose to receive the reward at a future date were those who possess understanding of financial concepts and computational skills that are necessary in intertemporal decisions (Hastings & Mitchell, 2011). A related study was conducted in Chile, which found that impatient individuals tend to have lower accumulated savings (Hastings & Mitchell, 2020).

Similarly, Martin et al. (2016) asserted that people's willingness to save for retirement is strongly influenced by their inclination towards intertemporal consumption. Those who were more inclined towards current consumption (those with high personal discount rate) chose to save less and were less prepared for their retirement. These findings are consistent with Berneheim, Skinner, and Weinberg (2001) who also found that people with lower retirement wealth were less prepared for their retirement. However, this negative relationship between personal discount rate and retirement wealth was reduced when they had some sort of retirement planning (Martin et al., 2016). Other studies have also revealed similar findings that time preference was prevalent in predicting retirement planning behaviours (Hershey & Mowen, 2000; Jacobs-Lawson & Hershey, 2005).

Another closely related concept is *time perspective*. Time perspective was originally conceptualised by Lewin (1951) who described the term as "the totality of the individual's views of his psychological future and past existing at a given time" (p. 75, in Earl, Bednall, & Muratore, 2015). This can be interpreted as one's integrative perspective of all temporal frames, in which the past and future will influence behaviour at the present moment (Zimbardo & Boyd, 2015). This view is consistent with Carstensen, Isaacowitz, and Charles (1999) who argued that individuals' perception of time is central to the decisions that people make, and in their selections and pursuit of social goals. The authors also argue that when people focus on the present as opposed to the past or the future, there will be an emphasis on intuition and subjectivity rather than on analytical and logical reasoning.

Zimbardo and Boyd (2015) developed a measurement called the Zimbardo Time Perspective Inventory (ZTPI), which can determine if a person is concerned about future goals and rewards or about instant gratification. Those who are more concerned about the future would be willing to forgo present enjoyment, while those who are more focused on the present time would not be concerned about future consequences. According to Zimbardo and Boyd (2015), those who focused on the present moment believe that external forces would control one's life. Meanwhile, the last category of people are those who emphasise on the past, who can either be positively inclined (thinking about nostalgic and warm experiences) or negatively inclined (affected by unpleasant or repulsive experiences).

Indeed, the psychology of time is such an abstract concept that many find difficult to comprehend. In developing his book on Future Time perspective, Nuttin (1985) proposed another two facets of time psychology apart from *time perspective*, which are *time attitude* and *time orientation*. The three aspects of time (time perspective, attitude, and orientation) are dissimilar yet closely connected in that they all refer to temporal experiences and views of the past, present, and future (Neukam, 2002). Nuttin (1985) explained that *time attitude* is "the positive or negative attitude towards the past, the present, and the future." Hence, an individual may have a positive or optimistic view of his future, in that it offers more opportunities than in the past, simultaneously also having a negative attitude towards the present moment. The third time element is *time orientation*, which refers to

> the preferential direction in a person's behaviour and thought, that is, whether the individual is oriented toward objects and events in the past, present, or future. Thus, one may assume for instance that most young people are future-oriented, whereas older people are past-oriented.

In the context of retirement planning, time is indeed an essence. Retirement will certainly occur sometime in the future, but the journey to reach that stage may be a long way forward for most people. For a fresh graduate who has just started working, retirement may be thirty to forty years down the road. Planning for such events may be daunting, and it is no wonder that most people would prefer to prioritise financial goals that would occur within a shorter time period.

3.6.2.3 Financial planning (Cognition)

Retirement planning is one of the key areas of personal finance, alongside risk management and insurance planning, investment planning, tax planning, and estate planning. In this regard, a study by Martin, Guillemette, and Browning (2016) found that retirement planning strategies reduced the negative effects between personal discount rate and retirement wealth. The financial planning strategies were measured by asking whether respondents consulted a financial planner and/ or whether they personally calculated their retirement income needs. The study found that those who had either personally planned for their retirement or used the help of a financial planner had a higher change in retirement wealth. Having a retirement plan would improve the reduction in retirement savings caused by a high personal discount rate.

Hershey et al. (2013) developed a three-dimensional framework to understand financial planning for retirement. The dimensions are capacity, willingness, and opportunity. Capacity relates to the knowledge, ability, and skills to plan for retirement. Willingness refers to the motives, attitudes, and emotions that drive a person to plan for retirement. Lastly, opportunity refers to external environment that facilitates effective retirement planning, such as the availability of retirement saving tools and the role of financial planners. Topa et al. (2018) extended Hershey's model by including psychosocial factors into the model. Among others, Topa's model suggests that an individual's involvement in the retirement planning process (under the dimension of willingness) and the engagement with a financial advisor (under the dimension of opportunity) would enhance the outcomes of financial planning for retirement.

The importance of financial planning was also supported by Kim and Hanna (2015) who found that households who were more financially sophisticated (using a proxy of use of a financial planner) were more likely to have adequate retirement savings than those who did not use the services of a financial planner. However, the authors also acknowledged that not everyone can afford to render the services of a Certified Financial Planner due to high fees charged for financial plans. This implies that individuals who have the opportunity and access to financial planners will tend to have better retirement outcomes than those without the opportunity. It can be argued that financial planning falls under the psychological domain of *cognition* as it entails using knowledge and understanding based on thoughts and experiences.

3.6.2.4 Goal setting (Motivation)

Generally, the literature posits that goals are an important precursor to planning behaviours (Friedman & Scholnick, 1997; Locke, Durham, Poon, & Weldon,

1997; Petkoska & Earl, 2009). In regards to retirement planning, Neukam (2002) suggested that there are two opposing motives driving individuals' retirement saving behaviour. *Inhibitory or fear factors* are those that impede one from planning for their future retirement, while *goal or achievement motives* are those that encourage one to formulate his or her plans. Some people fail to plan due to fearful beliefs of the uncertainties of the future, such as having insufficient savings for retirement and having to depend on social welfare or friends and family (Neukam, 2002). On the other hand, others are driven to save for retirement due to certain goals that they wish to achieve, such as a comfortable retirement, retirement vacations, etc. It is therefore argued that goal-setting comes under the psychological domain of *motivation* and drives people to plan for their retirement.

Other studies have also found evidence of a significant link between goal clarity and retirement planning (Hershey et al., 2007; Neukam, 2002). Goal clarity signifies how strongly delineated a person's goals are and reflects how much thought has been put in to achieving those goals, and is measured as how deep into thought one has visualised how life will be during retirement and whether clear goals have been set (Stawski et al., 2007). Past studies have observed that goal clarity significantly predicted pre-retirement planning behaviours, which ultimately led to higher amounts of retirement wealth (Stawski & Hershey, 2001). Stawski et al. (2007) found evidence of a sequential relationship linking goal clarity towards planning activities, of which consequently predicted the saving amounts contributed. Meanwhile, findings by Hershey et al. (2007) revealed that retirement goal clarity influenced the level of planning activity. An explanation to this relationship is because having well-defined retirement goals will provide a solid foundation to analyse one's financial needs during or upon retirement, leading to proper engagement and implementation of retirement plans. Past studies have clearly found that those with clear retirement objectives saved more aggressively compared to those with poorly defined goals (Hershey et al., 2007; Topa et al., 2018). Other studies found that the strength of financial goals positively influenced retirement savings contributions (Neukam & Hershey, 2003).

In the context of Malaysia, Zabri, Ahmad, and Lian (2016) measured goal clarity by asking respondents whether they set specific goals for retirement, whether they had a clear vision about how life would be in retirement, the extent to which they thought about retirement, and whether they discussed their retirement plans with their spouse or friends. Generally, the respondents in their study reported having clear retirement goals. However, how well these goals translate into positive retirement outcomes were not explored in the study.

Having discussed the research themes in retirement planning studies and the antecedents of retirement issues, particularly on the main dimensions of psychological determinants of retirement planning, the next section will discuss the policy recommendations in regards to retirement planning in Malaysia.

3.7 Policy recommendations

Policymakers and researchers have recognised that one of the main determinants of consumers' financial vulnerabilities, including inadequacies of retirement savings, is financial illiteracy. According to S&P Global Financial Literacy Survey (2014), only 36% of Malaysian adults are financially literate. Recognising the low levels of financial literacy among Malaysians, yet increasingly high demand and expectations of consumers today, the EPF introduced the Retirement Advisory Service (RAS) to assist EPF contributors to better plan for their retirement. Under the RAS, EPF officers are trained to give personalised advisory services to members that visit the EPF offices. The officers can offer advice on basic financial and retirement planning. By providing this service, officers disseminate financial advice and help educate EPF members on their retirement saving and advise them on how to plan for any shortfalls in their retirement savings. The RAS officers can also provide options to members on ways to increase their savings and pro-mote the PRS to members. In this vein, EPF should ensure that the RAS officers are duly trained with the relevant certifications such as the Registered Financial Planner (RFP) or Certified Financial Planner (CFP), provided by the MFPC and Financial Planning Association Malaysia (FPAM), respectively. Such qualifications would ensure that they would be able to provide more holistic and comprehen-sive financial advice to EPF members.

Perhaps not known to many is the fact that EPF contributors can opt to increase their contributions exceeding the statutory rate, and at any time, they can top-up their savings contributions. Rather than opting for PRS, adding up contributions to their EPF accounts would be another good option since there are not that many complex tasks involved adding up contributions to EPF as opposed to investing in PRS. The only option to be considered is perhaps the decision on whether to invest in the conventional or Shariah fund and the amounts to be invested. In addition, the Inland Revenue Board (IRB) should consider increasing the tax relief amounts for EPF and PRS contributions so that tax payers would be more encouraged to save for their retirement, especially for voluntary retirement schemes such as the PRS.

Employers should play a more proactive role in providing financial education, particularly in regards to retirement planning, to their employees. Newly hired employees should be given free financial education, and the employers should appoint dedicated financial planners to conduct financial education workshops. As Clark and d'Ambrosio (2003) found, financial education significantly altered the retirement planning behaviour of employees who attended the financial education workshop. Hence, the expected outcomes of financial education programmes are to increase financial literacy and instil positive retirement planning behaviours among employees.

Past studies have found that financial planning and goal clarity are important factors that influence retirement saving. The role of financial planners is there-fore vital to help people initiate voluntary retirement plans. Setting clear goals and seriously thinking about retirement is imperative in the retirement planning process. The MFPC and Financial Planning Association Malaysia (FPAM) thus play a key role in disseminating and alleviating awareness about the financial planning industry so that people are more receptive to the services of a financial planner or financial advisor. A key consideration is to foster trust and relationship between the planner and the client so that a long-lasting relationship can be built among them.

Thaler and Benartzi (2007) have long examined behavioural economics issues and recommended several suggestions to tackle the behavioural biases in retirement saving. Among the suggestions given is to automatically enrol employees

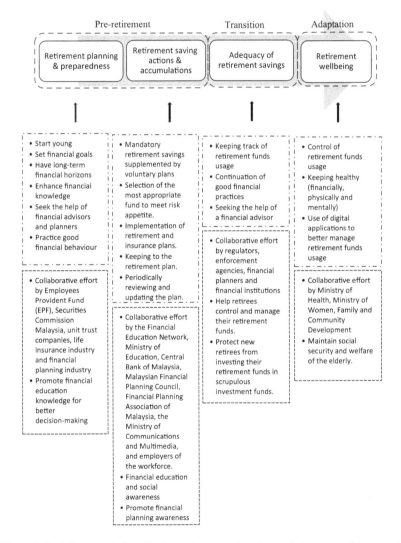

Figure 3.19 A framework for effective retirement planning and the responsible agencies.

in DC plans, which are allocated in the default conservative asset allocations. In the case of Malaysia, the PRS is voluntary and is not enforced upon employees. However, to encourage employees to participate, employers should make the enrolment easy and assisted by dedicated appointed financial advisors to take care of the needs of employees. This can be viewed as an additional benefit provided by firms to their employees. Another suggestion put forth by Thaler and Benartzi (2007) is to impose an auto escalation rate of contribution as income increases. Rather than having a fixed amount contributed, there could be an option for automatic escalation of contributions with salary increment.

To deal with the issue of time perspective, community service messages via radio, television, and social media should be broadcasted to instil the values of planning for the future rather than instant gratification. Currently, there are already efforts using community service messages that are being broadcasted to promote the importance of financial planning.[2] Plausibly, the use of an iconic celebrity to influence the mindset and behaviour of people would be more advantageous and effective. Thus, Malaysian celebrities and public figures should play a more prominent role by working together with policymakers and industry players to foster good financial behaviour among Malaysian consumers.

Extending the typology of research retirement planning based on Figure 3.18, Figure 3.19 maps out the recommended retirement planning strategies that can be adopted by Malaysian consumers and the relevant agencies that can assist in ensuring a sustainable retirement for the elderly in Malaysia.

Notes

1 Under the "Belanjawanku" (EPF, 2019) launched by the EPF and the Social Wellbeing Research Centre (SWRC), a couple in retirement living in the Klang Valley would need a minimum of RM3,090 monthly to fund their living expenses.
2 TV3 has broadcasted the message "Failing to plan is planning to fail", which is a general but useful community service message that applies to the mass public.

References

Almenberg, J. & Dreber, A. (2015). Gender, stock market participation and financial literacy. *Economics Letters, 137,* 140–142.

Al-Tamimi, H.A. & Kalli, A. (2009). Financial literacy and investment decisions of UAE investors. *The Journal of Risk Finance, 10*(5), 500–516.

Atkinson, A. & Messy, F.A. (2012). *Measuring Financial Literacy: Results of the OECD/ International Network on Financial Education (INFE) Pilot Study.*

Baranzini, M. (2005). Modigliani's life-cycle theory of savings fifty years later. *PSL Quarterly Review, 58*(233–234), 109–172.

Benartzi, S. & Thaler, R. (2007). Heuristics and biases in retirement savings behavior. *Journal of Economic perspectives, 21*(3), 81–104.

Bernheim, B.D., Skinner, J., & Weinberg, S. (2001). What accounts for the variation in retirement wealth among US households? *American Economic Review, 91*(4), 832–857.

Bloom, D.E., Chatterji, S., Kowal, P., Lloyd-Sherlock, P., McKee, M., Rechel, B., ... & Smith, J.P. (2015). Macroeconomic implications of population ageing and selected policy responses. *The Lancet, 385*(9968), 649–657.

Boisclair, D., Lusardi, A., & Michaud, P.C. (2017). Financial literacy and retirement planning in Canada. *Journal of Pension Economics & Finance, 16*(3), 277–296.

Browning, M. & Lusardi, A. (1996). Household saving: Micro theories and micro facts. *Journal of Economic literature, 34*(4), 1797–1855.

Burnett, J., Davis, K., Murawski, C., Wilkins, R., & Wilkinson, N. (2018). Measuring the adequacy of retirement savings. *Review of Income and Wealth, 64*(4), 900–927.

Carstensen, L.L., Isaacowitz, D.M., & Charles, S.T. (1999). Taking time seriously: A theory of socioemotional selectivity. *American Psychologist, 54*(3), 165.

Chee, L.K. (1997). The Malaysian Government Pension Scheme: Whither its future direction. *Jurnal Ekonomi Malaysia, 31*, 87–106.

Clark, R.L. & d'Ambrosio, M. (2003). Financial education and retirement savings. Retrieved on 14 August 2019 fromre https://papers.ssrn.com/sol3/papers.cfm?abstract_id=390642

De Vaus, D., Wells, Y., Kendig, H., & Quine, S. (2007). Does gradual retirement have better outcomes than abrupt retirement? Results from an Australian panel study. *Ageing & Society, 27*(5), 667–682.

Department of Statistics Malaysia (2016b). Current Population Estimates, Malaysia 2014–2016. Retrieved on 5 November 2019 from www.dosm.gov.my/v1/index.php?r=column/pdfPrev&id=OWlxdEVoYlJCS0hUZzJyRUcvZEYxZz09

Department of Statistics Malaysia (2018). Retrieved on 1 December 2019 from www.dosm.gov.my/v1/index.php?r=column/pdfPrev&id=aDV6TWxoU0NlNVBYN1hXM1Y0L2Jadz09

Department of Statistics Malaysia (*n.d.*). Malaysia's Population Pyramid 2010–2040. Retrieved on 1 December 2019 from https://dosm.gov.my/v1/index.php?r=column/cdatavisualization&menu_id=WjJMQ1F0N3RXclNGNWpIODBDRmh2UT09&bul_id=a0ZQRGIrV3k1R0FJeDBCYnFUZVU4Zz09

Department of Statistics Malaysia OSM (2016a). Population Projection (Revised). Retrieved on 5 November 2019 from www.dosm.gov.my/v1/index.php?r=column/pdfPrev&id=Y3kwU2tSNVFDOWp1YmtZYnhUeVBEdz09

Disney, R. & Gathergood, J. (2013). Financial literacy and consumer credit portfolios. *Journal of Banking & Finance, 37*(7), 2246–2254.

Earl, J.K., Bednall, T.C., & Muratore, A.M. (2015). A matter of time: Why some people plan for retirement and others do not. *Work, Aging and Retirement, 1*(2), 181–189.

Employees' Provident Fund (2014–2001). *EPF Annual Reports.* Retrieved on 1 December 2019 from www.kwsp.gov.my/about-epf/news-highlights/publications

Employees' Provident Fund (2015). *Annual Report 2015 – Empowering our Retirement.* Retrieved on 5 November 2019 from www.kwsp.gov.my/documents/20126/144335/Facts_at_a_Glance_2015.pdf/52e95602-137b-9369-02a7-e99e5ac7225b.

Employees' Provident Fund (2015). *Empowering our Retirement. EPF Annual Report.* Retrieved on 5 November 2019 from www.kwsp.gov.my/documents/20126/144335/Facts_at_a_Glance_2015.pdf/52e95602-137b-9369-02a7-e99e5ac7225b

Employees' Provident Fund (2016). *Annual Report 2016 – Achieving A Better Future.* Retrieved on 19 November 2019 from www.kwsp.gov.my/documents/20126/144342/Facts_at_a_Glance_2016.pdf/242c3315-2bec-e3fb-51e5-52206c21ef4b?t=1543963104020

Employees' Provident Fund (2016). *Annual Report 2016 – Giving Value Back*. Retrieved on 30 August 2019 from www.kwsp.gov.my/o/kwsp-theme/css/assets/pdf/annual-report/2016/3._GIVING_VALUE_BACK.pdf

Employees' Provident Fund (2017). *Annual Report 2017 – Facts at a Glance for 2017*. Retrieved on 30 August 2019 from www.kwsp.gov.my/o/kwsp-theme/css/assets/pdf/annual-report/2017/2._Overview_of_Results.pdf

Employees' Provident Fund (2018). *Annual Report 2018 – Live Life Now*. Retrieved on 18 December 2019 from www.kwsp.gov.my/documents/20126/974925/1.+Facts+At+A+Glance.pdf/cbf4777c-8415-202b-64f0-692e1f35955a?t=1564377638113

Employees' Provident Fund (2018). *Annual Report*. Retrieved on 19 November 2019 from www.kwsp.gov.my/documents/20126/974925/1.+Fakta+Sekilas+Pandang.pdf/3ea62364-a346-4638-a898-98c36e936b3f?t=1564377603313

Employees' Provident Fund (2019). *Belanjawanku – Klang Valley 2019*. Retrieved on 23 December 2019 from www.kwsp.gov.my/documents/20126/131635/Panduan_Belanjawanku.pdf/76872674-983a-3860-19a3-c47d2d2d2ab6

Employees' Provident Fund (*n.d.*). *Retirement Withdrawal*. Retrieved on 20 October 2019 from www.kwsp.gov.my/member/withdrawals/partial/age-50

Engen, E.M., Gale, W.G., Uccello, C.E., Carroll, C.D., & Laibson, D.I. (1999). The adequacy of household saving. *Brookings Papers on Economic Activity*, 1999(2), 65–187.

Fisher, P.J. & Montalto, C.P. (2010). Effect of saving motives and horizon on saving behaviors. *Journal of Economic Psychology*, *31*(1), 92–105.

Focus Malaysia (2019). PRS sets record-breaking 2018 with new members. Retrieved on 18 February 2020 from www.focusmalaysia.my/Snippets/prs-sets-record-breaking-2018-with-new-members

Folk, J.Y. (2019). Factors affecting age cohorts on life cycle retirement planning. *Asian Journal of Advanced Research and Reports*, 1–17.

Friedman, S.L. & Scholnick, E.K. (1997). *The Developmental Psychology of Planning: Why, How, and When Do We Plan?* Mahwah, NJ: Erlbaum.

Ghilarducci, T., Papadopoulos, M., & Webb, A. (2017). Inadequate retirement savings for workers nearing retirement. *Schwartz Center for Economic Policy Analysis and Department of Economics, The New School for Social Research, Policy Note Series*.

Hanna, S.D., Kim, K.T., & Chen, S.C.C. (2016). Retirement savings. In *Handbook of Consumer Finance Research* (pp. 33–43). Springer, Cham.

Hastings, J. & Mitchell, O.S. (2020). How financial literacy and impatience shape retirement wealth and investment behaviors. *Journal of Pension Economics & Finance*, *19*(1), 1–20.

Hastings, J., Mitchell, O.S., & Chyn, E. (2011). Fees, framing, and financial literacy in the choice of pension manager. In *Financial Literacy: Implications for Retirement Security and the Financial Marketplace*, eds. Mitchell, O.S. and Lusardi, A. Oxford, NY: Oxford University Press, 101–115.

Hershey, D.A. (2004). Psychological influences on the retirement investor. *CSA: Certified Senior Advisor*, 22, 31–39.

Hershey, D.A. & Mowen, J.C. (2000). Psychological determinants of financial preparedness for retirement. *The Gerontologist*, *40*(6), 687–697.

Hershey, D.A., Jacobs-Lawson, J.M., & Austin, J.T. (2013). Effective financial planning for retirement. In *The Oxford Handbook of Retirement*, ed. Wang M. Oxford, NY: Oxford University Press, 402–430.

Hershey, D.A., Jacobs-Lawson, J.M., McArdle, J.J., & Hamagami, F. (2007). Psychological foundations of financial planning for retirement. *Journal of Adult Development*, 14(1–2), 26–36.

Holzmann, R. (2015, May). Addressing Longevity Risk through Private Annuities: Issues and Options. In Conference paper presented at the 13th International Workshop on Pension Insurance and Savings Paris Dauphine (Vol. 28).

Index Mundi (*n.d.*). *Indonesia – Gross Savings (% of GDP)*. Retrieved on 28 April 2020 from www.indexmundi.com/facts/indonesia/gross-savings

Index Mundi (*n.d.*). *Indonesia – Households and NPISHs final consumption expenditure (% of GDP)*. Retrieved on 28 April 2020 from www.indexmundi.com/facts/indonesia/household-final-consumption-expenditure

Index Mundi (*n.d.*). *Malaysia – Gross Savings (% of GDP)*. Retrieved on 5 March 2020 from www.indexmundi.com/facts/malaysia/gross-savings

Index Mundi (*n.d.*). *Malaysia – Households and NPISHs final consumption expenditure (% of GDP)*. Retrieved on 5 March 2020 from www.indexmundi.com/facts/malaysia/household-final-consumption-expenditure

Index Mundi (*n.d.*). *Philippines – Gross Savings (% of GDP)*. Retrieved on 8 March 2020 from www.indexmundi.com/facts/phillipines/gross-savings

Index Mundi (*n.d.*). *Philippines – Households and NPISHs final consumption expenditure (% of GDP)*. Retrieved on 17 April 2020 from www.indexmundi.com/facts/philippines/household-final-consumption-expenditure

Index Mundi (*n.d.*). *Singapore – Gross Savings (% of GDP)*. Retrieved on 17 April 2020 from www.indexmundi.com/facts/singapore/gross-savings

Index Mundi (*n.d.*). *Singapore – Households and NPISHs final consumption expenditure (% of GDP)*. Retrieved on 17 April 2020 from www.indexmundi.com/facts/singapore/household-final-consumption-expenditure

Index Mundi (*n.d.*). *Thailand – Gross Savings (% of GDP)*. Retrieved on 8 March 2020 from www.indexmundi.com/facts/thailand/gross-savings

Index Mundi (*n.d.*). *Thailand – Households and NPISHs final consumption expenditure (% of GDP)*. Retrieved on 8 March 2020 from www.indexmundi.com/facts/thailand/household-final-consumption-expenditure

Inland Revenue Board of Malaysia (2019). *Tax Relief for Resident Individual*. Retrieved on 9 January 2020 from www.hasil.gov.my/bt_goindex.php?bt_kump=5&bt_skum=1&bt_posi=3&bt_unit=1&bt_sequ=1

Jacobs-Lawson, J.M. & Hershey, D.A. (2005). Influence of future time perspective, financial knowledge, and financial risk tolerance on retirement saving behaviors. *Financial Services Review-Greenwich-*, 14(4), 331.

Jappelli, T. & Modigliani, F. (1998). The age-saving profile and the life-cycle hypothesis. *Long-Run Growth and Short-Run Stabilization: Essays in Memory of Albert Ando*.

Jappelli, T. & Padula, M. (2013). Investment in financial literacy and saving decisions. *Journal of Banking & Finance*, 37(8), 2779–2792.

Kahneman, D. (2003). Maps of bounded rationality: Psychology for behavioral economics. *American Economic Review*, 93(5), 1449–1475.

Kasper, H., Mathur, A., Ong, F.S., Shannon, R., & Yingwattanakul, P. (2019). Contextual influences on financial preparedness of middle-aged workers: A four-country comparative life course study. *Journal of Global Scholars of Marketing Science*, 29(4), 423–439. 10.1080/21639159.2019.1613909

Keynes, J.M. (1936). *The General Theory of Employment, Investment, and Money*. London and New York, quoted from https://sites.google.com/site/biblioeconomicus/ KeynesJohnMaynard-TheGeneralTheoryOf EmploymentInterestAndMoney. pdf.

Khazanah Research Institute (2015). Population Ageing: Can We "Live Long and Prosper"? Retrieved on 10 April 2020 from www.krinstitute.org/kris_publication_ Population_Ageing_Can_We_Live_Long_and_Prosper.aspx

Kim, B.K. & Zauberman, G. (2009). Perception of anticipatory time in temporal discounting. *Journal of Neuroscience, Psychology, and Economics, 2*(2), 91–101. https:// doi.org/10.1037/a0017686

Kim, K.T. & Hanna, S.D. (2015). Does financial sophistication matter in retirement preparedness? *Journal of Personal Finance*, 14(2), 9–20. Retrieved from SSRN: https:// ssrn.com/abstract=2651293

Knoef, M., Been, J., Alessie, R., Caminada, K., Goudswaard, K., & Kalwij, A. (2016). Measuring retirement savings adequacy: Developing a multi-pillar approach in the Netherlands. *Journal of Pension Economics & Finance, 15*(1), 55–89.

Kumar, S., Tomar, S., & Verma, D. (2019). Women's financial planning for retirement systematic literature review and future research agenda. *International Journal of Bank Marketing, 37*(1), 120–141.

Lewin, K. (1951). *Field Theory in the Social Sciences: Selected Theoretical Papers*. New York: Harper.

Locke, E.A., Durham, C.C., Poon, J.M.L., & Weldon, E. (1997). Goal setting, planning, and performance on work tasks for individuals and groups. In S.L. Friedman & E.K. Scholnick (eds.), *The Developmental Psychology of Planning: Why, How, and When Do We Plan?* (pp. 239–262). Lawrence Erlbaum Associates Publishers.

Lusardi, A. (2008). Financial literacy: An essential tool for informed consumer choice? (No. w14084). *National Bureau of Economic Research*.

Lusardi, A. & Mitchell, O.S. (2017). How ordinary consumers make complex economic decisions: Financial literacy and retirement readiness. *Quarterly Journal of Finance, 7*(03), 1750008.

Lusardi, A. & Mitchelli, O.S. (2007). Financial literacy and retirement preparedness: Evidence and implications for financial education. *Business Economics, 42*(1), 35–44. 10.2145/20070104

Lusardi, A. & Tufano, P. (2015). Debt literacy, financial experiences, and overindebtedness. *Journal of Pension Economics & Finance, 14*(4), 332–368.

Mahdzan, N.S., Mohd-Any, A.A., & Chan, M.K. (2017). The influence of financial literacy, risk aversion and expectations on retirement planning and portfolio allocation in Malaysia. *Gadjah Mada International Journal of Business, 19*(3), 267.

Mahdzan, N.S. & Tabiani, S. (2013). The impact of financial literacy on individual saving: An exploratory study in the Malaysian context. *Transformations in Business and Economics, 12*(1/28), 41–55.

Malaysian Accounting Standards Board (MASB) (*n.d.*). *Accounting and Reporting by Retirement Benefit Plans*. Retrieved on 13 April 2019 from www.masb.org.my/article. php?id=280

Malaysian Financial Planning Council (MFPC) (*n.d.*). *6 Stages of Retirement Planning*. Retrieved on 13 February 2019 from https://mfpc.org.my/wp-content/uploads/ 2018/12/01@Slide-Note-6-Stages-of-Retirement-Planning.pdf

Martin Jr, T.K., Guillemette, M.A., & Browning, C.M. (2016). Do retirement planning strategies alter the effect of time preference on retirement wealth? *Applied Economics Letters, 23*(14), 1003–1005.

McKenzie, C.R. & Liersch, M.J. (2011). Misunderstanding savings growth: Implications for retirement savings behavior. *Journal of Marketing Research, 48*(SPL), S1–S13.

Modigliani, F. (1986). Life cycle, individual thrift, and the wealth of nations. *The American Economic Review, 76*(3) 297–313.

Modigliani, F. & Brumberg, R. (1954). Utility analysis and the consumption function: An interpretation of cross-section data. *Franco Modigliani, 1*, 388–436.

Motika, M. (2019). Personality traits and low wealth at retirement. *Eastern Economic Journal, 45*(3), 464–476.

Muratore, A.M. & Earl, J.K. (2015). Improving retirement outcomes: The role of resources, pre-retirement planning and transition characteristics. *Ageing & Society, 35*(10), 2100–2140.

Mustafa, A., Yusof, S.K., Silim, A., Adiman, R., & Hassan, N.L. (2017). Factors influencing retirement planning behaviour of lecturers in polytechnics. *Advanced Journal of Technical and Vocational Education, 1*(4), 09–13.

Neukam, K.A. (2002). Fear and goal-based planning motives: A psychological model of financial planning for retirement (Doctoral dissertation, Oklahoma State University).

Neukam, K.A. & Hershey, D.A. (2003). Financial inhibition, financial activation, and saving for retirement. *Financial Services Review, 12*(1), 19.

O'Donoghue, T. & Rabin, M. (1999). Doing it now or later. *American Economic Review, 89*(1), 103–124.

OECD (*n.d*). *Saving rate*. Retrieved on 8 August 2020 from https://data.oecd.org/natincome/saving-rate.htm

Pang, G. & Warshawsky, M. (2014). Retirement savings adequacy of US workers. *Benefits Quarterly, 30*(1), 29-38.

Peach, R.W. & Steindel, C. (2000). A nation of spendthrifts? An analysis of trends in personal and gross saving. *Current Issues in Economics and Finance, 6*(10), 1-6.

Petkoska, J. & Earl, J.K. (2009). Understanding the influence of demographic and psychological variables on retirement planning. *Psychology and Aging, 24*(1), 245.

Public Service Department (*n.d.*). Penambahbaikan Skim Faedah Persaraan. Portal Rasmi Bahagian Pasca Perkhidmatan JPA. Retrieved on 2 June 2020 from www.jpapencen.gov.my/penambahbaikan_faedah_persaraan.html

Rahim, M.S., Yusof, M.A., & Ismail, M.S. (2011). The reporting of employee retirement benefits in Malaysia prior to FRS119. *International Journal of Business and Social Science, 2*(5), 249–258.

Reitzes, D.C. & Mutran, E.J. (2004). The transition to retirement: Stages and factors that influence retirement adjustment. *The International Journal of Aging and Human Development, 59*(1), 63–84.

Robinson, O.C., Demetre, J.D., & Corney, R. (2010). Personality and retirement: Exploring the links between the Big Five personality traits, reasons for retirement and the experience of being retired. *Personality and Individual Differences, 48*(7), 792–797.

S&P Global FinLit Survey (2014). *Financial Literacy Around the World: Insights from the Standard & Poor's Ratings Services Global Financial Literacy Survey*. Retrieved on 21 August 2020 from https://gflec.org/initiatives/sp-global-finlit-survey/

Sevim, N., Temizel, F., & Sayılır, Ö. (2012). The effects of financial literacy on the borrowing behaviour of Turkish financial consumers. *International Journal of Consumer Studies, 36*(5), 573–579.

Shefrin, H. (2002). *Beyond Greed and Fear: Understanding Behavioral Finance and the Psychology of Investing*. Oxford University Press on Demand.

Shefrin, H.M. & Thaler, R.H. (1988). The behavioral life-cycle hypothesis. *Economic Inquiry, 26*(4), 609–643.

Simon, H.A. (1955). A behavioral model of rational choice. *The Quarterly Journal of Economics, 69*(1), 99–118.

Soman, D., Ainslie, G., Frederick, S., Li, X., Lynch, J., Moreau, P., … & Wertenbroch, K. (2005). The psychology of intertemporal discounting: Why are distant events valued differently from proximal ones? *Marketing Letters, 16*(3–4), 347–360.

Stawski, R.S., Hershey, D.A., & Jacobs-Lawson, J.M. (2007). Goal clarity and financial planning activities as determinants of retirement savings contributions. *The International Journal of Aging and Human Development, 64*(1), 13–32.

Stawski, R. & Hershey, D.A. (2001, October). Goal clarity as a predictor of financial planning for retirement. *Gerontologist, 41*, 142–143.

Thaler, R.H. & Benartzi, S. (2007). The behavioral economics of retirement savings behavior. AARP Public Policy Institute (PPI). Retrieved on 20 August 2020 from www.albacharia.ma/xmlui/bitstream/handle/123456789/31865/2007_02_savings.pdf?sequence=1

Thaler, R.H. (1999). Mental accounting matters. *Journal of Behavioral Decision Making, 12*(3), 183–206.

Thaler, R.H. & Benartzi, S. (2004). Save more tomorrow™: Using behavioral economics to increase employee saving. *Journal of Political Economy, 112*(S1), S164–S187.

Thaler, R.H. (1981). Some empirical evidence on dynamic inconsistency. *Economics Letters, 8*, 201–207.

The Edge (2015). *Malaysia's EPF says 80% of workers have savings below poverty line as they turn 55. Sheridan Mahavera*. Retrieved on 7 June 2020 from www.theedgemarkets.com/article/malaysias-epf-says-80-workers-have-savings-below-poverty-line-they-turn-55

The Star Online (2012). *PM Launches New Voluntary Private Retirement Scheme*. Retrieved on 21 August 2020 from www.thestar.com.my/news/nation/2012/07/18/pm-launches-new-voluntary-private-retirement-scheme

Topa, G. & Valero, E. (2017). Preparing for retirement: How self-efficacy and resource threats contribute to retirees' satisfaction, depression, and losses. *European Journal of Work and Organizational Psychology, 26*(6), 811–827. 10.1080/1359432X.2017.1375910

Topa, G., Lunceford, G., & Boyatzis, R.E. (2018). Financial planning for retirement: A psychosocial perspective. *Frontiers in Psychology, 8*, 2338.

Tversky, A. & Kahneman, D. (1979). Prospect theory: An analysis of decision under risk. Econometrica, *47*(2), 263–291.

Van Rooij, M., Lusardi, A., & Alessie, R. (2011). Financial literacy and stock market participation. *Journal of Financial Economics, 101*(2), 449–472.

Wärneryd, K.E. (1999). *The Psychology of Saving*. Edward Elgar Publishing, No. 1694, November.

World Bank (*n.d.*). *Life Expectancy at Birth, Total (Years)*. Retrieved on 21 August 2020 from https://data.worldbank.org/indicator/sp.dyn.le00.in

World Health Organization (2011). *Global Health and Aging*. Retrieved on 21 August 2020 from www.who.int/ageing/publications/global_health.pdf

Zabri, S.M., Ahmad, K., & Lian, A.A.L.H. (2016). The awareness of private retirement scheme and the retirement planning practices among private sector employees in Malaysia. *International Journal of Economics and Financial Issues, 6*(6S), 120–124.

Zauberman, G. (2003). The intertemporal dynamics of consumer lock-in. *Journal of Consumer Research, 30*(3), 405–419.

Zimbardo, P.G. & Boyd, J.N. (2015). Putting time in perspective: A valid, reliable individual-differences metric. *Time Perspective Theory; Review, Research and Application* (pp. 17–55). Springer, Cham.

4 Falling prey to financial fraud

Investigating the causes of victimisation

4.0 Introduction

The problem of financial frauds and scams in Malaysia that will be discussed in this chapter is the third issue on consumer financial vulnerabilities explored in this book. Following this introductory section, the second section of this chapter begins by explaining the financial fraud and scam scenarios in Malaysia, including a discussion on the financial frauds and scams definition as well as statistics and empirical data in regards to them. Data from the Divisions of Commercial Crime Investigation Department, Royal Malaysian Police will be presented and discussed to show some trends in financial crimes among Malaysians. The different patterns of financial frauds and scams, specifically to Malaysian consumers, will also be discussed. A brief review of the literature is presented in the third section of this chapter, which locates the main arguments explaining why there are still many Malaysians falling victims to these frauds even though various information, as well as their modus operandi, have been disseminated. The factors that influence Malaysian consumer behaviour to believe in the financial fraud schemes, focusing on psychological and behavioural aspects will also be discussed. Finally, the chapter ends by analysing the policy and legal implications from the findings and provide suggestions for consumers and other relevant stakeholders, including the financial services sector, and policymakers to better protect consumers and the society from any type of financial frauds and scams.

4.1 Financial fraud issues – the Malaysian scenario

4.1.1 Evidence of financial fraud cases in Malaysia

Financial fraud is defined as an illegal activity of providing false information to someone so that they will invest in something. It is also generally referred to as a varied range of deceptive practices involving financial transactions by criminals or scammers for the purpose of personal gain. These practices can include fictitious opportunities or misleading information where fraudsters can contact their potential victims via different channels such as emails, phone calls, or face-to-face interaction (Bank Negara Malaysia, 2010). It is also known as a violation of security laws or deceptive practice in the investment markets. Fraudsters will normally entice investors to make investment decisions on the basis of false information, which frequently results in losses.

Previous studies have shown that the effect of this crime clearly falls onto different stakeholders, including individuals, group of societies, financial institutions, and perhaps most damaging of all, government or financial regulators. For example, Zunzunegui et al. (2017) reported that victims of financial frauds will have poor life quality such as inferior physical and mental health as well as more sleeping problems compared to their similar age counterparts. Hofstetter, Mejía, Rosas, and Urrutia (2018), on the other hand, studied the effects of financial fraud schemes on formal financial institutions. They found that deposits in the financial institutions were inversely related to the growth of these fraudulent schemes. In addition, they reported that individuals pulled resources away from the financial institutions in order to invest in those schemes. The effects of financial frauds on financial regulators were discussed separately by Baucus and Mitteness (2016) and Bruhn (2019). However, both studies lead to the same conclusion. They argue that many investors who participated in fraudulent schemes have mistakenly believed that they were investing with legal and ethical institutions who were pursuing wealth creation for them. This incident leads them to have less trust in the financial system and the credibility of government and financial regulators. Therefore, it is important to explore financial fraud scenarios in order to minimise its negative effects on different parties and stakeholders.

In Malaysia, financial frauds and scams have become a prevalent and damaging problem among the society. In 2017 for example, approximately 28,575 Malaysians were victims of at least one of the many different types of financial fraud offences tracked by the Commercial Crime Department of Royal Malaysian Police, amounting to a loss of RM1.94 billion. During the years 2010 to 2017, 173,252 police reports were received regarding the financial crime cases. Of these, Selangor recorded the highest number with a total of 39,548 reports (equivalent to 22.8%), followed by Kuala Lumpur (25,490), and Johor (25,423). Out of the 14 states nationwide, Perlis recorded the lowest crime cases with a total of 1,675 reports followed by Kelantan (4,233) and Terengganu (4,306). The number of reported cases then decreased from year 2010 until 2013 before it continuously increased and reached the highest peak in year 2017. The full list is shown in Table 4.1. Apart from the Royal Malaysian Police, Securities Commission, Central Bank of Malaysia, Malaysia Co-operative Societies Commission, Malaysian Communications, and Multimedia Commission as well as the Ministry of Domestic Trade and Consumer Affairs are also involved in regulating the financial and financial activities of companies and individuals that provide services to consumers. At the same time, these bodies also maintain the integrity of financial markets in Malaysia.

Between the year 2010 and 2017, financial fraud and scam cases were registered as the highest number of cases reported to the Royal Malaysian Police. A total of 121,127 cases were recorded during this period. Other cases that

Table 4.1 Financial crime cases by state in Malaysia (2010 to 2017)

State	2010	2011	2012	2013	2014	2015	2016	2017	Total
Perlis	112	224	197	208	135	206	309	284	1,675
Kedah	1,025	1,046	821	725	624	830	1,309	1,911	8,291
P.Pinang	1,559	1,384	1,155	943	688	945	1,822	1,622	10,118
Perak	1,753	1,718	1,299	1,294	1,507	1,484	2,126	2,404	13,585
Selangor	5,848	4,936	3,775	3,246	3,945	4,198	6,743	6,857	39,548
K.Lumpur	3,115	3,506	2,707	2,278	2,717	3,164	4,690	3,313	25,490
N.Sembilan	1,104	982	946	872	561	843	934	1,490	7,732
Melaka	1,202	686	816	960	661	923	974	1,429	7,651
Johor	3,608	3,162	2,968	2,769	2,591	3,109	3,772	3,444	25,423
Pahang	1,015	1,054	947	996	964	776	997	1,362	8,111
Terengganu	715	608	468	430	468	509	540	568	4,306
Kelantan	479	498	329	330	675	539	696	687	4,233
Sabah	1,254	1,191	1,128	901	870	1,088	1,050	1,597	9,079
Sarawak	1,216	1,028	830	706	542	972	1,109	1,607	8,010
Total	**24,005**	**22,023**	**18,386**	**16,658**	**16,948**	**19,586**	**27,071**	**28,575**	**173,252**

Source: Divisions of Commercial Crime Investigation Department (2019), Royal Malaysian Police.

were recorded as the highest contributor to this period of statistics are breach of criminal trust, VCD/DVD pirated case, and cybercrime. All of the three cases each recorded a total of 22,811 cases for breach of criminal trust, 9,025 cases for VCD/DVD, and 7,104 cases for cybercrime. Similar to Table 4.1, all cases recorded a declining trend between year 2010 and 2013 except for loan shark cases before it increased back up to year 2017. Table 4.2 shows a comparison of statistics between the different types of crime cases.

Although statistics of the number of financial crimes show a declining trend over the years 2010 to 2013, but touching on the issue of total loss, the amount showed an increasing trend and reached the highest record in year 2015 where the amount of total losses recorded amounted to RM12.323 billion. Based on Table 4.3, it can be seen that financial fraud and scam cases contribute to the highest total loss of RM7.539 billion, followed by a breach of criminal trust cases (RM4.608 billion) for the period between year 2010 and 2017. The majority of other cases also recorded an increase in their total losses every year. As reported in the previous tables, the financial fraud trend in Malaysia for years between 2010 and 2017 has shown a mixed trend with a significant increment in the total number of cases and losses in the last three years.

Financial fraud and scam cases involve different types of sophistication methods that come with different names and titles. With the advancement of technology and information system, criminals are getting smarter and can manipulate the use of technology for the wrong purpose especially involving the use of emails, social media, and other telecommunication tools. For example, in a press statement dated 8 October 2018, the Communications and Multimedia Minister of Malaysia, revealed that from January to 3 October 2018, a total of 8,313 cybercrime cases were reported to the Royal Malaysian Police, with approximately RM300 million total losses. The loss amount recorded over a similar period in 2017 was about RM184.2 million (*Daily Express*, 2018). Similarly, Table 4.4 shows the statistics of computer security incidents reported by the Malaysia Computer Emergency Response Team (MyCERT) between year 2010 and 2019. A total of 103,520 cases were recorded during this period. Out of nine incident classifications, fraud recorded the highest number of cases with a total of 44,389 reports. This statistic indicates that this more advanced digital era has also led to an increase in cases of financial fraud through computer security attacks. Therefore, consumers need to use these technologies wisely and put extra caution in sharing information, especially information that is related to personal data.

4.1.2 Different patterns of the most common financial frauds and scams in Malaysia

This section will provide some definitions and details on the different patterns of financial frauds and scams that are commonly reported to the Royal Malaysia Police. This includes Pyramid and Ponzi schemes, African scam, Parcel scam,

Table 4.2 Financial crime by type of offense (2010 to 2017)

Type of Offenses	2010	2011	2012	2013	2014	2015	2016	2017	Total
Financial Frauds and Scams	13,622	14,267	12,164	11,776	11,640	14,186	20,684	22,788	**121,127**
Breach of Criminal Trust	3,480	3,071	2,773	2,557	2,554	2,613	3,165	2,598	**22,811**
Misuse of Property	268	207	154	105	84	92	144	72	**1,126**
Cybercrime	2,239	1,682	942	257	287	441	718	538	**7,104**
Forgery	418	316	235	157	116	149	190	160	**1,741**
Counterfeit Money	1,456	504	152	234	214	215	233	281	**3,289**
Loan Shark (Ah Long)	278	267	448	478	734	951	1,414	1,187	**5,757**
Other Cases of Commercial Crime	220	147	108	120	153	135	124	265	**1,272**
VCD/DVD Case	2,024	1,562	1,410	974	1,166	804	399	686	**9,025**
Total	**24,005**	**22,023**	**18,386**	**16,658**	**16,948**	**19,586**	**27,071**	**28,575**	**173,252**

Source: Divisions of Commercial Crime Investigation Department (2019), Royal Malaysian Police.

Table 4.3 Value of losses by type of offense (2010 to 2017)

Type of Offenses	2010 (RM)	2011 (RM)	2012 (RM)	2013 (RM)
Financial Frauds and Scams	599,422,770	839,025,124	1,131,215,263	655,333,545
Breach of Criminal Trust	279,837,153	278,117,667	461,839,752	1,070,049,185
Misuse of Property	3,043,133	3,739,069	2,462,432	1,940,699
CyberCrime	11,509,647	6,825,366	13,848,651	3,952,232
Forgery	15,287,364	67,806,478	6,784,170	36,598,283
Counterfeit Money	275,760	59,570	33,343	93,672
Loan Shark (Ah Long)	555,694	1,086,890	3,252,240	5,740,670
Other Cases of Commercial Crime	8,051,457	1,164,915	0	101,700
Total	**917,982,979**	**1,197,825,079**	**1,619,435,850**	**1,773,809,986**

Source: Divisions of Commercial Crime Investigation Department (2019), Royal Malaysian Police.

Love scam, Inheritance scam, E-banking scam and Macau scam, financing or loan scam, phone scam, and credit card fraud.

4.1.2.1 Ponzi and Pyramid schemes

A Ponzi or Pyramid scheme is well known as a get-rich-quick scheme. This type of scheme often promises its investors an investment plan that offers high rates of return with little or no risk. Since the early 1900s, the "get rich quick" term has been used to describe shady investments.[1] With little risk and with little skills, effort, or time, this type of scheme will create an impression that a constant flow of new money or a high rate of return can be obtained by its participants. In reality, no actual investment was made, rather, the money received from its participants was used by the founders for their personal gain and to pay those who invested earlier. The scheme will start to collapse when large numbers of existing investors cash out or when it becomes hard to recruit new investors. In Malaysia, any types of get-rich-quick schemes like the pyramid or Ponzi schemes, which offer exorbitant returns on investment, are considered illegal by the Malaysian jurisdiction. In year 2016, from January until June, the Royal Malaysian Police received 485 reports involving get-rich-quick schemes, with losses amounting to RM116,116,658. A 152% increase in the monetary amount worth RM81,489,073 was recorded compared to a similar period in year 2014 and 2015 (*New Straits Time*, 2016a).

2014 (RM)	2015 (RM)	2016 (RM)	2017 (RM)	Total (RM)
788,552,932	1,080,717,917	1,068,240,985	1,376,809,136	**7,539,317,672**
420,683,729	1,136,514,724	502,663,663	458,444,367	**4,608,150,240**
1,637,186	1,786,774	3,142,228	1,523,919	**19,275,439**
23,099,574	9,587,816	9,573,653	7,079,867	**85,476,806**
7,767,297	14,071,123	6,129,554	13,557,788	**168,002,057**
154,602	478,783	251,628	1,007,820	**2,355,178**
4,536,720	32,375,720	16,210,445	60,099,287	**123,857,666**
1,506,884	47,278,583	2,521,550	25,492,182	**86,117,271**
1,247,938,923	**2,322,811,441**	**1,608,733,707**	**1,944,014,366**	**12,632,552,329**

Although pyramid schemes and Ponzi schemes are both known as get-rich-quick schemes, they are actually different from each other. A pyramid scheme mainly focuses on members' recruitment, while a Ponzi scheme is a form of fraud that pays existing investors with money or funds collected from new investors. In a pyramid scheme, members who successfully recruit or enrol newcomers into the scheme will receive certain amounts of payments, rather than selling products or supply of investments. This pyramid scheme is highly unsustainable and often illegal. Most members are unable to profit when the recruitment multiplies and recruiting becomes impossible. Pyramid schemes have existed for many years under different names, and some multi-level marketing (MLM) businesses are also categorised as pyramid schemes. A Ponzi scheme, on the other hand, leads victims to believe that the high returns they earned are coming from different profitable investments made by the fraudsters. The victims remain unaware that the source of funds they receive are coming from other investors. The illusion of a Ponzi scheme as a sustainable business can be maintained as long as these three conditions exist. First, the scheme can still find new investors to contribute for new funds. Second, all investors do not demand full repayment at the same time. Third, most investors still believe that the scheme is genuine.

Ponzi and pyramid schemes are related because they are both forms of financial fraud and scam. Nevertheless, Ponzi schemes are based on the principle of "Robbing Peter to pay Paul", where money put for investment by investors who come later will be used by the scheme to pay earlier investors. In other words, the

Table 4.4 Reported cybercrime cases based on classification (2010 to 2019)

Incident	2010	2011	2012	2013	2014	2015	2016	2017	2018	2019	Total
Content Related	39	59	20	54	35	33	50	46	111	298	745
Cyber Harassment	419	459	300	512	550	442	529	560	356	260	4,387
Denial of Service	66	78	23	19	29	38	66	40	10	19	388
Fraud	2,212	5,328	3,991	4,485	4,477	3,257	3,921	3,821	5,123	7,774	44,389
Intrusion	2,160	3,699	4,326	2,770	1,125	1,714	2,476	2,011	1,160	1,359	22,800
Intrusion Attempt	685	734	67	76	1,302	303	277	266	1,805	104	5,619
Malicious Codes	1,199	1,012	645	1,751	716	567	435	814	1,700	738	9,577
Spam	1,268	3,751	526	950	3,650	3,539	545	344	342	129	15,044
Vulnerabilities	42	98	78	19	34	22	35	60	92	91	571
	8,090	15,218	9,976	10,636	11,918	9,915	8,334	7,962	10,699	10,772	103,520

Source: Malaysia Computer Emergency Response Team (MyCERT) (2019), CyberSecurity Malaysia.

Ponzi scheme operator will become an entity in the middle, taking money from one party, keeping some of it, and pays profit to investors who had invested in the scheme earlier. Initially, the scheme will pay very high returns to initial investors in order to entice them to put more money and to attract more investors to join the scheme. When other investors begin to participate, the scheme will start paying the early investors through the proceeds of investments by later investors. Pyramid schemes, on the other hand, are based on network marketing, where an individual who wishes to join the scheme is required to make a membership fee payment. In return, the scheme promises its new members that for every additional member they recruit, they will be given a share of the membership fee. The pyramid scheme operators will try to make the scheme operation look like a legitimate business, but no genuine product or service is actually involved. The primary focus is on new participants' recruitment. The scheme fails simply because when it gets too big, there are no more people to be recruited; therefore, the last group of investors who joined the scheme will lose their money.

Legitimate MLM schemes are often being confused with pyramid schemes. Unlike pyramid schemes, legitimate MLM plans have real products or services being sold. According to the Direct Sales and Anti-Pyramid Scheme Act (1993) Malaysia, pyramid schemes, however, focus on recruiting new people, rather than selling products. Any products or services promoted by pyramid schemes are used to simply hide their fraud structure. Products or services offered by pyramid schemes normally have a very high markup, which makes them totally overpriced. In addition, profit made from the pyramid MLM scheme is often based on the number of people who participated or recruited. However, a legitimate MLM will make profit based on sales or services provided to the customers. Therefore, it is best to avoid schemes that offer passive income or easy money, emphasise on recruiting members rather than selling genuine products or services, and promise high returns in a short time period (SEC Investor, *n.d.*).

4.1.2.2 *African scam*

African scams or frauds are often initiated by syndicates made up of Africans. Since the first wave of the scam came from Nigeria, the scam is also known as "Nigerian scam." The most commonly used modes of African scam operation are through someone from overseas who offers the victims a share in a payment or a large sum of money on condition that they help them with money transfer out of their country (Australian Competition and Consumer Commission, *n.d.*). They are often found using Internet networks, especially social media sites like Facebook, Twitter, or email to find and trick victims. For example, in 2014, the Commercial Crime Department, Royal Malaysia Police recorded 1,028 cases involving losses of over RM52.3 million related to African scams. In 2015, the Department reported a significant increase in the total number of cases (1,521 cases) and losses (RM71 million) involving the scams. This shows an increase of 47.9% and 36% for cases and losses, respectively (New Straits Time, 2016b).

Despite its Nigerian origin, this African scam is now operated in various places all over the world. The scammers will often use countries that are currently in the news for coups or civil wars to create stories to victims that their money was trapped in banks during the events. The victims are promised a large sum of money if they successfully help them bring out the money from the country. Alternatively, the scammers will use a large inheritance money as a story. The story will continue by telling the victims that due to their government restrictions or taxes in their country, it becomes difficult for them to access the money. These scammers will then request the victims to help them to transfer their personal fortune out of the country. They will first ask the victims' bank account details before they use the information to steal money from the account. Otherwise, the victims are requested to pay some fees or charges to help them transfer or release the money out of the country through the victims' bank. These fees start out as small amounts before the scammers continuously ask for more money in order for the victims to claim their share or rewards. Motivated by the large sum of money promised, the victims will continue to make payment until they finally realise that they are caught in a scam and the promised money will never be sent.

4.1.2.3 Parcel scam

Scammers in parcel scam cases will usually identify the victims through social media. The scammer will normally convince the victim that he has fallen in love with the victim and then wishes to send the parcel to the victim as a token of love. Once the package is delivered to the country where the victim resides, someone claiming to be a customs officer or company courier will notify and contact the victim to inform that the parcel has arrived. The victim is later asked to pay tax or insurance on the package that was found to contain undisclosed money or valuables. The victim will also receive calls from a local individual saying that the payment needs to be paid into an account that is usually owned by someone locally. The victim will only realise that he or she is being cheated when the promised goods are not received and the syndicate continues to demand for money from the victims for various reasons. There were 1,847 cases involving parcel delivery in year 2016 reported by the Commercial Crime Department, Royal Malaysia Police (New Straits Time, 2017a).

4.1.2.4 Love scam

Love scam or romance scam refers to a confidence trick that aims to gain victims' affection via fake online romantic relationships in order to get access to victims' money or wealth. In Malaysia, many are falling prey to this type of scam, especially women. For example, a total loss of RM61.9 million involving 1,652 love scam cases were reported by the Commercial Crime Department, Royal Malaysia Police (*New Straits Times*, 2018a).

The modus operandi used in this type of scam is not much different than a parcel scam. In many instances, dating websites, apps, or social media are used by the scammers to trap victims. Scammers will pretend to be a prospective companion to the victims who are looking for romantic partners. Scammers will then exchange communication with the victim over a certain period of time until the scammer feels that the victim has fallen in love with them. There are many narratives used by the scammers before they can get access to the victims' money, gifts, or personal details. One of the most popular methods used in Malaysia is the scammers usually claim that they live abroad and want to visit and marry the victim. Upon arrival, they will claim that they have been detained by the authorities and require help from the victim to pay a certain sum of money to allow them to be released. These love scammers are very skilful in earning trust from their victims. They are good with their word arrangement and are also often sweet talkers, which help them to easily deceit their victims who will eventually surrender money or personal details to them.

4.1.2.5 Inheritance scam

Inheritance scam is associated with a claim of a large amount of bequest from a wealthy benefactor or a distant relative. A potential victim will be contacted by the scammer who usually disguises as a banker, lawyer, or a foreign official via email or a social networking message. The scammer will then inform the victim about a wealthy deceased person who left no other beneficiaries and has chosen the victim as his or her heir to receive the inheritance. The scammer might alternatively say that the victim is a distant relative and can inherit the fortune of a wealthy person who has died without a will. The scammers will often claim that the wealth or money is outside the country and would charge a fee to manage the transfer of the inheritance to the victim. The scammers will then request the victim to give them his or her personal details as well as the fee payment before they can transfer the wealth ownership to the victim's name or money to the victim's account. In order to convince the victim, some fake supporting documents from certain government agencies like courts, the judiciary, or central bank are provided. The victims only realise that they have been fooled when the person who acts as a middleman goes missing and the promised property or wealth does not exist. The Royal Malaysian Police has advised Malaysians not to believe in any emails, messages, or phone calls claiming that they have inherited money, property, or wealth belonging to an unknown individual. These messages may contain fraudulent syndicates who are looking for their preys (The Borneo Post, 2018).

4.1.2.6 E-banking scam

E-banking scam refers to a fraud where the scammer tricks the victim into giving his or her private banking information for the purpose of stealing money or gaining other benefits. The reported cases are mostly cases of illegal withdrawals from bank accounts. Most cases are due to customer negligence for revealing their personal identification numbers (PINs) and passwords to a third party. In most cases, the victim receives a short message service (SMS) mentioning that the victim has won a cash prize. In order to claim the prize, the victim is directed to open an Internet banking account and follow the instructions provided by the scammers, including revealing a PIN number and bank verification code that they receive through SMS.

4.1.2.7 Macau scam

Macau scam is a form of criminal phone fraud where scammers often gain access to victim's private and personal financial information via a telephone system by using a special social engineering technique. In most cases, the victim will be contacted by a syndicate member who will disguise himself as a bank officer and inform the victim that he/she has a credit card in arrears. Alternatively, the syndicate may also disguise themselves as police officers and contact the victim and claim that the victim was involved in a money laundering case. According to the Royal Malaysian Police, the syndicate will use a technique known as the spoofing caller identity where this technique allows syndicate members to determine what numbers will appear on the screen of the victim's phone. Normally, the number that appears on the victim's cell phone is a number of a real bank or the Royal Malaysian Police headquarters in Bukit Aman, Kuala Lumpur. In this case, the victim is deceived by the next call and will obey all instructions given to them until the end where they are directed to transfer their money to the syndicate's account. In 2017, 4,500 such cases were recorded at a loss reaching RM 113.1 million. This amount shows a significant increase compared to the last five years' figure of 2012, which recorded only 821 cases with RM22.4 million losses (Utusan Online, 2018a).

4.1.2.8 Financing or loan scam

Financing or a loan scam involves syndicates that pretend to be an established credit company offering cash loans. The modus operandi used by the scam is to offer the victims loans that do not exist. Victims, on the other hand, will believe them and may be desperate to apply for the loan. After the victim has sent their documents to the syndicate, the scammer will then contact the victim, state that the loan has been approved, and ask the victim to pay a tax where the scammer will use a fake Inland Revenue Board (IRB) certificate and send it to the victim. In addition to that, the scammer would then request the victim to pay insurance to cover the loan agreement before the loan amount can be credited. According to the Royal Malaysian Police, a total of 513 cases were reported during 2017 involving losses of approximately RM32.187 million. As of 3 October 2018, a total of 286 fraud cases in 2018 were reported involving a loss of RM37.284 million. This figure clearly shows that while the number of fraud cases is less than those recorded in 2017, the value of the losses is even greater (Malaysian Communications and Multimedia Commission, 2018).

4.1.2.9 *Phone scam*

A phone scam is one of the techniques used by fraudsters to defraud people out of their money, targeting households across the country. Fraudsters will normally call members of the household pretending to be from a trusted organisation like the police, a bank, a government office, a court, or from a utilities company. They will try to get the victims' personal or financial information and will encourage them to hand over their money or trick them into transferring money to accounts they control. One of the most common methods used by the fraudsters is to pose as the victims' bank or the police. These fraudsters will claim that there has been fraud on the victims' bank account, and the victims need to act quickly to protect the money. They will suggest the victims to transfer their money to a so-called "safe account," which is under their control and will steal the money immediately after it has been transferred. Fraudsters can sound extremely professional to convince that their call is genuine and will even threat the victims that they may be put in prison if they refuse to do so. Fraudsters may already have some information about the victims' name and address in order to claim that they are representing a legitimate organisation that the victims know. It is really important to be cautious of any unsolicited phone calls, especially when they ask to transfer money to a new account for fraud reasons because banks or the police will never ask to make such actions. According to the Ministry of Home Affairs, Malaysians lost over RM224 million to online and phone scams in year 2018 (Malaymail Online, 2019).

4.1.2.10 *Credit card fraud*

Credit card fraud involves transactions that charge the purchase or expenses of goods and services without the permission of the cardholder. According to Bank Negara Malaysia (BNM), such transaction often occurs as a result of stolen, lost, or unreceived credit cards. It may also happen due to other fraudulent conditions such as counterfeit or credit card issued on a fraudulent application (Bank Negara Malaysia, 2020). The modus operandi used in this type of scam is a fraudster who will contact victims requesting them to confirm a credit card transaction and ask whether the credit card transaction had taken place. Once the victim informs the fraudster that he or she did not make the transaction or has such credit card, the fraudster will advise the victim to contact the victim's bank's "credit card management department" or BNM by providing the victim with a fake telephone number. This number will direct the victim to a so-called "bank officer" that will request the victim to confirm the credit card details so they can further investigate. If the victim provides the fraudster with all credit card details over the phone, they will use them to carry out fraudulent activities such as stealing money through the victim's credit card account. According to BNM, in 2018, the overall payment card fraud losses increased to 82.72 million from 61.53 million in 2017. Cases involving credit cards were the majority, which accounted for 92.1% of total fraud losses (Bank Negara Malaysia, 2018).

4.1.3 *Financial fraud and scam modus operandi*

The common modus operandi on how the fraud usually happens is presented by a flowchart in Figure 4.1. This flowchart is an adaptation of the structure and process of victimisation in the financial frauds and scams proposed by Whitty (2013) and Burgard and Schlembach (2013). Whitty (2013) developed a model called the Scammers Persuasive Technique Model. She provides a description of the various stages on how fraudsters develop a relationship with the victim prior to any financial requests until the victims are involved in the fraud or scam themselves. In a similar vein, Burgard and Schlembach (2013) analysed the structures and processes of online frauds and proposed a fraud framework that consists of three stages, namely getting hooked on, staying attuned, and cooling out. In the first or getting hooked on stage, fraudsters will try to make relevant information necessary until the victim is convinced that the situation is real. Once the victim is convinced, in the staying attuned stage, the fraudster will keep the victim comfortable to the situation without giving room to doubt. If, finally, the victim learns that he or she was duped, the victim will find ways back into reality through different ways like reporting the incident to the police, share with others, keep their experiences secret, or suffer physically or emotionally. This stage is called the cooling out phase.

Drew and Cross (2016) in their article proposed a "Prey Model" that summarises the skills and techniques used by fraudsters in performing investment fraud. According to the model, the fraudster begins by conducting research to determine the particular points of the victim's vulnerability, which is called "Profiled." Once the relationship and trust between the potential victim and fraudster have been established (Relational), the victim can easily be duped, which typically involves the fraudster using personal information of the victim to gain unauthorised access to the victim's bank account (Exploitable). At the final stage, fraudsters will ensure that the interaction between him or her and the victim continued, so the victim's involvement in the fraudulent scheme can be reinforced and extended (Yielding). Drew and Cross (2016) argued that financial literacy curriculum that supports prevention of financial fraud efforts should be beyond attainment and the application of financial knowledge and generic warnings about the frauds. The curriculum needs to explicitly include the modus operandi and persuasion techniques used by fraudsters as highlighted in Figure 4.1.

4.2 A theoretical perspective on consumer financial frauds and scams

The vulnerability of consumers towards different types of financial frauds and scams is the main reason for the increase in the number of scams in Malaysia. Previous studies agree that the convincing approach by the scammers alone will not ensure long-term success of the frauds. There are many different factors,

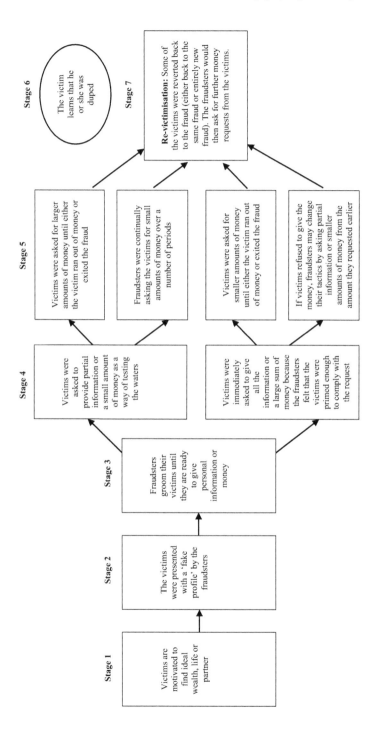

Figure 4.1 The Scammers Persuasive Techniques Model.

Source: Adapted from Whitty (2013) and Burgard and Schlembach (2013).

both internal and external, contributing to the survival of financial frauds and scams in Malaysia. As a result, the incremental effect of each factor on consumer vulnerability towards financial frauds and scams has called for more attention from researchers and authorities to be investigated. Despite the high numbers of financial frauds and scams in Malaysia and its dreadful consequences, very little research has been conducted on the psychological and behavioural factors that leave Malaysian consumers susceptible to deceptive sales practices or frauds. This section focuses on the theories of consumer vulnerability to frauds and scams when a consumer is persuaded to proceed with the transaction even after he or she notices a problematic term in the contract.

4.2.1 Self-control theory

In the self-control theory, Gottfredson and Hirschi (1990) asserted that an essential element of a victim falling into any financial crime is the absence of self-control. According to the theory, people who lack self-control have a higher chance of having risk-taking behaviours. They also put little emphasis on the long-term consequences of their decisions. Consequently, this type of behaviour will make them more vulnerable to exploitation, thereby increases their risk to fraud victimisation. Gottfredson and Hirschi (1990) also argue that self-control is usually learned and developed in the early stages of life and once learned or developed, people become highly resistant to change.

Holtfreter, Reisig, and Pratt (2008) assess the effects of self-control hypothesis theory on the likelihood of fraud targeting and victimisation on 922 adult respondents in Florida, United States. The study finds that individuals who lack self-control are more likely to be victimised due to their inclination towards making impulsive decisions. Using a Dutch large-scale online victimisation longitudinal survey data, Van Wilsem's (2013) study further supported the self-control theory. He reveals that people with low self-control are more vulnerable to financial fraud as they engage more in risk-enhancing activities, such as online purchasing, which lead to higher victimisation risks. Similarly, Pratt, Turanovic, Fox, and Wright (2014) studied the relationship between self-control theory and victimisation using a meta-analysis of 66 empirical related studies. Their results suggest that the effect of self-control is significantly stronger when predicting non-contact forms of victimisation such as online and fraud victimisation. This finding is consistent with Van Wilsem (2013) who argues that people with low self-control are normally active with online shopping and like to participate in online forums. Mesch and Dodel (2018) in a more recent study investigated the role of low self-control, online activities, and the disclosure of personal information on the risk of being a target of fraud. Their results show that individuals with low self-control are more likely to be involved in risky activities online and disclose personal information, which leads to a higher risk of being a target of a fraud or scam. Therefore, understanding the role of self-control in fraud victimisation will help to reduce consumer fraud victimisation.

4.2.2 *Diffusion theory*

Diffusion is always referred to as a process by which an innovation is communicated over time among members of a social system. The diffusion theory was proposed by Rogers (1962) that describes and explains how, why, and at what rate new ideas and technology spread. This theory proposes that four main elements influence the spread of a new idea or in this case, a financial fraud: the innovation or new idea of the fraud itself, communication channels, time, and a social system. Based on this theory, Nash, Bouchard, and Malm (2013) analysed a Ponzi scheme in British Columbia, Canada, that defrauded 2,285 investors for a total of $240 million over a five-year period. According to them, the fraudsters were successful in convincing multiple people to spread the fraud through a social network. They find that interpersonal ties as the main reason for the fraud to be maintained over those five years. Similarly, Rantala (2019) studied the spreading of a large Ponzi scheme in Finland by applying the diffusion theory. The study finds that the growth and survival of investment frauds, specifically the Ponzi scheme in the country, are due to the role of social network. The observed social network in the study refers to a scale-free connectivity structure through word-of-mouth. This network has significantly facilitated the diffusion of the Ponzi scheme fraudulent investment idea in Finland. The study also revealed that victims tend to invest more if their social network introducer has comparatively higher income, age, and education.

4.2.3 *Agency theory*

The main notion of agency theory (Jensen & Meckling, 1979) is based on the relationship between principals and agents. In the relationship between principal and agent, problem arises when the two parties have different interests and information. In the context of commercial and financial fraud, this theory has been applied by Shapiro (1990) who suggests that fraud exists because of a violation and manipulation of trust relationships between agents and clients. In this case, the fraudster plays the role of an agent while the victim is the principal. Victim is in need of information to look for a good investment opportunity or expertise and passes control to the agent, thus creating an asymmetric relationship between the two. The agent will take advantage of the given trust and trap the victim into his or her fraudulent scheme. Benson and Simpson (2009) take this trust relationship one step further by adding the element of deception. They argue that the victim hires the agent based on professional skills; however, the agent lacks the required skills. Therefore, the agent can easily deceive and abuse the trust of the victim and exploit the victim due to information asymmetry. This will lead the agent to introduce any fraudulent investment scheme or scam to the victim. In a more recent study, Pouryousefi and Frooman (2019) developed an agency-theoretic approach to the study of information between fraudsters and victims. They highlight the role of fraudsters as agents who have access to private information and exercise considerable control over them to design a consumer scam for their victims.

4.2.4 Routine activity theory

The routine activity theory, which was first proposed by Cohen and Felson (1979) as a sub-field of crime opportunity theory, focuses on the element of crime. According to the theory, the occurrence of a crime depends on three essential things that converge in space and time, namely the presence of a motivated offender, an attractive target, and the absence of a capable guardian. The lack of any of the three elements is sufficient to prevent a crime. Briefly, this theory argues that opportunity is the root cause of victimisation and opposes any claims saying that crime is a result of social causes, such as poverty and inequality. For example, potential sexual assault targets should change their daily routines such as using different routes to work in order to decrease their chances of becoming targeted for the second time. Pratt, Holtfreter, and Reisig (2010) apply the routine activity theory on United States consumers in order to understand how personal characteristics and online routines increase people's exposure to motivate financial fraudulent activities. The study shows that internet activities have motivated and expanded opportunities for fraudsters to target online consumers. Therefore, they suggest that consumers who perceive higher risks of facing financial fraud or scams should reduce their potential exposure through behavioural adaptations such as spending less time online and making fewer internet purchases. In a different study, Whitty (2019) found that routine activities are essential to understand why individuals are tricked by cyber-scams. Nevertheless, she also argues that socio-demographic and consumer personality should also be considered in scam victimhood prevention.

Following the discussion on theories related to consumer financial frauds and scams, Table 4.5 presents some of the authors who have based their studies on the aforementioned theories.

4.3 Empirical evidence on financial fraud victimisation

4.3.1 Research background on consumer financial frauds

Research related to consumer financial frauds has been the subject of extensive, multidisciplinary discussion. This section will summarise the research backgrounds or themes identified from the previous literature related to the fraud. Structure of information, social engineering, social network, prevalence of fraud, internet influence, scale development, and enforcement have been proposed by researchers, behavioural economists, and psychologists as fraudster–victim relationship background. Table 4.6 outlines the background or themes identified from the literature, the concepts examined, and their definitions and measurements used in the studies. In summary, previous studies suggest that there are many similarities in content and techniques used by different groups

Table 4.5 Sources of studies related to theories on consumer financial frauds and scams

Theory	Authors
Self-Control Theory (Gottfredson and Hirschi, 1990)	Holtfreter, Reisig, and Pratt (2008) Bossler and Holt (2010) Van Wilsem (2013) Pratt, Turanovic, Fox, and Wright (2014) Mesch and Dodel (2018)
Diffusion Theory (Rogers, 1962)	Nash, Bouchard, and Malm (2013) Rantala (2019)
Agency Theory (Jensen and Meckling, 1979)	Shapiro (1990) Benson and Simpson (2009) Pouryousefi and Frooman (2019)
Routine Activity Theory (Cohen and Felson, 1979)	Pratt, Holtfreter, and Reisig (2010) Whitty (2019)

Table 4.6 Concepts of consumer financial fraud and scam being studied and their definitions

Background	Definition of Concept	Authors
Structure of information	Role of scam perpetrators as agents who have access to private information and exercise considerable control over the terms and design of scam relationships, of which the victims are the uninformed principals	Pouryousefi and Frooman (2019)
	Relying on information provided by professionals (i.e. the scammers) that lead to huge capital investment in fraudulent scheme	Nash et al. (2018)
Social engineering	Application of social engineering and persuasion tactics used by offenders in perpetrating fraudulent investment schemes	Drew and Cross (2016)
	Consideration of perceived benefits and risks in financial decision making in the context of pervasiveness of persuasion techniques	Wood et al. (2018)
	Range of persuasion methods that prevent victims from developing doubts and suspicions	Laroche et al. (2019)
Social network	Various forms of harms suffered by victims due to trust in social ties	Nash et al. (2017)
	Spread of investment information based on inviter–invitee relationships	Rantala (2019)
	Nature of relationship between the victims and the perpetrators and the success of fraud diffusion in comparison to a classic diffusion model	Nash et al. (2013)
	Characteristics of a Ponzi scheme through structure of investors network	Zhu et al. (2017)

(*continued*)

Table 4.6 Cont.

Background	Definition of Concept	Authors
Prevalence	Estimation of elder financial fraud-scam victimisation in the United States	Burnes et al. (2017)
	Differences between victims and non-victims based on visceral processing and dispositional differences	Fischer et al. (2013) Button et al. (2014)
	Comprehensive and comparable statistics on financial and online fraud in the United States	Bai and Koong (2017)
Internet influence	Vulnerability to online scams based on individual differences and contextual factors	Williams et al. (2017)
	The influence of online activities, personal information disclosures, and self-control on online fraud victimisation	Mesch and Dodel (2018)
	The influence of psychological, socio-demographic characteristics, and online routine activities in predicting victimhood	Whitty (2019)
Scale development	Measure individual's susceptibility to fraudulent offers (i.e. scam compliance)	Modic, Anderson, and Palomäki (2018)
Enforcement/ intervention	How imperfect enforcement may increase the odds of becoming a victim to scam	Miles and Pyne (2017)
	Identification of at-risk consumers to enhance consumer protection	Bosley et al. (2019)

of financial fraudsters that target different groups of victims via different types of information, techniques, and social networks. In addition, the Internet and online activities have further exacerbated the situation. The prevalence of financial frauds varies among different groups of people and location. Serious effort in combating financial frauds through effective measures, enforcement, and intervention has significantly reduced the depraved effect of it.

4.3.2 Factors influencing financial fraud victimisation

Factors influencing financial fraud victimisation involve a mixture of financial literacy, risk taking, personalities, trust, greed, overconfidence, third-party incentive, low reporting, and online activities. These factors can be grouped into four dimensions, namely cognitive, dispositional, motivational, and technology. Table 4.7 summarises the dimensions and factors adopted by different researchers.

4.3.2.1 Cognitive factors

Financial literacy refers to knowledge or a set of skills that allows an individual to make effective and informed decisions on investment. Understanding basic

Table 4.7 Factors influencing consumer financial frauds and scams

Dimensions	Specific Factors	Authors
Cognitive	Financial literacy	Amoah (2018)
		Engels et al. (2020)
Dispositional	Risk taking	Van Wyk and Benson (1997)
		Amoah (2018)
	Personalities	Van de Weijer and Leukfeldt (2017)
		Whitty (2019)
	Trust	Lewis (2012)
		Wilkins et al. (2012)
		Blois and Ryan (2013)
		Nash et al. (2018)
		Laroche et al. (2019)
	Greed	Langenderfer and Shimp (2001)
		Lea, Fischer, and Evans (2009)
		Lewis (2012)
		Whitty (2013)
		Baker and Puttonen (2017)
	Overconfidence	Gamble et al. (2013)
		Fischer et al. (2013)
Motivational	Third-party incentive	Deason et al. (2015)
		Sanusi et al. (2015)
	Low reporting	Button et al. (2009)
		Blois and Ryan (2013)
		Whitty (2013)
		Carey and Webb (2017)
Technology	Online activities	Walther (1996)
		Sulaiman et al. (2016)
		Ghani and Halim (2017)
		Ahmed and Ibrahim (2018)

financial concepts allow people to distinguish the difference between true and fallacious investments. When lack of financial literacy or knowledge is so widespread, scammers are likely to take advantage of the situation. Many consumers do not realise that they are trapped in the fraudulent investment schemes until the investments revealed that the promised return was unreasonable. In fact, some consumers still believe that promised return was possible even after the frauds were discovered due to lack of understanding on basic financial concepts (Amoah, 2018; Engels, Kumar, and Philip, 2020).

4.3.2.2 Dispositional factors

In psychology, the dispositional dimension refers to internal attribution, or inferring that personal factors are the cause of an event or behaviour. Van Wyk and Benson (1997) and Amoah (2018) found that individuals who tend to engage themselves in risk-taking behaviour are more susceptible to financial fraud. Using a large representative sample of Dutch individuals, Van de Weijer and Leukfeldt

(2017) revealed that individuals with low emotional stability are more likely to become victims of cybercrime and financial scams. Similarly, Whitty (2019) found that individuals with a lack of perseverance and low on external locus of control were more exposed to cyber-frauds. These findings further support the role of personality in financial crime victimization.

Many studies also consider trust as an essential factor in influencing victims to fall into fraudulent transactions. For example, Blois and Ryan (2013), Nash, Bouchard, and Malm (2018) and Laroche, Steyer, and Théron (2019) suggested that over-trust in a community or an organisation will prevent the victim from developing doubts and suspicions, thus making them vulnerable to scammers. Nash et al. (2017) further argued that trust is deeply rooted in social relations and embedded in financial decision-making among members of the society. Therefore, this will create opportunity for the scammers to deceive and abuse the trust they received from the victims. According to Lewis (2012), one of the major mistakes made by the victims in the financial frauds and scams was in trusting the wrong people, and the reasons may lie in the personalities of the fraudsters themselves and the nature of the scams. He argued that scammers are good at disguising as the "nice guy." They are normally charming, captivating, and presentable with good dress sense. They always try to be good listeners and exhibit considerable generosity that leads to a complete trust of their clients. For example, a well-known and massive investment scammer Bernard Madoff never used any high-pressure sales techniques to influence his current and potential clients. He instead relied on word-of-mouth and techniques of impression management such as demonstrated investment expertise, charitable giving, and appearance of wealth to entice new investors (Wilkins, Acuff, & Hermanson, 2012). This technique successfully made the victims mistakenly believe that the fraudulent scheme was legitimate.

The emergence and rapid growth of fraudulent investment schemes today is a reflection of the attitude and interest of Malaysian consumers to get rich quick. This is called greed by Lea, Fischer, and Evans (2009) and Whitty (2013). Naturally, people are attracted to financial gain and have a desire to become financially better off. One of the main reasons for victims to hand over the money to scammers for fraudulent investments is because they are too greedy. Too eager to earn a lot of money and fuelled by promises of high returns and low risks in investment might be a better description. According to Baker and Puttonen (2017), greed can cloud someone's judgement and leave that person to easily be exploited by scammers. Greedy investors might also make the mistake of trusting someone that appears to lie in the character of fraudulent schemes and leave them worse off financially (Lewis, 2012). Similarly, as suggested by Langenderfer and Shimp (2001), once the victim's greed is activated, his or her ability to think of the deal as legitimate is reduced or even eliminated. They also reveal that potential victims who are motivated by greed are more likely to ignore any red flags of the scam than those who are not so motivated. A writer also demonstrated the destructive nature of greed. As quoted by the late Jonathan Gash in his *The Great California Game* novel: "Fraud is the daughter of greed," theoretically, it is possible to get rich quickly if one is prepared to accept very high levels of risk such as participating in the gambling industry. However, the industry offers more shortcomings rather than benefits to participants.

Gamble, Boyle, Yu, and Bennett (2013) found that overconfidence in one's financial knowledge is a significant risk factor for someone becoming a victim of financial fraud. According to them, increasing awareness on someone's limitations may help to protect against any financial frauds. Similarly, Fischer, Lea, and Evans (2013) show that excessive self-confidence is a risk factor for falling into scams in the United Kingdom. In a similar vein, many researchers claim that the high incidence of people falling into fraudulent investment schemes is largely a result of the lack of basic financial literacy on the part of the consumers.

4.3.2.3 Motivational factors

In a different context, Deason, Rajgopal, and Waymire (2015) argued that financial incentives promised by scammers to third parties who successfully obtain or invite new victims to the scheme also play a significant role in motivating victims to be involved in different types of fraudulent investment schemes. Based on a sample of 376 fraudulent investment schemes prosecuted by the U.S. Securities and Exchange Commission (SEC) between 1988 and 2012, the returns promised by those scammers to third parties to obtain victims are sizable. According to them, on average, the annual return promised to the third parties who successfully bring new victims was 437%. Likewise in Malaysia, Sanusi, Rameli, and Isa (2015) suggested that fraud schemes in the banking institutions are also originated by third parties like property valuers and lawyers. According to them, this is due to the nature of the banking activities that provide a wide range of activities and products, which are open to many opportunities for third-party fraudsters to participate in such frauds.

Low reporting by the victims is another possible factor contributing to the growth in fraudulent investment schemes in Malaysia. The literature on fraud victimisation offers a number of reasons for low reporting of fraudulent cases (Button, Lewis, and Tapley, 2009; Blois and Ryan, 2013; Carey and Webb, 2017). Among others, the victims may not know they have been defrauded; the victims feel that they are partly responsible; the victims feel embarrassed to report their cases; the victims experience low or little financial loss and the attitude of statutory bodies. According to Whitty (2013), these behaviours can also be called as a lack of self-control. Victims are reluctant to admit that the frauds and scams were not genuine. According to Button, Lewis and Tapley (2009), some frauds are designed to be legally ambiguous. Even if the victim realises that it is a scam, under existing law, it is difficult to have any enforcement on it. Further, some victims are confused over the rightful parties of whom they should report to, for example, whether it should be the police, the central bank, or national consumer tribunal agencies. Another important factor in low reporting by the victims of frauds is related to the criminal justice process. A common misperception among people is that the criminal justice agencies do not take them seriously. A study of the Madoff Ponzi scam in the United States by Blois and Ryan (2013) found that one of the most important reasons for low reporting was slow action of legal bodies to respond to the victimisation. This situation may be aggravated if the victims refuse to admit that they have been scammed or try to resolve issues on their own. Fraudsters will exploit this opportunity to continue and expand their fraudulent investment activities (Carey & Webb, 2017).

4.3.2.4 Technological factors

Finally, the growing interest in the fraudulent investment schemes in Malaysia is also contributed by the influence of the internet and social media. According to Walther (1996), in some online environments, individuals develop more intimate relationships than they would experience in face-to-face conditions. Every year, the Central Bank of Malaysia will update a list of known companies and websites that are not authorised or approved under the relevant laws and regulations administered by the Malaysian Government. Table 4.8 provides a comparison of the list for the year 2012 to 2016. The table reports that the number of new schemes continue to flourish every year as the numbers of companies and websites added to the list are increasing. Ghani and Halim (2017) argued that the rapid development of information technology has made information about such schemes easy to access and promoted. Similarly, Sulaiman, Moideen, and Moreira (2016), and Ahmed and Ibrahim (2018) who studied the Ponzi schemes and investment scams in Malaysia found that the scammers adopt many sophisticated methods via the Internet to dupe unsuspecting victims. Therefore, they suggest that the regulators, domestic and international, who were aware of the prolif-eration of Internet investment schemes, should issue frequent reminders of the dangerous attraction of these Internet schemes.

4.3.3 Who is more vulnerable to financial fraud?

Certain groups of people are more vulnerable to financial fraud than others. The vulnerable investor in the fraud and scam activities can be described as someone

Table 4.8 The number of unauthorised companies and websites listed by Bank Negara Malaysia

Year	Number of Websites	% Change
2012	81	–
2013	131	61.73%
2014	197	50.38%
2015	247	25.38%
2016	277	12.15%
2017	408	47.29%
2018	425	4.17%

Source: Bank Negara Malaysia (2019).

who is interested in securing his or her financial future (Lokanan, 2014). Previous studies show that the most vulnerable groups are elders, retirees, and men. According to DeLiema, Shadel, and Pak (2020), elders and retirees become more vulnerable to fraud perpetrators when they have no relatives or trustworthy friends to advise them on how to manage or protect their assets. In addition, promises of high returns for a low-risk investment schemes further entice this vulnerable group of people to invest in products, although they have very little knowledge about it. Similarly, Lokanan (2014) and DeLiema, Deevy, Lusardi, and Mitchell (2020) argued that because older and retired persons may be sitting on large amounts of cash and are at or past the peak of their wealth accumulation, they are often the targets of fraud. In addition, another group of elders and retirees may also have limited money for their spending; therefore, they may seek supplemental income in their post-retirement phase, which are increasingly being targeted for fraud activities (Bosley & Knorr, 2018).

In a recent study, DeLiema, Shadel, and Pak (2020) proposed that elders, retirees, and men are relatively more materialistic than general investors; therefore, they are more tempted by unreasonable investment returns promised by scammers. Trahan, Marquart, and Mullings (2005) argued that men chose to enter an inherently risky business venture for the sole purpose of acquiring more money than they already had; therefore, they are vulnerable to financial frauds more than women. On a different note, Lea, Fischer, and Evans (2009) and Whitty (2019) proposed that overconfidence among elders, retirees, and men in their knowledge and ability to recognise scams leads them to undermine many fraudulent schemes. Their belief of invulnerability puts them into higher risks of becoming scammed. Similarly, James, Boyle, and Bennett (2014) suggested that elders are more at risk for susceptibility to scams compared to their younger counterparts because of their soft manners to telemarketers or scammers. This finding is also supported by Whitty (2019).

Studies in the Malaysian context in regards to financial frauds and scams are very limited. Nevertheless, mixed findings regarding the most vulnerable group to fraudulent schemes are found in the literature. For example, Nawawi (2018), Saad, Abdullah, and Murah (2018) and Sinar Harian (2019) reported that in Malaysia, elders and women are the most susceptible to scammers. The spreads of cyber romance scams are the main reasons why women are main target of those scammers. In terms of race, Jariah, Husna, Tengku Aizan, and Ibrahim (2012) found that Malays are relatively better in their financial behaviour compared to their Chinese and Indian counterparts. In addition, Penny, Chew, Raja, and Lim (2016) showed that Chinese respondents deal with online shopping more frequently than the Malay and Indian respondents. Nevertheless, Kahar, Yamimi, Bunari, and Habil (2012) showed that in general, all Malaysians regardless of their races are naive in dealing with financial frauds and scams. Similarly, Saad, Abdullah, and Murah (2018) highlighted that Chinese and Malay women are equally vulnerable to financial scams. Therefore, there is no significant evidence to support the claim that race plays a role in falling into victimisation of financial frauds or scams.

4.4 Suggestions and policy recommendations

The Malaysian government and regulators have put significant efforts to combat financial frauds and scams from spreading. For example, the divisions of commercial crime investigation department, Royal Malaysian Police is consistently dealing with financial crime cases under different measures to ensure that consumers feel safe and secure in their daily financial transactions. Similarly, BNM and Securities Commissions (SC) have taken the initiative to provide awareness and empower members of the public and investors to become more informed, confident, and self-reliant in making financial or investment decisions. BNM introduced the Financial Fraud Alert program that provides consumers with a list of unauthorised companies and websites together with BNM Telelink call centre that facilitates consumers on matters related to the financial sector. Similarly, SC introduced Invest Smart programs that provide direct interaction between SC and investors in ensuring them not to fall into any fraudulent investment schemes. Apart from these two main regulators, the Ministry of Domestic Trade and Consumer Affairs also introduced the SSM BizTrust standard, which certifies that the awarded business entity has complied with the characteristics of the trust principles, online security, and protection of information. This will help consumers to identify the right business entity to deal with. Other bodies such as Malaysian Communications and Multimedia Commission through MyCERT and Malaysia Co-operative Societies Commission are also working together with other regulators to ensure that financial frauds and scams in Malaysia are kept to the minimum. Overall observation has shown that although many efforts have been made, much more are needed to be implemented and achieved in order to improve, enhance, and strengthen the regulation and policy towards combating financial frauds and scams in Malaysia.

According to the Ministry of Communications and Multimedia, Malaysians should pay serious attention to all threats that come from fraudsters and scammers because they may lose their savings and money amounting to hundreds or thousands of ringgit from them (*Daily Express*, 2018). One of the major problems of financial frauds and scams in Malaysia arises from the attempt to earn profit quickly without putting into consideration relevant risks involved due to their lack of financial literacy. Ideally, investors avoid any unnecessarily high-risk types of investments or engage in unrecognised investment bodies or institutions. Therefore, financial knowledge will be the right tool to tackle this problem through an effective and aggressive public education. As the fraudsters sometimes target only a certain group of people, the government could intensify financial awareness and education campaigns through social media and other financial technology tools on how to identify illegal financial schemes. This will help in better targeting and reducing the huge costs associated with government intervention in the public financial literacy education. Drew and Cross (2016) also suggested that the financial literacy curriculum should not focus only on financial facts and information. Persuasion techniques and social engineering used by the scammers should also be taught to them in order to protect them from any fraudulent activities.

The essential role of any consumer is curiosity, which can act as a line of defence against any financial frauds and scams. The consumers should attend financial literacy and awareness programmes in order to gain more knowledge on commercial fraud activities. Consumers should also attempt to study and check with the relevant authorities before participating or falling prey into any different types of investment schemes or scams. Reforming such attitude and behaviour of consumers will create better resilience and promote efficiency against any type of frauds and thus, should be accorded high priority.

The other issue that needs to be looked at is the enforcement measure under existing and current regulations. It has been argued that frequent monitoring by regulators may uncover more fraud and can reduce the number of people who will be victimised by the fraudsters such as tracking prior offenders to make sure they do not return to their prior ways. Today, Malaysia has adopted many new technologies such as artificial intelligence that makes it much easier to identify and target fraudsters as well as victims. The use of technology in law implementations and enforcements can provide a more comprehensive solution to the issues of financial frauds and scams for consumers in Malaysia. While the government's role is pivotal to prevent financial frauds and scams, active co-operation of other market participants is also significantly required. Cohesive policy to improve co-operation between public and private market players should also be created to facilitate the commercial and financial operations in the country. For example, a more comprehensive crime control policy can be established in order to reduce the rate of commercial frauds and scam as well as lower the financial loss and damage among consumers. Community leaders could also help to prevent any financial crime via community-based activities like sharing experience and spreading information related to commercial frauds and scams through community-based communication tools like group chats or websites.

Finally, there is a need to evaluate and promote the updated status of financial frauds and scams, legal enforcement, and consumer behaviours through effective research settings. It is also necessary that seamless movement and promotion of anti-financial frauds and scams awareness all over the country are ensured. Besides, there needs to be a greater effort towards integration between public and private sectors as well as the government and community to fight against any type of fraud.

Note

1 According to the Collins English Dictionary, a get-rich-quick scheme refers to a scheme that promises to make a person extremely wealthy over a short period of time, often with little effort and at no risk. Retrieved 26 July 2019 from www.collinsdictionary. com/dictionary/english/get-rich-quick-scheme

References

Abidin, Z.S.Z. (2016). *Factors Influencing People to Involve in Get-Rich-Quick Scheme: A Case Study in the West Coast of Sabah* (Doctoral dissertation, Universiti Malaysia Sabah).

Ahmed, H. & Ibrahim, I.R. (2018). Financial consumer protection regime in Malaysia: Assessment of the legal and regulatory framework. *Journal of Consumer Policy*, 41(2), 159–175.

Ahmed, T. & Oppenheim, C. (2006, May). Experiments to identify the causes of spam. In *Aslib Proceedings*, 58(3), 156–178. Emerald Group Publishing Limited.

Albrecht, C., Morales, V., Baldwin, J.K., & Scott, S.D. (2017). Ezubao: A Chinese Ponzi scheme with a twist. *Journal of Financial Crime*, 24(2), 256–259.

Amoah, B. (2018). Mr Ponzi with fraud scheme is knocking: Investors who may open. *Global Business Review*, 19(5), 1115–1128.

Australian Competition and Consumer Commission (n.d.). *Nigerian Scams*. Retrieved on 19 July 2019 from www.scamwatch.gov.au/types-of-scams/unexpected-money/ nigerian-scams

Bai, S. & Koong, K.S. (2017). Financial and other frauds in the United States: A panel analysis approach. *International Journal of Accounting and Information Management*, 25(4), 413–433.

Baker, H.K. & Puttonen, V. (2017). *Investment Traps Exposed: Navigating Investor Mistakes and Behavioral Biases.* Emerald Publishing Limited.

Bank Negara Malaysia (2010). *What Is Financial Fraud?* Retrieved on 15 June 2019 from www.bnm.gov.my/microsites/fraudalert/01_what.htm

Bank Negara Malaysia (2018). *Financial Stability and Payment Systems Report 2018.* Retrieved on 11 November 2019 from www.bnm.gov.my/files/publication/fsps/en/ 2018/ fs2018_book.pdf

Bank Negara Malaysia (2019, updated 27 May). *List of Known Companies and Websites That Are Not Authorised Nor Approved under the Relevant Laws and Regulations Administered by Bank Negara Malaysia.* Retrieved from www.bnm.gov.my/ documents/2019/FCA_20190527_EN.pdf

Bank Negara Malaysia (2020). *Unauthorised Use of Credit or Debit Card.* Retrieved on 13 January 2020 from https://fraudalert.bnm.gov.my/0205_card.htm

Baucus, M.S. & Mitteness, C.R. (2016). Crowdfrauding: Avoiding Ponzi entrepreneurs when investing in new ventures. *Business Horizons*, 59(1), 37–50.

Benson, M.L. & Simpson, S.S. (2009). *White Collar Crime: An Opportunity Perspective.* Routledge.

Bertelsen, O.W. & Bødker, S. (2003). Activity theory. In Carroll, J.M. (ed.). *HCI Models, Theories and Frameworks: Toward a Multidisciplinary Science*, 291–324.

Blois, K. & Ryan, A. (2013). Affinity fraud and trust within financial markets. *Journal of Financial Crime*, 20(2), 186–202.

Bosley, S. & Knorr, M. (2018). Pyramids, Ponzis and fraud prevention: Lessons from a case study. *Journal of Financial Crime*, 25(1), 81–94.

Bosley, S.A., Bellemare, M.F., Umwali, L., & York, J. (2019). Decision-making and vulnerability in a pyramid scheme fraud. *Journal of Behavioral and Experimental Economics*, 80, 1–13.

Bossler, A.M. & Holt, T.J. (2010). The effect of self-control on victimization in the cyberworld. *Journal of Criminal Justice*, 38(3), 227–236.

Bruhn, A. (2019). Trust in, trust out: A real cost of sudden and significant financial loss. *Accounting and Finance*, 59, 359–381.

Burgard, A. & Schlembach, C. (2013). Frames of fraud: A qualitative analysis of the structure and process of victimization on the Internet. *International Journal of Cyber Criminology*, 7(2), 112–124.

Burnes, D., Henderson Jr, C.R., Sheppard, C., Zhao, R., Pillemer, K., & Lachs, M.S. (2017). Prevalence of financial fraud and scams among older adults in the United States: A systematic review and meta-analysis. *American Journal of Public Health*, *107*(8), e13–e21.

Button, M., Lewis, C., & Tapley, J. (2009). Fraud typologies and the victims of fraud: Literature review. Retrieved on 3 October 2020 from https://researchportal.port.ac.uk/portal/files/1926122/NFA_report3_16.12.09.pdf

Button, M., Nicholls, C.M., Kerr, J., & Owen, R. (2014). Online frauds: Learning from victims why they fall for these scams. *Australian and New Zealand Journal of Criminology*, *47*(3), 391–408.

Carey, C. & Webb, J.K. (2017). Ponzi schemes and the roles of trust creation and maintenance. *Journal of Financial Crime*, *24*(4), 589–600.

Choplin, J.M., Stark, D.P., & Ahmad, J.N. (2011). A psychological investigation of consumer vulnerability to fraud: Legal and policy implication. *Law and Psychology Review*, *35*, 61.

Cohen, L.E. & Felson, M. (1979). Social change and crime rate trends: A routine activity approach. *American Sociological Review*, *44*(4), 588–608.

Collins (2019). *Get rich quick definition*. Retrieved on 7 February 2020 from www.collinsdictionary.com/dictionary/english/get-rich-quick-scheme (26 July 2019).

Cropanzano, R. & Mitchell, M.S. (2005). Social exchange theory: An interdisciplinary review. *Journal of Management*, *31*(6), 874–900.

Daily Express (2018). *Serious Steps to Curb Cyber Crime*. Retrieved on 3 June 2020 from www.dailyexpress.com.my/news.cfm?NewsID=128775

Deason, S., Rajgopal, S., & Waymire, G.B. (2015). *Who Gets Swindled in Ponzi Schemes?* Retrieved on 19 November 2019 from https://cear.gsu.edu/files/2015/09/Session-8-White-Paper.pdf

DeLiema, M., Deevy, M., Lusardi, A., & Mitchell, O.S. (2020). Financial fraud among older americans: Evidence and implications. *The Journals of Gerontology: Series B*, *75*(4), 861–868.

DeLiema, M., Shadel, D., & Pak, K. (2020). Profiling victims of investment fraud: Mindsets and risky behaviors. *Journal of Consumer Research*, *46*(5), 904–914.

Divisions of Commercial Crime Investigation Department (2019). *Statistik kertas siasatan jabatan siasatan jenayah komersil (JSJK)*. Retrieved on 23 March 2020 from www.data.gov.my/data/ms_MY/dataset/statistik-kertas-siasatan-jsjk-mengikut-kontinjen-2010–2017

Drew, J.M. & Cross, C. (2016). Fraud and its PREY: Conceptualising social engineering tactics and its impact on financial literacy outcomes. In *Financial Literacy and the Limits of Financial Decision-Making* (pp. 325–340). Palgrave Macmillan.

Emerson, R.M. (1976). Social exchange theory. *Annual Review of Sociology*, *2*(1), 335–362.

Engels, C., Kumar, K., & Philip, D. (2020). Financial literacy and fraud detection. *The European Journal of Finance*, *26*(4–5), 420–442.

Engeström, Y., Miettinen, R., & Punamäki, R.L. (eds.). (1999). *Perspectives on Activity Theory*. Cambridge University Press.

Evola, K. & O'Grady, N. (2009). As fraud schemes proliferate – Are you the next investor to crash and burn? *Journal of Investment Compliance*, *10*(2), 14–17.

Fischer, P., Lea, S.E., & Evans, K.M. (2013). Why do individuals respond to fraudulent scam communications and lose money? The psychological determinants of scam compliance. *Journal of Applied Social Psychology*, *43*(10), 2060–2072.

Gamble, K.J., Boyle, P., Yu, L., & Bennett, D. (2013). Aging, financial literacy, and fraud. Netspar Discussion Paper No. 11/2013–066. Retrieved on 10 September 2019 from https://papers.ssrn.com/sol3/papers.cfm?abstract_id=2361151

Gash, J. (1992). *The Great California Game: A Lovejoy Mystery*. Penguin books: UK.

Ghani & Halim (2017). Pseudo-investment scheme in Malaysia: Issues and problems. *Journal Sultan Alauddin Sulaiman Shah*, 4(1), 60–66.

Gottfredson, M.R. & Hirschi, T. (1990). *A General Theory of Crime*. Stanford University Press.

Hofstetter, M., Mejía, D., Rosas, J.N., & Urrutia, M. (2018). Ponzi schemes and the financial sector: DMG and DRFE in Colombia. *Journal of Banking and Finance*, 96, 18–33.

Holtfreter, K., Reisig, M.D., & Pratt, T.C. (2008). Low self-control, routine activities and fraud victimization. *Criminology*, 46(1), 189–220.

James, B.D., Boyle, P.A., & Bennett, D.A. (2014). Correlates of susceptibility to scams in older adults without dementia. *Journal of Elder Abuse & Neglect*, 26(2), 107–122.

Jariah, M., Husna, S., Tengku Aizan, T.A.H., & Ibrahim, R. (2012). Financial practices and problems amongst elderly in Malaysia. *Pertanika Journal of Social Sciences & Humanities*, 20(4), 1065–1084.

Jensen, M.C. & Meckling, W.H. (1979). Theory of the firm: Managerial behavior, agency costs and ownership structure. In *Economics social institutions* (pp. 163–231). Springer.

Kahar, R., Yamimi, F., Bunari, G., & Habil, H. (2012). Trusting the social media in small business. *Procedia-Social and Behavioral Sciences*, 66, 564–570.

Langenderfer, J. & Shimp, T.A. (2001). Consumer vulnerability to scams, swindles and fraud: A new theory of visceral influences on persuasion. *Psychology and Marketing*, 18(7), 763–783.

Laroche, H., Steyer, V., & Théron, C. (2019). How could you be so gullible? Scams and over-trust in organizations. *Journal of Business Ethics*, 160(3), 641–656.

Lea, S.E., Fischer, P., & Evans, K.M. (2009). *The Psychology of Scams: Provoking and Committing Errors of Judgement*.

Lee, J. & Soberon-Ferrer, H. (1997). Consumer vulnerability to fraud: Influencing factors. *Journal of Consumer Affairs*, 31(1), 70–89.

Lewis, M.K. (2012, December). New dogs, old tricks. Why do Ponzi schemes succeed? *Accounting Forum*, 36(4), 294–309.

Lokanan, M. (2014). The demographic profile of victims of investment fraud: A Canadian perspective. *Journal of Financial Crime*, 21(2), 226–242.

Malaymail Online (2019). *Malaysians lost over RM410m to online, phone scams since 2018, deputy minister says*. Retrieved on 10 June 2019 from www.malaymail.com/news/malaysia/2019/11/06/malaysians-lost-over-rm410m-to-online-phone-scams-since-2018-deputy-ministe/1807390

Malaysian Communications and Multimedia Commission (2018). *Elakkan diri daripada menjadi statistik jenayah siber*. Retrieved on 20 January 2020 from www.mcmc.gov.my/media/press-clippings/elakkan-diri-daripada-menjadi-statistik-jenayah-si

Mc Ghee, J.L. (1983). The vulnerability of elderly consumers. *The International Journal of Aging and Human Development*, 17(3), 223–246.

Mesch, G.S. & Dodel, M. (2018). Low self-control, information disclosure and the risk of online fraud. *American Behavioral Scientist*, 62(10), 1356–1371.

Miles, S. & Pyne, D. (2017). The economics of scams. *Review of Law and Economics*, 13(1), 1–18.

Modic, D., Anderson, R., & Palomäki, J. (2018). We will make you like our research: The development of a susceptibility-to-persuasion scale. *PloS one*, *13*(3), 1–21.

Muda, M., Aziz, M.Y.A., & Rozali, M.H. (2003). *Kajian Kegiatan Sekim Cepat Kaya di Semenanjung Malaysia*. Retrieved on 2 March 2020 from http://ddms.usim.edu.my/handle/123456789/7859

Mugarura, N. (2017). The use of anti-money laundering tools to regulate Ponzi and other fraudulent investment schemes. *Journal of Money Laundering Control*, *20*(3), 231–246.

Malaysia Computer Emergency Response Team (MyCERT) (2019). Incident Statistics. Retrieved on 2 September 2019 from www.mycert.org.my/portal/statistics-content?menu=b75e037d-6ee3-4d11-8169-66677d694932&id=0d39dd96-835b-44c7-b710-139e560f6ae0

Nash, R., Bouchard, M., & Malm, A. (2013). Investing in people: The role of social networks in the diffusion of a large-scale fraud. *Social Networks*, *35*(4), 686–698.

Nash, R., Bouchard, M., & Malm, A. (2017). Social networks as predictors of the harm suffered by victims of a large-scale Ponzi scheme. *Canadian Journal of Criminology and Criminal Justice*, *59*(1), 26–62.

Nash, R., Bouchard, M., & Malm, A. (2018). Twisting trust: Social networks, due diligence and loss of capital in a Ponzi scheme. *Crime, Law and Social Change*, *69*(1), 67–89.

Nawawi, M.H. (January, 2018). *Macau Scam guna Melayu tipu Melayu*. Retrieved on 2 November 2019 from www.hmetro.com.my/mutakhir/2018/01/301236/macau-scam-guna-melayu-tipu-melayu

New Straits Times (2016a). *Malaysians lost more than RM100m to get-rich-quick schemes this year*. Retrieved on 12 February 2020 from www.nst.com.my/news/2016/07/160533/malaysians-lost-more-rm100m-get-rich-quick-schemes-year

New Straits Times (2016b). *Malaysians lost RM44 million to African scammers so far this year*. Retrieved on 6 August 2019 from www.nst.com.my/news/2016/08/162781/malaysians-lost-rm44-million-african-scammers-so-far-year

New Straits Times (2017a). *Love scam: Spinning a web of deceit*. Retrieved on 6 August 2019 from www.nst.com.my/news/exclusive/2017/06/247760/love-scam-spinning-web-deceit

New Straits Times (2018a). *People still falling victim to love scam despite awareness campaign*. Retrieved on 6 August 2019 from www.nst.com.my/news/crime-courts/2018/09/411233/people-still-falling-victim-love-scam-despite-awareness-campaign

Penny, L., Chew, W.L., Raja, R., & Lim, H.A. (2016). Online shopping preference and M-payment acceptance: A case study among Klang Valley online shoppers. *Pertanika Journal of Social Sciences & Humanities*, *24*(3), 1121–1130.

Perri, F.S. & Brody, R.G. (2012). The optics of fraud: Affiliations that enhance offender credibility. *Journal of Financial Crime*, *19*(4), 355–370.

Pouryousefi, S. & Frooman, J. (2019). The consumer scam: An agency-theoretic approach. *Journal of Business Ethics*, *154*(1), 1–12.

Pozza Jr, C.L., Cox, T.R., & Morad, R.J. (2009). A review of recent investor issues in the madoff, standford and forte ponzi scheme cases. *Journal of Business & Securities Law*, *10*, 113.

Pratt, T.C., Holtfreter, K., & Reisig, M.D. (2010). Routine online activity and internet fraud targeting: Extending the generality of routine activity theory. *Journal of Research in Crime and Delinquency*, *47*(3), 267–296.

Pratt, T.C., Turanovic, J.J., Fox, K.A., & Wright, K.A. (2014). Self-control and victimization: A meta-analysis. *Criminology*, *52*(1), 87–116.

Rantala, V. (2019). How do investment ideas spread through social interaction? Evidence from a Ponzi scheme. *The Journal of Finance, 74*(5), 2349–2389.

Rogers, E.M. (1962). *Diffusion of Innovations* (1st ed.). New York: Free Press of Glencoe.

Royal Malaysian Police (2012). *Divisions of Commercial Crime Investigation Department Annual Report 2012*. Retrieved on 6 August 2019 from http://ccid.my/bm/annual_reports/

Saad, M.E., Abdullah, S.N.H.S., & Murah, M.Z. (2018). Cyber romance scam victimization analysis using routine activity theory versus apriori algorithm. *International Journal of Advanced Computer Science and Applications, 9*(12), 479–485.

Sanusi, Z.M., Rameli, M.N.F., & Isa, Y.M. (2015). Fraud schemes in the banking institutions: Prevention measures to avoid severe financial loss. *Procedia Economics and Finance, 28*, 107–113.

SEC Investor (n.d.). *Pyramid schemes*. Retrieved on 12 February 2020 from www.investor.gov/protect-your-investments/fraud/types-fraud/pyramid-schemes

Shapiro, S.P. (1990). Collaring the crime, not the criminal: Reconsidering the concept of white-collar crime. *American Sociological Review*, 346–365.

Sinar Harian (January, 2019). *Golongan berusia, pekerja swasta sasaran Macau Scam*. Retrieved on 12 February 2020 from www.sinarharian.com.my/article/8306/BERITA/Jenayah/Golongan-berusia-pekerja-swasta-sasaran-Macau-Scam

Snyder, M. & Swann Jr, W.B. (1978). Behavioral confirmation in social interaction: From social perception to social reality. *Journal of Experimental Social Psychology, 14*(2), 148–162.

Sulaiman, A.N.M., Moideen, A.I., & Moreira, S.D. (2016). Of Ponzi schemes and investment scams: A case study of enforcement actions in Malaysia. *Journal of Financial Crime, 23*(1), 231–243.

The Borneo Post (2018). *Careful of inheritance scam emails from abroad – PDRM*. Retrieved on 12 February 2020 from www.theborneopost.com/2018/09/26/careful-of-inheritance-scam-emails-from-abroad-pdrm/

Trahan, A., Marquart, J.W., & Mullings, J. (2005). Fraud and the American dream: Toward an understanding of fraud victimization. *Deviant Behavior, 26*(6), 601–620.

Utusan Online (2018a). *Macau Scam semakin membimbangkan*. Retrieved on 12 February 2020 from www.utusan.com.my/rencana/utama/macau-scam-semakin-membimbangkan-1.746650

Van de Weijer, S.G. & Leukfeldt, E.R. (2017). Big five personality traits of cybercrime victims. *Cyberpsychology, Behavior, and Social Networking, 20*(7), 407–412.

Van Wilsem, J. (2013). 'Bought it, but never got it' Assessing risk factors for online consumer fraud victimization. *European Sociological Review, 29*(2), 168–178.

Van Wyk, J. & Benson, M.L. (1997). Fraud victimization: Risky business or just bad luck? *American Journal of Criminal Justice, 21*(2), 163–179.

Walther, J.B. (1996). Computer-mediated communication: Impersonal, interpersonal and hyperpersonal interaction. *Communication Research, 23*(1), 3–43.

Whitty, M.T. (2013). The Scammers Persuasive Techniques Model: Development of a stage model to explain the online dating romance scam. *British Journal of Criminology, 53*(4), 665–684.

Whitty, M.T. (2019). Predicting susceptibility to cyber-fraud victimhood. *Journal of Financial Crime, 26*(1), 277–292.

Wilkins, A.M., Acuff, W.W., & Hermanson, D.R. (2012). Understanding a ponzi scheme: Victims' perspectives. *Journal of Forensic and Investigative Accounting, 4*(1), 1–19.

Williams, E.J., Beardmore, A., & Joinson, A.N. (2017). Individual differences in suscep-tibility to online influence: A theoretical review. *Computers in Human Behavior, 72,* 412–421.

Wood, S., Liu, P.J., Hanoch, Y., Xi, P.M., & Klapatch, L. (2018). Call to claim your prize: Perceived benefits and risk drive intention to comply in a mass marketing scam. *Journal of Experimental Psychology: Applied, 24*(2), 196.

Zhu, A., Fu, P., Zhang, Q., & Chen, Z. (2017). Ponzi scheme diffusion in complex networks. *Physica A: Statistical Mechanics and its Applications, 479,* 128–136.

Zunzunegui, M.V., Belanger, E., Benmarhnia, T., Gobbo, M., Otero, A., Béland, F., … & Ribera-Casado, J.M. (2017). Financial fraud and health: The case of Spain. *Gaceta Sanitaria, 31,* 313–319.

5 The paradox of life insurance protection

Why are consumers underinsured?

5.0 Introduction

This chapter discusses the issue of underinsurance in Malaysia which is the fourth issue on consumer financial vulnerability explored in this book. The ASEAN Insurance Pulse 2019 report shows that Malaysia has the lowest life and non-life real insurance premium growth rate among the ASEAN-5 countries (Schanz, Alms, & Company, 2019). Bank Negara Malaysia (BNM) reports that the current life insurance penetration rate (56%) is far below the targeted penetration rate of 75% by 2020. According to the Life insurance Association of Malaysia (LIAM) and the Employees' Provident Fund (EPF), the average protection gap per family member is high, and the retirement savings for Malaysians are not enough while life expectancy is increasing, thus giving rise to the risk of having wider protection shortfall. In actual fact, only 34 out of 100 Malaysians have some form of life insurance or takaful policy (Rao, 2019). The underinsurance issue has significant health and financial implications, and thus, timely policy intervention is needed to close the existing insurance protection gap in Malaysia.

To better understand the above concerns, this chapter begins by presenting the issue of low insurance penetration rate. It then presents the current status of the insurance and takaful growth using data from BNM, Department of Statistics Malaysia (DOSM), and other agency reports. The most common issues and challenges for the insurance and takaful industry in Malaysia are also briefly discussed. The third section of this chapter discusses various insurance and takaful schemes in Malaysia, including private–public partnership schemes such as mySalam. Subsequently, the fourth section reviews and briefly illustrates the insurance planning process.

A brief review of the relevant theories is presented in the fifth section, which provides justification explaining why many Malaysian consumers are not purchasing insurance and takaful products in spite of various awareness campaigns. A very small probability of not receiving the insurance compensation claim apart from high premiums can make this contract unpopular, holding other factors constant. Section 5.6 presents a discussion on empirical studies examining the issue of insurance and takaful penetration rates. The final section ends by discussing possible implications for policymakers, particularly the government and the insurance and takaful industry.

5.1 Insurance and takaful issues – the Malaysian scenario

5.1.1 Overview of insurance and takaful in Malaysia

Insurance has been practised for over a thousand years worldwide. Similar to some countries in the world, Malaysia has both conventional insurance and Shariah-compliant insurance (takaful). Basically, insurance is defined as a contract in which individuals pay a defined amount of premium and in return receive financial compensation for damage or loss of what they have insured. Takaful is a contract (aqad) in which a policyholder contributes money to a takaful fund agreeing to share risks and offer help to other policyholders in the event of death or permanent disability or any other such misfortunes (Kamil & Nor, 2014). The insurance industry in Malaysia offers life insurance, general insurance, and takaful. Life insurance consists of whole life, term, investment-linked, and annuity policies. General insurance includes motor, aviation, and transit insurance (MAT); fire insurance; medical and personal accident insurance (PA); marine insurance; and others (i.e. employer's liability insurance). Takaful consists of family takaful and general takaful.

There are 55 licensed insurance and takaful operators in Malaysia comprising of general, life, composite, takaful license holders and reinsurers (Table 5.1), servicing the country's 32 million population (Shen, 2018). However, foreign insurers hold around 76% market share as of 2016 compared to 60% in 2009. In July 2017, BNM reinforced the rule that was set in 2009 that foreign ownership need to be less than 70% as it aims to increase local participation in the industry.

The insurance sector in Malaysia has significantly contributed to the economic development of the country for the last few decades. The insurance and takaful industry in Malaysia is one of the largest among countries with similar economic development such as Indonesia, Vietnam, Thailand, and Philippines (Masud et al., 2019). This chapter and the following sections will focus on the most common and relevant insurance and takaful plans to the consumer financial

Table 5.1 Number of insurers and takaful operators in Malaysia

Categories	Numbers
Life insurer + reinsurer	11+1
General insurer + reinsurer	19+5
Composite insurer + reinsurer	3+1
Family takaful operator	3
General takaful operator	8
Retakaful operator	4
Total	55

Source: Bank Negara Malaysia (2019).

vulnerabilities concept such as life insurance, family takaful, and medical and health insurance. These insurance policies provide long-term protection against various risks and serves as a tool to accumulate funds and preserve wealth for future consumption. General insurance/takaful will not be discussed in detail as this line of insurance mainly protects assets such as car and residential homes and is usually short term in nature. Futhermore, some of these general insurance such as car insurance is mandated by law, hence, the problem of underinsurance is rather negligible.

5.1.2 Penetration rate of insurance and takaful in Malaysia

Penetration rate is defined as the activity or fact of increasing the market share of an existing product (Dash et al., 2018). Insurance penetration can be defined and measured using three ways: (i) the ratio of premiums to Gross Domestic Product (GDP), (ii) the ratio of premiums to Gross National Income (GNI), and (iii) the ratio of of total policies in force to the total population. According to ASEAN Insurance Pulse 2019 report and Swiss Re, the ASEAN region's insurance penetration rate fell far short of the global average (3.6% versus 6.1%). Using the third measurement of insurance penetration, BNM (2017) reported that the penetration rate for life insurance and family takaful in Malaysia stood at 56% and 15.2%, respectively. The life insurance penetration in Malaysia has increased by 30.7% in 20 years (1996: 25.3% and 2016: 56%). Reports by LIAM have expressed concern that the insurance penetration rate had lingered at 56%, while life insurance real premium growth rate remained unchanged at around 4.8% over the past few years (Shen, 2018). From 2013 to 2018, Malaysia had the lowest life and non-life real premium average growth rate among the ASEAN-5 countries (see Figure 5.1). Nonetheless, the life insurance real premium growth rate in Malaysia is higher than the world average.

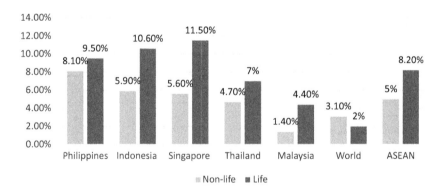

Figure 5.1 Life and non-life real premium growth (2013–2018, annual averages, in %).
Source: Swiss Re (2019).

The low penetration rate of insurance and takaful among Malaysians remains critical. Less than 41% of Malaysians own at least one individual/group life insurance policy or family takaful, while only about 32% own more than one policy (Bernama, 2019). The life insurance penetration rate among the B40 group remained at 30.3% in 2018, while the national working population penetration rate for life insurance and family takaful stands at 56%, respectively, which is relatively low compared to many developed countries (Bank Negara Malaysia, 2019). These indicators suggest that the Malaysian insurance market is still substantially under-penetrated.

Figures 5.2 and 5.3 illustrate that the insurance and takaful fund assets have increased over the years. The percentage of GNI for insurance fund assets decreased between years 2013 and 2016. While for takaful fund assets, the percentage of GNI remained the same between years 2013 and 2016. In terms of percentage of total assets of the financial system, insurance fund assets remained at about 5.2% for years 2013 to 2016, while takaful fund assets increased their percentage of total assets of the insurance and takaful industry from 9% to 12.1%. Although the total fund assets' increase over the years for insurance and especially takaful seem promising, the continuous decline in percentage of GNI could result in a significant shortfall in achieving the targeted insurance and takaful industry growth.

The insurance and takaful penetration rates in Malaysia are presented in Figures 5.4 and 5.5. The graphs roughly show that both insurance and takaful penetration rates have remained unchanged for the past few years. A similar trend following Figures 5.1 and 5.2 (low growth) is observed here.

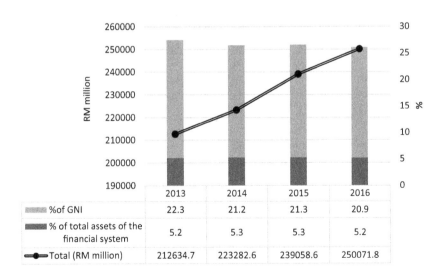

	2013	2014	2015	2016
%of GNI	22.3	21.2	21.3	20.9
% of total assets of the financial system	5.2	5.3	5.3	5.2
Total (RM million)	212634.7	223282.6	239058.6	250071.8

Figure 5.2 Insurance fund assets.
Source: Bank Negara Malaysia (2016a).

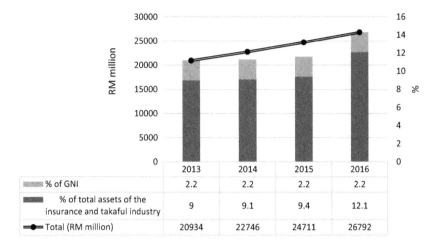

Figure 5.3 Takaful fund assets.
Source: Bank Negara Malaysia (2016b).

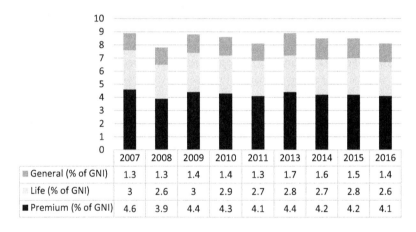

Figure 5.4 Insurance penetration rate (2007–2016).
Source: Bank Negara Malaysia (2016a).

Table 5.2 shows that between years 2012 and 2017, the total sum insured in force for life insurance increased from RM1 trillion (approx.) to RM1.3 trillion over the six years but in terms of percentage of GNI, it declined from 112.9% to 108.8%. Between 2012 and 2016, the premium income from life insurance increased from RM24,929 million to RM31,431.6 million, while the percentage of GNI declined from 2.8% to 2.6%; the population increased from 29.5 million to 31.7 million; the employment increased from 12.7 million to 14.2 million;

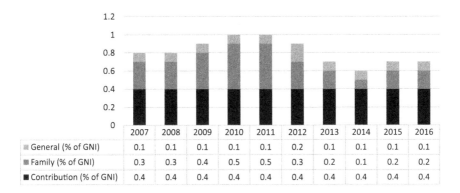

	2007	2008	2009	2010	2011	2012	2013	2014	2015	2016
General (% of GNI)	0.1	0.1	0.1	0.1	0.1	0.2	0.1	0.1	0.1	0.1
Family (% of GNI)	0.3	0.3	0.4	0.5	0.5	0.3	0.2	0.1	0.2	0.2
Contribution (% of GNI)	0.4	0.4	0.4	0.4	0.4	0.4	0.4	0.4	0.4	0.4

Figure 5.5 Takaful penetration rate (2007–2016).
Source: Bank Negara Malaysia (2016b).

Table 5.2 Life insurance growth and socio-economic indicators in Malaysia (2012–2016)

Year	Total sum insured in force		Premium income[1]		Population	Employment	Per capital income
	RM mil	% of GNI	RM mil	% of GNI	Million		RM
2012	1,021,907.0	112.9	24,929.0	2.8	29.5	12.7	30,667
2013	1,089,975.0	114.4	26,369.1	2.8	29.9	13.2	31,844
2014	1,165,339.8	108.9	28,725.4	2.7	30.7	13.9	34,839
2015	1,238,795.5	110.1	29,889.8	2.7	31.2	14.1	36,078
2016	1,300,254.9	108.8	31,431.6	2.6	31.7[p]	14.2[p]	37,738[p]
2017	1,380,000.0	NA	NA	NA	NA	NA	NA

Source: Department of Statistics Malaysia (2019).

[1] As per revenue accounts
p preliminary

and per capita income increased from RM30,667 to RM37,738 (BNM, 2016a). Looking at these statistics, it is clear that over the years, the number of insurance policyholders and amount of premium income have increased, while it has a downward trend when it comes to the percentage of GNI. If this trend continues, the chances of falling short to the targeted insurance penetration rate could be even higher in the long run.

Compared to life insurance, the penetration rate for family takaful is relatively much lower. This is illustrated in Figure 5.6 which depicts that the penetration rate for family takaful is around 0.3% compared to more than 2% for life insurance (measured using the first measurement method, i.e. ratio of premiums to GDP).

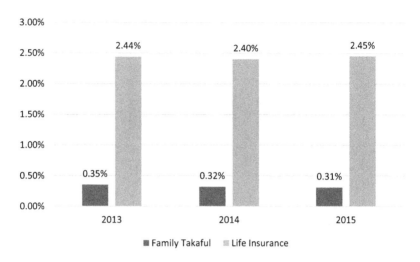

Figure 5.6 Life insurance and family takaful penetration rates for Malaysia (2013–2015).
Source: Ismail & Tan (2018).

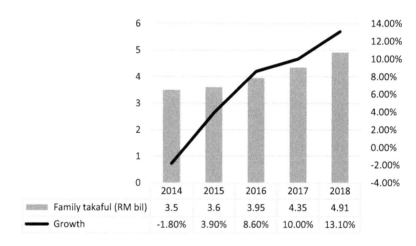

Figure 5.7 Family takaful total gross contribution and growth.
Source: Lim (2019, March 11).

However, the family takaful operators in Malaysia continued to record positive growth in new business, with new premiums and contributions. Whole life, endowment, mortgage-related term insurance, and takaful products continued to dominate the share of new premiums/contributions, collectively making up 64.8% of total new premiums/contributions (Bank Negara Malaysia, 2019).

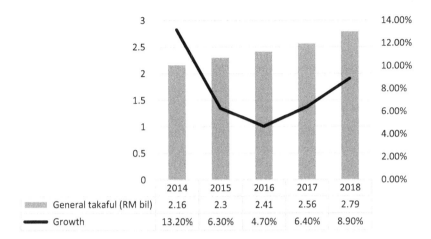

	2014	2015	2016	2017	2018
General takaful (RM bil)	2.16	2.3	2.41	2.56	2.79
Growth	13.20%	6.30%	4.70%	6.40%	8.90%

Figure 5.8 General takaful total gross contribution and growth.
Source: Lim (2019, March 11).

Figure 5.7 shows the total gross contribution and growth of family takaful, while Figure 5.8 presents the total gross contribution and growth of general takaful.

5.1.3 Issues and challenges for the insurance and takaful industry

The insurance industry is one of the key pillars of the financial services sector. Also, it is a crucial element of the business and development matrix. A well-functioning insurance sector for any country plays an important role in economic development (Devarakonda, 2016). The emergence of new critical illnesses and the increase of life expectancy have increased the urgency to develop the country's insurance industry. The literature also indicates that more developed markets have higher shares of insurance in the economy (Ahmad & Yadav, 2019; Dash et al., 2018; Pradhan et al., 2016). Arena (2008) noted that both life and non-life insurance positively contribute to economic growth and transfer risk by allowing different risks to be managed more efficiently by mobilising domestic savings. The life insurance sectors play a critical role in personal risk management, savings opportunity, tax-deferred wealth accumulation, preservation, and transfer.

Despite having positive growth over the past years, both the insurance and takaful industry could not achieve the targeted 75% life insurance penetration rate by 2020. Apart from having some unique challenges, both industries face the following three common major challenges.

5.1.3.1 Low level of awareness

In general, the level of awareness among Malaysians about various insurance and takaful products and services is considerably low. Salleh and Laksana (2018) believed that the lack of awareness about protection and investment plans offered by the sectors slows down the growth of the industry. According to various insurance and takaful associations in Malaysia, there have been many types of awareness campaigns and events over the past few years promoting insurance and takaful products; however, the level of awareness remains low.

5.1.3.2 Low disposable income

A significant portion of Malaysians still falls under the low-income group known as the B40 group. As discussed in Chapter 1 (Table 1.3), the mean and median income of the B40 group in Malaysia are RM3,000 and RM2,848, respectively. As of 2018, only about 30.3% individuals among the B40 group have life insurance or family takaful coverage (BNM, 2019). Considering the current cost of living in Malaysia compared to the income, majority from the B40 group as well as many from the M40 group have difficulties purchasing any form of insurance or takaful plans. In 2018, the then Malaysian Finance Minister also highlighted this issue saying that the main cause for the low penetration rates is the pricing and affordability of policies.

5.1.3.3 Lack of technological advancement

Compared to the banking industry, the insurance and takaful industry is still at an early stage of providing e-services to their customers. Many Malaysians still prefer buying plans through agents, and policyholders may need to wait long to get their insurance claims. It is believed that the industry needs to continuously invest in developing appropriate self-service technologies to increase market base and to achieve the national targeted penetration rates.

5.2 Insurance and takaful schemes in Malaysia

5.2.1 Life insurance

Life insurance is a long-term bilateral contract that pays a lump-sum amount of money to the beneficiaries the event of death or total and permanent disability of the insured. In general, life insurance reduces the current consumption level and increases the aggregate savings in a country. In Malaysia, most of the life insurers offer a range of life insurance policies (see Table 5.3). They also allow customers to pay a set of fixed or variable premiums based on the desired coverage and various payment schedules such as annually, semi-annually, quarterly, and monthly. Usually, the maturity date is linked to a fixed number of years or whole life. A whole life insurance policy usually costs ten times more than the term life insurance policy. However, it provides lifetime protection, helps to accumulate non-taxable cash values, and supports families to settle debts like mortgage loans. While term life insurance policy, which is also known as pure protection policy, is less costly for the protection of certain number of years (e.g. 15 years), these term policies do not provide savings or investment component, and the pay out to the beneficiaries is exercised only at the event of the death of the policyholder during the covered period. Life insurance policies are highly recommended to those who have financial dependents and thus not usually recommended for retirees or children. Malaysians receive a tax relief of up to RM6,000 per year for premiums paid for life insurance and family takaful.

According to the LIAM, for many Malaysians, life insurance is not in their priority list of financial planning. Hence, life insurance remains under-penetrated among the Malaysian society.

It can be observed from Table 5.3 that there are many kinds of life insurance policies in Malaysia that not only provide numerous benefits including death, disability, critical illness, and medical coverage but also provide the opportunity for savings, tax-deferred wealth accumulation, preservation, and wealth transfer. Yet, statistics show that Malaysia has the lowest life insurance real premium growth among the ASEAN-5 countries (see Figure 5.1). Therefore, it is very crucial for the Malaysian life insurance industry to continuously launch promotion campaigns and introduce more attractive products and digital services to increase their market share.

5.2.2 Family takaful

Family takaful provides both protection and savings similar to whole life insurance policy. In Malaysia, family takaful normally covers education, medical critical illnesses, total and permanent disability, mortgage protection, and investment. On the other hand, general takaful, which is known as the counterpart of general insurance, is designed to meet the needs for protection of individuals and corporate bodies in the event of loss and damage due to disasters, floods, and other perils (Htay, Sadzali & Amin, 2015).

Consumers in Malaysia enjoy tax relief for having family takaful policies. In Malaysia, there are a few types of products under takaful such as family takaful, investment-linked takaful, child education takaful, and medical and health takaful. Family takaful provides benefits that include: (i) option for part-withdrawal and (ii) sharing surplus with takaful operator apart from having long-term investment and savings opportunity. Investment-linked takaful combines both protection and investment providing flexibility to choose between the level of protection and investment. It allows consumers to make single contributions (i.e. a single lump-sum payment) or regular contributions (i.e. monthly, quarterly, half-yearly, or yearly). This plan also allows contributors to switch between different investment-link funds and partial withdrawing facility at any point of time. Child Education Takaful Plan (CETP) provides both protection and financing for a child's higher education. It provides financial support to the children when misfortunes happen to the policyholder. The contributor of CETP gets a tax relief of up to RM3,000 per year. A family takaful rider can be added to the plan to have additional types of coverage such as personal accident, medical, and critical illnesses. Apart from

Table 5.3 Types of life insurance in Malaysia

Types of life insurance	Description of the policy	Financial goals
Whole life insurance	It provides "life risks" coverage, requires higher premium payments compared to term life policy. Usually, the premium amount is fixed and provides an opportunity to accumulate non-taxable cash values.	Recommended for tax-deferred wealth accumulation, transfer, and preservation.
Term insurance	It is also meant for "life risks" protection but for a certain number of years (e.g. 15 years) and cheaper compared to other forms of life policy.	Recommended for income replacement during working years.
Endowment	It provides an opportunity for protection and savings, and the payout is exercised at the event of the death or permanent disability.	Recommended for savings, tax-deferred wealth accumulation, preservation, and transfer.
Investment-linked insurance	It combines both investment and protection in one policy dividing the premiums between protection and investment following the choice of the policyholder.	Recommended for savings, tax-deferred wealth accumulation, preservation, and transfer.
Life annuity	It pays a certain amount of money to the policyholders over a set specified period till death.	Recommended for tax-deferred wealth accumulation and retirement savings.
Mortgage reducing term assurance (MRTA)	It settles borrowers' property loans on the event of permanent disability, critical illness, or untimely death.	Recommended for asset transfer and estate planning.
Supplementary rider	It provides an opportunity to add few other coverages such as personal accident, medical, and critical illnesses to the basic insurance policy like term life plan.	Recommended for personal accident, medical, and critical illnesses coverage.

having ordinary child education takaful, an investment-linked child education takaful is available in Malaysia. Finally, medical and health takaful plans provide coverage for the cost of private medical treatment (e.g. hospitalisation, surgery, etc.) in the event of illnesses or accidents.

5.2.3 Medical and health insurance/takaful

Medical and health insurance/takaful is the most basic insurance plan that provides coverage for the treatment of illness or injury owing to diseases or an accident. This plan is designed to cover the cost of private treatments such as hospitalisation and surgical expenses. The most common types of medical and health insurance as well as takaful offered in Malaysia include:

i   medical card or hospital and surgical cover (any hospitalisation expenses due to illness, injury and accident)
ii critical illness plan (a lump-sum amount is paid to the insured upon diagnosis of a critical illness such as heart attack, cancer, stroke, etc.)
iii hospital income insurance (daily income during hospitalisation)
iv e-Medical pass takaful (Shariah-compliant medical card and surgery cover, and cashless admission, no lifetime limit, no medical check-up required)
v   e-CancerCare insurance (cash payout for early-stage cancers, 150% cash payout upon diagnosis of advanced cancer, coverage from 21 cent a day, no medical check-up required)

In Malaysia, health and medical treatment coverage can be obtained by purchasing a stand-alone medical and health insurance/takaful or and add-on policy to the basic life insurance/family takaful plan. Both life insurance and family takaful offer supplementary benefits (riders), which provide opportunity to add other coverages such as personal accident, medical, and critical illnesses to the basic plan.

5.2.4 mySalam

mySalam is a health insurance program launched by the Malaysian government on 24 January 2019. It is a public–private partnership scheme, which aims to offer medical benefits to 3.69 million Malaysians from the low-income group (B40), from 1 January 2019 for a period of five years. This scheme uses the protection premium of RM112 per eligible individual per year from the government to provide free health protection for 36 critical illnesses. According to the mySalam scheme, the recipients of mySalam will get a lump sum of RM8,000 for the diagnosis of critical illnesses such as heart attack, cancer, stroke, and others. Besides, an amount of RM50 daily will be paid to the individual recipient during hospitalisation. This scheme aims to reduce the financial vulnerability caused by medical and health expenses and improve the financial well-being of the B40 group in Malaysia.

5.2.5 PeKa B40 scheme

The Malaysian Ministry of Health introduced a scheme known as PeKa B40 in 2019. It provides health needs to individuals and their spouses aged 40 years and above, and aims to cover the lower income group in Malaysia (B40 group). It pays benefits upon the diagnosis of non-communicable diseases (NCDs) such as cancer. According to ProtectHealth, a wholly owned subsidiary under the Ministry of Health Malaysia (MOH), the PeKa B40 recipients will receive the following benefits: (i) health screening, (ii) health equipment aid, (iii) completing cancer treatment incentive, and (iv) transport incentive. The PeKa B40 recipients need to first complete health screening to determine eligibility to receive incentives for health equipment aid, cancer treatment incentive, and transport incentive. According to the Malaysian Finance Minister in 2018, the main causes for the low insurance penetration rate are the pricing and affordability of policies. Hence, the introduction of PeKa B40 and mySalam schemes will reduce the financial vulnerability of the B40 group in Malaysia caused by their inadequate or low medical and health plans.

5.3 Insurance planning

5.3.1 Insurance planning process

Insurance planning is a series of activities involved in the protection, saving, and wealth accumulation and preservation in the event of misfortune. It is an important part of personal financial planning as it may lead individuals to be financially vulnerable against unexpected events (e.g. death, critical disease, accident, etc.). Therefore, it is necessary to fully understand the insurance planning process to evaluate the adequacy of protection and reduce the protection gap. The insurance planning process is illustrated in Figure 5.9.

5.3.2 Challenges in insurance and takaful planning

Individuals often face various challenges in purchasing insurance or takaful plans. *First*, insurance as well as takaful products are complicated in nature, and many people do not have the required knowledge to understand the contracts. *Second*, purchasing insurance in Malaysia is often time-consuming because it involves a series of activities such as enrollment, document acquisition, and others. *Third*, in many occasions, consumers lack the trust in insurance and takaful agents, knowing the fact that insurance agents work for commission and thus, may not propose policies that are for the best interest of the client. *Fourth*, and most importantly, some individuals do not have insurance plans as they feel that they are constrained by their current income flow, and thus they do not have easily available funds to protect against low probability events. *Fifth*, many people who want to possess insurance to gain investment opportunities find insurance/takaful products unattractive due to low investment return. *Finally*, the issue of lack of skilled insurance agents and skills gap in human resources may demotivate many consumers from possessing insurance/takaful plans. Figure 5.10 conceptualises the challenges in insurance and takaful planning among consumers.

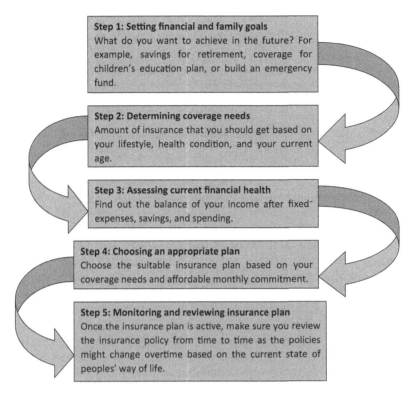

Figure 5.9 Insurance planning process.

Figure 5.10 Challenges in insurance and takaful planning.

5.4 A theoretical perspective on insurance and takaful planning

This section discusses various theories that explain insurance and takaful purchasing behaviour. This behaviour does not always conform to many standard economic theories of decision-making. Hence, studies investigate anomalies empirically and identify causes or behavioural biases for the irrationality, which opens up the possibility of introducing policies for better decision-making. The theories discussed below include the theory of risk aversion, life-cycle hypothesis (LCH), behavioural life-cycle hypothesis (BLCH), availability bias, and prospect theory.

5.4.1 Risk aversion

Risk attitude is related to behavioural intentions associated with personal finance. It is believed that the higher the level of risk aversion, the lower the behavioural intentions should be to engage in planned portfolio management (Bailey & Kinerson, 2005; Mayfield, Perdue, & Wooten, 2008). Usually, risk-averse individuals are reluctant to engage in long-term investment activities that involve uncertainty. Insurance is considered a long-term investment, but it reduces risk and uncertainty; hence, it can be posited that risk-averse individuals will buy more insurance plans compared to risk takers. Risk provides an illustrative set of decisions made in the presence of uncertainty, and insurance markets are particularly amenable to the observation of risk-taking decisions (Richter, Schiller, & Schlesinger, 2014). Usually, risk-averse investors are more vulnerable to a situation with an unknown payoff, and thus they are willing to accept predictable but lower payoff which in turn makes insurance or takaful products more attractive and vice versa. In turn, the presence of many high risk takers in a country may make the insurance products less popular. However, if risk-averse customers could sense any form of uncertainty of not receiving the expected claim payments from the insurers, then they would be reluctant to engage in the plans.

5.4.2 Life-cycle hypothesis and behavioural life-cycle hypothesis

LCH claims that individuals spread their lifetime consumption over their life by accumulating savings during earning years and maintaining consumption levels after retirement. The outcome of such conjecture is that the consumption is treated as a function of age, where individuals borrow in the early stages of life, and then save during the prime years of working life, and upon retirement at old age, dis-save. Another variant of this theory is based on the linear association among the variables such as aggregate consumption, income, and wealth, as discussed by Modigliani and Tarantelli (1975) and Ando and Modigliani (1963). Both insurance and takaful plans are part of the life cycle of financial planning and savings. Hence, the LCH helps people to understand insurance needs and plan ahead. In the early years, individuals tend not to purchase insurance due to (the misperception of having) low health risk, zero dependents, and other factors, while at a later age, underinsurance makes them financially vulnerable. Hence, protection plans are highly recommended for individuals at the early stage of their own financial life cycle. However, individuals are not always rational in purchasing insurance and takaful plans, and the causes of irrational behaviour are explained by the BLCH.

5.4.3 Availability bias

Availability bias by Tversky and Kahneman (1973) refers to the human tendency of perceiving that certain incidents will have a higher probability of happening if it had just recently occurred. The implication of this bias is that promoting insurance plans right after the occurence of an event would increase the chances of life insurance/takaful being sold to customers. For instance, the demand for health and life insurance is expected to be higher right after the Covid-19 crisis compared to a few years after the crisis. As argued in the literature, a recent event influences people's decision-making behaviour more than an older event. Therefore, any recent event would be of help to an insurance agent to convince the potential buyers as it is known that insurance/takaful policies are sold, rather than bought.

5.4.4 Prospect theory

Normative economic approaches are usually used to explain insurance decisions. However, a study by Wakker, Thaler, and Tversky (1997) documented that when an insurance or takaful plan has a small probability of default, the consumers demand big discounts in premium payment. This relationship is explained using the prospect theory by Tversky and Kahneman (1979) in which it is pointed out that small probabilities get overweighed. The implication of this theory in penetrating insurance or takaful is that the insurers and the policymakers must work together to ensure zero default in paying consumer claims. The word-of-mouth phenomenon has a huge influence in the Malaysian market; hence, a single default in paying out consumer insurance claims would create a big negative impact on customers' insurance or takaful buying behaviour.

5.5 Empirical studies on insurance and takaful

5.5.1 Research concepts on insurance and takaful

The concepts of insurance and takaful have been investigated in various branches of social science. The most studied concepts in insurance and takaful include insurance and takaful planning; insurance or takaful penetration; legal and regulatory frameworks for insurance and or takaful products; demand for life insurance and family takaful; insurance and takaful purchasing behaviour; and awareness about insurance products, services, and benefits. Table 5.4 outlines the concepts identified from the literature, their definitions, and measurements used in prior studies.

Table 5.4 Insurance and takaful concepts being studied and their definition/measurement

Concepts	Definition/Measurement	Authors
Insurance or takaful planning	A range of activities that involve having protection, savings and wealth accumulation, wealth preservation, and transfer at the event of death or misfortunes.	Lahsasna (2016)
	Insurance planning involves researching various insurance policies, assessing financial health, and seeking advice from trusted insurance agents.	Crichton (2008); Shectman (1982)
Insurance or takaful penetration	Penetration refers to the size of premium related to GDP.	Kaur (2015)
	The growth of insurance market or in insurance premium.	Pradhan, Arvin, Norman, Nair & Hall (2016); Alhassan, & Fiador (2014)
Legal and regulatory framework of insurance and/or takaful	Regulatory frameworks strengthen the overall industry and enhance its sustainability in the long run. Risk-based capital framework, risk-based capital framework for takaful operators (RBCT), life insurance and family takaful framework (LIFE framework).	Fauzi et al. (2016); BNM (2019)
Demand for life insurance and family takaful	Premiums that individuals are willing and afford to pay for a life insurance plan.	Mahdzan & Victorian (2013)
	Life insurance is a long-term investment and a bilateral contract of defined protection and benefits.	Emamgholipour, Arab, & Mohajerzadeh (2017)
	The demand for life insurance depends on one's dependency structure.	Kjosevski (2012); Sherif & Hussnain (2017)
	The growth of the insurance industry can be explained by the demand functions of life insurance or family takaful.	Truett & Truett (1990)
Insurance and takaful purchasing behaviour	Factors influencing consumers' insurance buying intention or behaviour.	Aziz, Md Husin, & Hussin, Afaq (2019)
	Measuring behaviour of participating in insurance or takaful schemes using behavioural factors and theories.	Husin & Ab Rahman (2013); Othman, Mohamad, & Ismail (2018)
Awareness	The knowledge about the insurance or takaful product and services. The benefits of having insurance protection.	Allain, Friedman, & Senter (2012); Soualhi & Al Shammari (2015)

From Table 5.4, it can be noted that prior empirical studies on insurance and takaful mostly explored the determinants of insurance or takaful products' buying intentions or behaviours. Most of the previous studies that investigated the concept of legal and regulatory frameworks for insurance or takaful products have highlighted many issues that demotivate consumers to participate in various insurance or takaful schemes. The concept of awareness has drawn huge attention to researchers. According to many previous studies, one of the most important factors that slows down the growth of the insurance industry is the lack of awareness among households about the importance of having insurance (e.g. Husin & Ab Rahman, 2013). The concept of insurance penetration has also been investigated across the world and found to have several influencing psychological and behavioural factors. The above concepts shed light on the various issues involved in insurance or takaful research.

5.5.2 *Factors influencing insurance and takaful purchasing behaviour*

The notable socio-demographic and psychological factors linked to insurance and takaful purchasing decisions are presented and discussed in this section. A range of socio-demographic factors such as life expectancy, marital status, age, education, dependency ratio, employment status, and income are found to be influential in individuals' insurance buying behaviour. Evidences also show that various psychological factors such financial literacy, trust, worry and fear, risk perception, social norms, religious belief, and money management influence insurance and takaful purchasing behaviour. Table 5.5 summarises the factors adopted by different researchers. The following sections will discuss all the factors outlined in the table.

5.5.2.1 *Socio-demographic factors*

The demand for various insurance and takaful policies has found to be influenced by various social-demographic factors such as *life expectancy, marital status, age, education, dependency ratio, employment status, and income*. Some prior studies suggested that the longer individuals expect to live, the higher the demand for life insurance (i.e. Nesterova, 2008). However, some other studies found no significant relationship between life expectancy and demand for life insurance (e.g. Lim & Haberman, 2004). Simultaneously, some studies found a negative relationship between life expectancy and demand for life insurance (Beck & Webb, 2003; Brown & Kim, 1993). In Malaysia, *life expectancy* is found to have a significant negative relationship with the demand for family takaful (Sherif & Shaairi, 2013).

Dorfman and Adelman (2002) found that married people buy more life insurance compared to unmarried ones due to concern on the well-being of the surviving spouse. Similarly, Allcock et al. (2019) identified that those who were married early have the highest coverage of health insurance. However, Mahdzan and Victorian (2013) found that in Malaysia, single people buy more life insurance policies compared to married and divorced individuals. Literature has registered *age* of the people as an important factor in buying insurance policies. According to Atreya et al. (2015), age groups above 45 are more likely to buy flood insurance. Loke and Goh (2012) found that young Malaysian adults are less

Table 5.5 Factors influencing insurance and takaful purchasing behaviour

Dimensions	Specific factors	Authors
Socio-demographic factors	Life expectancy	Akhter, Pappas, & Khan (2017); Sherif & Shaairi (2013); Wahid et al. (2019); Nesterova, 2008; Rahim & Amin (2011).
	Marital status	Mahdzan & Victorian (2013); Dorfman and Adelman (2002); Allcock et al. (2019).
	Age	Atreya, A., et.al. (2015); Loke & Goh (2012); Savvides (2006).
	Education	Mahdzan & Victorian (2013); Nowotny, Scott, and Gibbons (2013); Li, Moshirian, Nguyen, and Wee, 2007; Allcock et al. (2019).
	Dependency ratio	Mahdzan and Victorian (2013); Dorfman & Adelman (2002); Allcock et al. (2019).
	Employment status	Ishak (2017); Aziz et al. (2019); Liebenberg, Carson & Dumm (2012); Skinner & Dubinsky (1984); Loke and Goh (2012).
	Income	Delafrooz and Paim (2011); Raza, Farhan, & Akram (2011); Milevsky (2006); Haron, Razali, and Mohamad (2019).
Psychological factors	Financial literacy	Mahdzan & Victorian (2013); Lusardi, Mitchell, and Curto (2010); Delafrooz and Paim (2011); Manaf & Amiruddin (2019). Rahman, Azma, Masud, & Ismail (2020); Azma, Rahman, Adeyemi, & Rahman (2019); Lin, Hsiao, & Yeh (2017); Zakaria et al. (2016); Shafii, Abiddin, & Ahmad (2009).
	Money management	Bharucha (2019); Mahdzan and Victorian (2013); Lea, Webley, and Walker (1995); Bharucha (2019); Henry, Weber, & Yarbrough (2001); Hsiao & Yeh (2017).
	Religious belief	Sherif & Shaairi (2013); Salleh (2012); Zakaria et al. (2016); Othman et al. (2018); Hassan & Abbas (2019); Ajzen and Fishbein (1980); Souiden & Jabeur (2015); Dusuki & Abdullah (2007); Noland (2005); Salleh (2012); Delener (1994); Md. Taib, Ramayah, & Razak (2008); Browne & Kim (1993); Farooq, Chaudhry, Alam, & Ahmad (2010); Chui & Kwok (2009); Husin & Ab Rahman (2013).
	Social norms	Aziz et al. (2017); Lo (2013); Razak & Abduh (2012); Siang & Weng (2011); Amin (2013); Husin et al. (2016); Amron et al. (2018).
	Worry and fear	Borkovec, Alcaine, & Behar (2004); Baron, Hershey, & Kunreuther (2000); Borkovec & Newman (1998); Zick, Smith, Mayer, & Botkin (2000); Hsee & Kunreuther (2000); Kunreuther (1996); Loewenstein, Weber, Hsee, & Welch (2001).

(*continued*)

Table 5.5 Cont.

Dimensions	Specific factors	Authors
	Risk perception	Amaefula, Okezie, & Mejeha (2012); Annamalah (2013); Amin (2012); Azma, Rahman, Adeyemi, & Rahman (2019); Rahman, Azma, Masud, & Ismail (2020); Doosti & Karampour (2017); Botzen & van den Bergh (2012); Lo (2013); Rahman et al. (2020); Keese (2010); Barros & Botelho (2012); Qureshi (2019); Raza et al.(2019); Amin & Chong (2013).
	Trust	Guiso (2012); Aziz et al. (2019); Shukor (2020); Dercon, Gunning, & Zeitlin (2019); Lee (2009); Nash, Bouchard, & Malm (2018); Cai, Chen, Fang, & Zhou (2009); Cole et al. (2011); Jamshidi & Hussin (2016); Zhang, Zhu, & Liu (2012); Aziz, Md Husin, Hussin, & Afaq (2019).

likely to buy life insurance compared to older adults. On the other hand, some studies argued that age has an inverse relationship with life insurance demand as the cost of coverage increases with the people's age (Savvides, 2006).

Studies show that the level of *education* influences one's insurance purchasing decision. Allcock et al. (2019) suggested that women with higher levels of education are more likely to be insured. A study by Mahdzan and Victorian (2013) found that in Malaysia, people with higher level of education are more willing to purchase life insurance and family takaful (Sherif & Shaairi, 2013), while another Malaysian study argued that the level of education is an insignificant determinant of life insurance demand as individuals receive necessary information and guidance from agents instead of the formal education system (Tan, Wong, & Law, 2009). However, in general, higher education enhances awareness about uncertainties and thus influences individuals' decision of purchasing higher insurance coverage (Nowotny, Scott, & Gibbons, 2013). Likewise, the number of dependents on the household head directly affects life insurance purchasing decisions. For instance, some Malaysian empirical studies found that *dependency ratio* has a positive influence on the demand for life insurance or family takaful (Mahdzan & Victorian, 2013; Sherif & Shaairi, 2013; Tan, Wong, & Law, 2009).

Employment status influences people's purchasing decision, as based on the results from a previous study which suggest that employment status is an important predictor of life insurance demand (e.g. Liebenberg, Carson, & Dumm, 2012). Many prior studies have suggested that both part-time and full-time working individuals are more likely to own life insurance. It is also noted that the possibility of buying more life insurance coverage is high when both husband and wife are working (e.g. Skinner & Dubinsky, 1984). A study by Loke and Goh (2012) found that in Malaysia, white-collar workers or professionals are more likely to buy life insurance compared to blue-collar workers or unemployed individuals.

This is because *income* is found to be an important factor that significantly affects households' ability to spend on buying insurance policies (Tan, Wong, & Law, 2009). Evidences show that in Malaysia, the demand for life insurance and family takaful increases when households' incomes rise, as higher income makes insurance premiums more affordable (Mahdzan & Victorian, 2013; Redzuan, Abdul Rahman, & Aidid, 2009).

The above discussion shows that various empirical studies have been carried out to understand the relationship between social-demographic factors and demand for insurance policies (e.g. life insurance, family takaful) particularly in the context of Malaysia. However, the evidence shows that the impact of social-demographic factors may not hold in every setting, yet understanding the nature of the factors and their impacts on demand for insurance policies in general would help policymakers and insurance or takaful companies to formulate appropriate policies.

5.5.2.2 Psychological factors

Psychological factors influencing the demand for insurance or takaful policies consist of various cognitive factors (e.g. financial literacy, money management, religious belief), motivational factors (e.g. social norms, worry and fear), and dispositional factors (risk perception, trust). An increasing number of empirical studies have suggested that households' life insurance or family takaful purchasing behaviour is not only influenced by the basic demographic factors but also by the psychological factors (Lin, Hsiao, & Yeh, 2017; Mahdzan & Victorian, 2013; Souiden & Jabeur, 2015). The following sections will discuss the relationship between various psychological factors and demand for life insurance or family takaful.

FINANCIAL LITERACY

Financial literacy is one of the cognitive factors that helps people to analyse available information and make better financial decisions. Literally, it refers to individuals' ability to understand financial concepts (i.e. compound interest, time value of money) and calculations to make sound financial decision (Rahman, Azma, Masud, & Ismail, 2020). In general, financially literate households are better in managing their income and achieving their financial goals. Prior studies also suggest that higher financial literacy would lead people to secure their financial well-being by having proper financial planning including sufficient savings, well-diversified investment portfolios, and adequate insurance policies (Azma, Rahman, Adeyemi, & Rahman, 2019; Mahdzan & Victorian, 2013; Zakaria, Azmi, Hassan, Salleh, Tajuddin, Sallem, & Nor, 2016).

Lin, Hsiao, and Yeh (2017) found that financial literacy has a significant positive relationship with the demand for life insurance policies. A study by Zakaria et al. (2016) found that in Malaysia, financial literacy directly influences the intention of public universities' staff to purchase life insurance or family takaful policies. However, Mahdzan and Victorian (2013) found an insignificant association between financial literacy and demand for life insurance. These contradictory findings suggest that intention to purchase life insurance or family takaful may not translate into actual behaviour. Moreover, financial literacy may not always play a significant role when it comes to buying life insurance or family takaful. Many empirical studies also argued that individuals with high financial literacy are more likely to accumulate and preserve their wealth by participating in various investment and insurance plans (e.g. Lusardi, Mitchell, & Curto, 2010; Shafii, Abiddin, & Ahmad, 2009).

Studies also suggest that financial literacy enhances people's ability to manage their day-to-day finance and protect them from having severe losses resulting from their poor financial decisions. Indeed, financial literacy helps people to understand the importance of having adequate insurance protection. It encourages individuals to be involved in the insurance planning process as it may prevent individuals from becoming financially vulnerable against unexpected events (e.g. death, critical disease, accident, etc.). Financial literacy helps individuals to overcome various challenges in purchasing insurance or takaful policies, e.g. understanding the contracts, and/or finding appropriate investment-linked insurance policies.

MONEY MANAGEMENT

Money management refers to a set of skills that help individuals to manage their money in an effective way such as putting money aside for regular bill payments, maintaining bank accounts, etc. Lea, Webley, and Walker (1995) suggested that individuals' money management skills are associated with the teachings received about money management from their parents (e.g. pocket money received during childhood). Studies have suggested that individuals who have weak personal money management skills are more likely to get involved in unnecessary debt and less likely to plan before making large purchases (e.g. Lea, Webley, & Walker, 1995). In fact, many individuals do not realise that they are poor money managers until they end up having outstanding bills and struggle to make the repayments. According to Bharucha (2019), money management factors are associated with individuals' financial planning. It helps people to make better financial planning, including accumulating and preserving wealth through purchasing life insurance. It is also argued in the literature that individuals' high income leads to better money management skills such as maintaining bank accounts, using direct debits for paying bills, having high level of savings and others.

In regards to the demand for life insurance, Lin, Hsiao, and Yeh (2017) found that individuals in Taiwan who have high concerns about money management have a higher tendency to buy life insurance products. The study also suggested that money management as a component of financial literacy is significantly and positively linked to the possession of life insurance. This is not surprising as empirical evidence shows that good money managers would like to accumulate wealth and plan ahead before making large purchases (Henry, Weber, & Yarbrough, 2001; Lea, Webley, & Walker, 1995; Lin, Hsiao, & Yeh, 2017). It was argued that individuals who took the effort to manage their money have a higher tendency to protect their wealth using insurance and takaful. Prior studies also suggest that weak money management skills would lead to individuals becoming financially vulnerable due to bad borrowing behaviour, lack of personal budgeting, lack of savings, and lack of planning in purchasing and paying instalments.

RELIGIOUS BELIEFS

Religious beliefs refer to one's trust in God regardless of religion (Souiden & Jabeur, 2015). It is considered as a main part of the religiosity variable. Empirical studies have suggested that religious beliefs strongly influence individuals' attitudes and behaviours (Dusuki & Abdullah, 2007; Souiden & Rani, 2015). Noland (2005) also argued that one's religious beliefs influence his/her behaviour regardless of the religion. Furthermore, Salleh (2012) suggested that people's strong religious values increase their belief in God . According to Delener (1994), highly religious people tend to strictly follow the religious teachings and are comparatively more conservative in their buying behaviour. One's beliefs are the most important underlying factors that influence the intention and behaviour (Md. Taib, Ramayah, & Razak, 2008). Hence, religious beliefs are found to be important determinants of purchase intention and behaviour.

Numerous empirical studies on insurance confirm that the demand for life insurance, particularly in Muslim countries, heavily depends on religion and religious beliefs (e.g. Browne & Kim, 1993; Farooq, Chaudhry, Alam, & Ahmad, 2010). Studies have found that individuals who have high religious beliefs are less likely to buy life insurance as there is a belief that buying life insurance means doubting God's protection (Chui & Kwok, 2009; Sherif & Shaairi, 2013). An increasing number of studies also noted that the demand for life insurance in non-Muslim countries is higher than Muslim countries. These results are not unexpected, given that Muslim scholars (*ulama*) have three different views about subscribing to insurance products that affect individuals' demand for life insurance. Among them, the first school of thought accepts insurance as a permissible product as long as its contracts are free from *riba*. The second group of scholars accepts general insurance but rejects life insurance on the grounds of having *gharar* (uncertainty) and *maisir* (gambling) in the contract. However, the third group completely rejects the insurance practice as a whole, arguing that it involves *gharar*, *maisir*, and *riba*.

To address the issues involved in insurance practices and eliminate misconceptions about life insurance, like other Muslim nations, Malaysia introduced takaful in year 1984, which provides Muslims the sense of understanding that preparing for vulnerabilities in life is encouraged in Islam. In general, holistic religious beliefs play an important role in encouraging people to accept insurance or takaful. In Malaysia, Muslims are more likely to buy family takaful instead of conventional life insurance (Husin & Ab Rahman, 2013). This implies that Malaysian Muslim consumers would be willing to purchase protection policies provided that the contracts are developed following Shariah principles.

Social norms refer to a set of informal rules on how people should behave in a group or a society (Aziz et al., 2017; Lo, 2013). Social norm is one of the motivational factors triggered by social pressure to perform certain behaviour. Basically, most individuals want to be part of the society by fulfilling a set of societal expectations. Social norm is one of the most important indicator of subjective norm, and subjective norm is found to be significantly associated with intention and behaviour (e.g. Razak & Abduh, 2012; Siang & Weng, 2011). Subjective norm refers to the expectation that leads to the performance of behaviour (Amin, 2013). Social norm is also known as social dilemma, which may lead individuals to be irrational in making various decisions to show the belongingness to the society. For instance, Amron, Usman, and Mursid (2018) found that individuals are more likely to buy insurance products upon receiving pressure from the society.

In studies of life insurance and family takaful demand, subjective norm has been found to be a strong predictor leading to positive life insurance or family takaful buying behaviour. For instance, Husin et al. (2016) suggested that conventional media influence the intention to buy insurance services. Similarly, Amron et al. (2018) found that subjective norm positively and significantly influenced the intention to purchase insurance. However, Husin et al. (2016) found no significant relationship between subjective norms and the intention to purchase family takaful. In regards to the demand for takaful products, Amin (2012) found that Malaysian students who follow social norms have high willingness to use takaful products. In other words, the empirical evidence suggests that various stakeholders of a society including family members, friends, community leaders, religious teachers, and the media would be able to influence individuals' insurance or takaful products purchasing behaviour. Therefore, it can be argued that social norms can help to address the existing underinsurance problem in Malaysia.

Worry refers to unpleasant emotions that involves negative thinking about future events. Borkovec, Alcaine, and Behar (2004) defined worry as "a pervasive human experience and the defining characteristics of generalised anxiety disorder". It is also known as an important predictor of personal action. In an experimental study, Baron, Hershey, and Kunreuther (2000) found that individuals' decision about taking protection against risks is strongly associated with worry and fear. Empirical studies have suggested that worry and fear can be influenced by several other factors such as age, gender, marital status, news reports, expertise, personal experience, and others (Baron, Hershey, & Kunreuther, 2000; Borkovec & Newman, 1998; Zick, Smith, Mayer, & Botkin, 2000). For example, individuals who had experienced unpleasant events or repeatedly heard about the event would be more worried about the risks compared to those without the experience. This implies that worry and fear would motivate individuals to protect themselves and their loved ones against various risks by purchasing adequate insurance policies. Baron, Hershey, and Kunreuther (2000) justified the explanation by asserting that worry is a primary motivating factor for individuals to engage in more protective behaviour like subscribing to insurance.

In regards to demand for insurance, several empirical studies have suggested that individuals do not usually purchase insurance until they experience similar unpleasant events (Hsee & Kunreuther, 2000; Kunreuther, 1996). The above findings are not unexpected, as Loewenstein, Weber, Hsee, and Welch (2001) have suggested that the vast majority of individuals are willing to insure themselves against any risky situation as a result of fear they experienced in connection with a particular risk. This behaviour will indirectly support the efforts of the government to reduce the number of underinsured citizens. Therefore, understanding the role of worry and fear in shaping individuals' risk perception and intention would be useful in reducing their vulnerabilities through having adequate insurance protection.

RISK PERCEPTION

Risk perception is one of the factors under the dispositional psychological domain, which indicates how people position risk while making decisions. It refers to an individual's view about risk (Azma, Rahman, Adeyemi, & Rahman, 2019; Rahman, Azma, Masud, & Ismail, 2020). Risk perception is found to have influence on individuals' behaviour. Doosti and Karampour (2017) found that individuals' financial decision-making and other risk-related behaviours are strongly related to risk perception. Botzen and van den Bergh (2012) found that individuals who perceive flood as a risky event would tend to buy insurance coverage for flood. This would imply that individuals who perceive the risks of having critical diseases or be involved in deadly accidents as low are less likely to buy life insurance or family takaful, and vice versa. Empirical evidence also suggests that people with low risk perception are less likely to invest in low probability events (Lo, 2013; Rahman et al., 2020). Individuals with low risk perceptions tend not to buy insurance or takaful considering the low probability of unexpected events (e.g. critical disease, accident, etc.). Moreover, Keese (2010) noted that factors such as level of education, income, religion, and marital status influence individuals' risk perception. For instance, two people who have different levels of education may perceive risks about the same goods differently, and thus end up having different decisions about purchasing the goods (Barros & Botelho, 2012). The above discussions based on empirical evidence shows that there is a positive relationship between individuals' risk perceptions about unexpected events and the demand for insurance.

However, studies have suggested that perceived risks about insurance or takaful itself is negatively linked to the intentions to purchase insurance/takaful policies. In other words, when individuals believe that insurance or takaful involves some form of risks, then they would be less likely to buy the insurance/takaful schemes. This justification is supported by a study by Raza, Ahmed, Ali, and Qureshi (2019) who found a negative association between perceived risk of insurance or takaful and the intention to purchase Islamic insurance schemes in Pakistan. Consumers often collect reviews from experienced buyers before buying any goods or services. Individuals usually have high perceived risk for any new or unknown products and services (Raza et al., 2019). Empirical evidences have suggested that there is an inverse relationship between perceived risk and the intention to purchase (Amin & Chong, 2013; Raza et al., 2019). This concludes that the intentions to buy insurance or takaful increases when perceived risk about the insurance or takaful schemes decreases. Hence, insurance and takaful operators could accelerate the demand for the insurance by addressing the concern of perceived risk related to their products and services.

TRUST

Dercon, Gunning, and Zeitlin (2019) defined trust as "the potential policyholder's perceived likelihood that a claim would be paid in the event of a loss." It is closely connected to the demand for insurance. It is an important dispositional factor causing individuals to be involved in various economic activities such as buying goods and services, investing money, and others (Lee, 2009). Trust is deeply rooted in social relations and embedded in financial decision-making (Nash, Bouchard, & Malm, 2018). Hence, the level of consumers' trust in agents and insurers plays an important role when it comes to buying insurance or takaful policies. In general, customers may be reluctant to buy insurance if they believe that they will have difficulties making a claim and/or being refused compensation of a claim by the insurer.

Empirical evidence on the demand for insurance has identified trust as an important determinants (Cai, Chen, Fang, & Zhou, 2009; Cole et al., 2011). Several studies have suggested that trust significantly influences individuals' behavioural intentions (Jamshidi & Hussin, 2016; Zhang, Zhu, & Liu, 2012). Likewise, Aziz, Md Husin, Hussin, and Afaq (2019) suggested that individuals would tend to buy family takaful schemes when they have trust in the policy. In other words, customers would more likely buy insurance/takaful policies once they come to know that the agents and insurers are working in the best interest of their clients. A study by Dercon et al. (2019) also found that consumers with high trust on insurers and agents are more likely to buy insurance products. This implies that the lack of trust in agents and the insurers may make the protection plans unpopular. Therefore, it is very important to build and enhance trust between consumers, insurance agents, and insurers to reduce the existing protection gap in the Malaysian society.

Based on the above discussion, it is noticed that psychological factors are crucial in determining the demand for insurance or takaful policies. Therefore, understanding psychological factors that influence the intention to purchase insurance or takaful products would be helpful for insurance and takaful operators to increase market share.

5.6 Policy recommendations for various stakeholders

Insurance and takaful have been categorised as unsought goods based on the continuum of product classification (Kotler & Keller, 2016). Consumers generally do not pay deliberate attention to buy these types of goods unless there is an emergency. It is also often heard that insurance is sold and not bought, which basically means that customers do not actively seek to purchase insurance/takaful but it is mainly the concerted efforts of agents to market and sell the products to customers. Empirical evidence suggests that numerous determinants account for the low penetration rate of takaful and insurance, such as socio-demographic factors (e.g. life expectancy, marital status, age, education, dependency ratio, employment status, and income) and psychological factors (e.g. financial literacy, trust in agents, worry and fear, risk perception, social norms, religious belief, and money management). A report by BNM shows that the current life insurance penetration rate falls far short from the national targeted penetration rate of 75% by 2020. Hence, it is inevitable for both the government and the industry to take effective actions in order to increase the penetration rate of takaful and insurance in Malaysia. Insurance or takaful purchasing behaviour does not always conform to standard economic theories of decision-making (irrational behaviour). Hence, findings of past studies that have identified the causes for irrational behaviours will help respective authorities to introduce policies for better decision-making among consumers.

5.6.1 Government level initiatives

The government plays a leading role in implementing policies and laws for the betterment of citizens. Although the Malaysian government targeted a penetration rate of 75% by 2020, existing strategies were not fully successful. Lack of awareness may be one of the key causes for the low penetration rate. Usually, governments create nudges as an effective tool for low awareness situations. Educational programmes can be conducted to educate people on the benefits and consequences of having life insurance. These programmes/contents can be published in national medias like TV, radio, newspapers, and in verified social media pages such as Facebook, Twitter, and Instagram. The importance of insurance in our daily lives can be included into the curriculum and co-curricular activities of primary and secondary schools as well as tertiary education so that young folks will have better understanding of insurance and takaful policies. Moreover, the government may include the concept of insurance protection for health and life risk into the financial literacy plan 2019–2023, which is currently missing.

In many instances, the cost of buying takaful and insurance policies is comparatively high due to the fact that foreign insurers have the lion share in the

Malaysian insurance industry (DBS Group Research, 2017). MNCs usually calculate premium and other associated costs equivalent to dollar amount. Besides, the key objective of MNCs is to maximise profits that may be remitted to the home country. The government should give privileges to the local insurers and takaful operators with financial incentives, and in return, the insurers could offer premium rate at affordable rates.

Most importantly, a mandatory health insurance policy can be introduced by the government in association with the EPF. The government can either deduct a certain amount as premium or introduce additional savings to EPF. Of course, the premium should differ based on age and protection needs. This will lead to the sense of health protection until death, enhancing the benefits of retirement funds. Besides, the newly introduced mySalam Scheme and National Health Protection Scheme (PeKa B40) by the government can be revised to provide life-long coverage instead of being limited to five years. In this case, 50% of the total social protection insurance premium can be borne by the B40 income groups, and the rest of the amount can be subsidised by the government. For those without income, the government should subsidise their health coverage. Finally, the government could focus on regulating MNCs by setting up a limit for cost of premium, that would be more affordable to various income groups in Malaysia.

5.6.2 Company level initiatives

From a business point of view, companies may revitalise their existing strategies to mitigate the current challenges. More precisely, the service offerings might need to be re-looked through the lens of prevailing challenges.

Due to the economic challenges and increasing expenditure in recent years, it is difficult to spare some income for health protection. The B40 income groups, especially, encounters difficulties in managing their family expenditure. Insurers may introduce customised products with affordable prices for different income groups. For instance, the cost of premium could be set lower for the B40 group. Furthermore, research should be carried out to investigate the affordable level of health insurance costs and benefits.

Generally, the contractual terms of an insurance/takaful policy are quite complex and difficult to comprehend for the layman. Despite being eligible, many people disregard buying health insurance or takaful due to the complex terms and conditions associated with buying and materialising the said claim. According to services marketing scholars, one of the fundamental criteria of service design is to simplify the service processes (Lovelock & Wirtz, 2011). Thus, the following aspects are essential in designing takaful and insurance product offerings:

• Terms and conditions must be self-explanatory so that consumers can easily understand the scheme and benefits. Communication materials including info graphics may highlight these issues so that people may be well-aware of different coverage types included in the plans and claims procedures.

- Simplify service provisions, documents requirement, buying and claim procedures.
- Straightforward claims should be paid out within a short stipulated time period.
- Underwriting procedures should be simplified by leaving mandatory information blank for the policy seekers. Customer service employees or agents can help them to fill out the necessary information.
- Company can enhance their an online systems for claims to be made by the insured or policyholder.
- In many instances, the branch of takaful and insurers is located at distance. The company can make the service point available in convenient locations and/or offer online services.
- Responsive, trustworthy and friendly service employees and agents are crucial. The company can initiate service feedback survey, which would help the company to train and guide these service employees when required.

Keeping pace with the technological development, insurers should continuously enhance smart technology in service design. User-friendly mobile apps should allow policyholders and beneficiaries place their claims or request for any service they require. Furthermore, takaful and insurance company can communicate and update their policyholders on various issues related to services with this mobile app.

Lack of trust is among the key aspects of low penetration rate of health insurance among the Malaysian citizens as multiple complexities are associated with takaful and insurance service policies. Precisely, complex purchasing and claims procedures, lack of responsiveness of service employees, and lack of proper awareness about the service provisions lead to distrust among the policyholders. Hence, an integrative marketing communication (IMC) programme should be

Table 5.6 Summary of policy implications for both government and company levels

Government wide	Company wide
• Education campaigns	• Introducing low premium scheme for
• Introduction of new curriculum	B40 group
• Specific strategy as financial literacy plan	• Simplifying service provisions,
• Foster local insurance and takaful companies	documents requirement, buying and claim procedures
• Mandatory health contribution scheme	• Easy and convenient location
• New regulations on the premium pricing for the low-income group	• Responsive and friendly service personnel
	• Updated technology adoption
	• Creating continuous awareness programmes using various social platforms

launched to increase awareness. In fact, advertisements, sponsorships, organising events, and participating in consumer trade expos should be among the key communication strategies by insurers. The company can share the service experience of existing policyholders in communication materials through digital platforms (i.e. Facebook, YouTube, and WhatsApp) and traditional media.

Overall, although there is no immediate solution for the current challenges, the above suggestions might help to resolve the issue of underinsurance among Malaysians.

References

Abduh, M. & Abdul Razak, D. (2012). Customers' attitude towards diminishing partnership home financing in Islamic banking. *American Journal of Applied Science, 9*(4), 593–599.

Ahmad, I. & Yadav, A. (2019). Impact of insurance sector on economic growth: A case of India. *ZENITH International Journal of Multidisciplinary Research, 9*(4), 332–340.

Ajzen, I. & Fishbein, M. (1980). *Understanding Attitudes and Predicting Social Behavior.* Prentice-Hall, Englewood Cliffs, NJ.

Akhter, W., Pappas, V., & Khan, S.U. (2017). A comparison of Islamic and conventional insurance demand: Worldwide evidence during the Global Financial Crisis. *Research in International Business and Finance, 42*, 1401–1412.

Alhassan, A.L. & Fiador, V. (2014). Insurance-growth nexus in Ghana: An autoregressive distributed lag bounds cointegration approach. *Review of Development Finance, 4*(2), 83–96.

Allain, D.C., Friedman, S., & Senter, L. (2012). Consumer awareness and attitudes about insurance discrimination post enactment of the Genetic Information Nondiscrimination Act. *Familial Cancer, 11*(4), 637–644.

Allcock, S.H., Young, E.H., & Sandhu, M.S. (2019). Sociodemographic patterns of health insurance coverage in Namibia. *International Journal for Equity in Health, 18*(16), 1–11.

Amaefula, C., Okezie, C.A., & Mejeha, R. (2012). Risk attitude and insurance: A causal analysis. *American Journal of Economics, 2*(3), 26–32.

Amin, H. (2012). An analysis on Islamic insurance participation. *Jurnal Pengurusan (UKM Journal of Management), 34*.

Amin, H. (2013). Factors influencing Malaysian bank customers to choose Islamic credit cards. *Journal of Islamic Marketing, 4*(3), 245–263.

Amin, H. & Chong, R. (2013). Determinants for ar-Rahnu usage intentions: An empirical investigation. *African Journal of Business Management, 5*(20), 8181–8191.

Amron, A., Usman, U., & Mursid, A. (2018). The role of electronic word of mouth, conventional media, and subjective norms on the intention to purchase Sharia insurance services. *Journal of Financial Services Marketing, 23*(3–4), 218–225.

Ando, A. & Modigliani, F. (1963). The "life cycle" hypothesis of saving: Aggregate implications and tests. *American Economic Review, 53*(1), 55–84.

Annamalah, S. (2013). Profiling and purchasing decision of life insurance policies among married couples in Malaysia. *World Applied Sciences Journal, 23*(3), 296–304.

Arena, M. (2008). Does insurance market activity promote economic growth? A cross-country study for industrialized and developing countries. *Journal of Risk and Insurance, 75*(4), 921–946.

Atreya, A., Ferreira, S., & Michel-Kerjan, E. (2015). What drives households to buy flood insurance? New evidence from Georgia. *Ecological Economics, 117,* 153–161.

Doosti, B.A. & Karampour, A. (2017). The impact of behavioral factors on propensity toward indebtedness case study: Indebted customers of Maskan Bank, Tehran province (Geographic regions: East). *Journal of Advances in Computer Engineering and Technology, 3*(3), 145–152.

Aziz, S., Md Husin, M., & Hussin, N. (2017). Conceptual framework of factors determining intentions towards the adoption of family takaful – An extension of decomposed theory of planned behaviour. *International Journal of Organizational Leadership, 6,* 385–399.

Aziz, S., Md Husin, M., Hussin, N., & Afaq, Z. (2019). Factors that influence individuals' intentions to purchase family takaful mediating role of perceived trust. *Asia Pacific Journal of Marketing and Logistics.* doi:10.1108/apjml-12-2017-0311

Azma, N., Rahman, M., Adeyemi, A.A., & Rahman, M.K. (2019). Propensity toward indebtedness: Evidence from Malaysia. *Review of Behavioral Finance, 11*(2), 188–200.

Bailey, J.J. & Kinerson, C. (2005). Regret avoidance and risk tolerance. *Journal of Financial Counseling and Planning, 16*(1), 23.

Bank Negara Malaysia (2016a). *Annual Insurance Statistics 2016.* Retrieved from www.bnm.gov.my/index.php?ch=statistic&pg=stats_insurance&ac=23&en

Bank Negara Malaysia (2016b). *Annual Takaful Statistics 2016.* Retrieved from www.bnm.gov.my/index.php?ch=statistic&pg=stats_takaful&ac=24&en

Bank Negara Malaysia (2017). *Financial Stability and Payment Systems Report 2017.* Retrieved from www.bnm.gov.my/files/publication/fsps/en/2017/cp03.pdf

Bank Negara Malaysia (2019). *Insurance and Takaful Sector.* Retrieved from www.bnm.gov.my/files/publication/fsps/en/2017/cp03.pdf.

Baron, J., Hershey, J.C., & Kunreuther, H. (2000). Determinants of priority for risk reduction: The role of worry. *Risk Analysis, 20*(4), 413–428. doi:10.1111/0272-4332.204041

Barros, L. & Botelho, D. (2012). Hope, perceived financial risk and propensity for indebtedness. *BAR-Brazilian Administration Review, 9*(4), 454–474.

Beck, T. & Webb, I. (2003). Economic, demographic and institutional determinants of life insurance consumption across countries. *World Bank Economic Review, 17*(1), 51–88.

Bernama (2019, September 10). Guan Eng: Govt likely to revise target for life insurance penetration rate. *The Straits Times.* Retrieved from www.nst.com.my/news/nation/2019/09/520377/guan-eng-govt-likely-revise-target-life-insurance-penetration-rate

Bharucha, J.P. (2019). Determinants of financial literacy among Indian youth. In *Dynamic Perspectives on Globalization and Sustainable Business in Asia* (154–167). IGI Global.

Borkovec, T.D. & Newman, M.G. (1998). Worry and generalized anxiety disorder. *Comprehensive Clinical Psychology, 6,* 439–459.

Borkovec, T.D., Alcaine, O., & Behar, E. (2004). Avoidance theory of worry and generalized anxiety disorder. In Heimberg, Turk & Mennin (eds.), *Generalized Anxiety Disorder: Advances in Research and Practice.* The Guildford Press: New York.

Botzen, W.W. & van den Bergh, J.C. (2012). Risk attitudes to low-probability climate change risks: WTP for flood insurance. *Journal of Economic Behavior & Organization, 82*(1), 151–166.

Brown, M.J. & Kim, K. (1993). An international analysis of life insurance demand. *Journal of Risk and Insurance, 60*(4), 616–634. http://dx.doi.org/10.2307/253382

Cai, H., Chen, Y., Fang, H., & Zhou, L.A. (2009). *Microinsurance, trust and economic development: Evidence from a randomized natural field experiment* (No. w15396). National Bureau of Economic Research.

Salleh, C.M. & Megat Laksana, N.N. (2018). Awareness of flood victims in the east-coast region of Malaysia towards the Takaful flood policy: A crosstabulation analysis based on demographic variables. *Management & Accounting Review, 17*(1), 63–78.

Chui, A.C. & Kwok, C.C. (2009). Cultural practices and life insurance consumption: An international analysis using GLOBE scores. *Journal of Multinational Financial Management, 19*(4), 273–290.

Cole, S., Sampson, T., & Zia, B. (2011). Prices or knowledge? What drives demand for financial services in emerging markets? *The Journal of Finance, 66*(6), 1933–1967.

Crichton, D. (2008). Role of insurance in reducing flood risk. *The Geneva Papers on Risk and Insurance-Issues and Practice, 33*(1), 117–132.

Damodaran, R. (2017). BNM targets national insurance penetration rate to breach 75 pct by 2020. Retrieved from www.nst.com.my/business/2017/10/297055/bnm-targets-national-insurance-penetration-rate-breach-75-pct-2020.

Dash, S., Pradhan, R.P., Maradana, R.P., Gaurav, K., Zaki, D.B., & Jayakumar, M. (2018). Insurance market penetration and economic growth in Eurozone countries: Time series evidence on causality. *Future Business Journal, 4*(1), 50–67.

DBS Group Research. (2017). Industry Focus: Malaysian Insurance. Retrieved from https://www.dbs.com.sg/treasures/aics/pdfController.page?pdfpath=/content/article/pdf/AIO/092017/170907_insights_changes_in_ownership_of_insurance_firms.pdf

Delafrooz, N. & Paim, L.H. (2011). Determinants of saving behaviour and financial problem among employees in Malaysia. *Australian Journal of Applied and Basic Science, 5*(7), 222–228.

Delener, N. (1994). Religious contrasts in consumer decision behaviour patterns: Their dimensions and marketing implications. *European Journal of Marketing, 28*(5), 36–53.

Department of Statistics Malaysia (2019). *Insurance.* Retrieved from www.dosm.gov.my/v1/index.php?r=column/cglossary2&menu_id=eWd2VFdIZ2xpdzBmT2Y0a0pweDcwQT09&keyword=N0ZVVUhuT3R6cThnVTVYaHlsZWV2dz09&release=1

Dercon, S., Gunning, J.W., & Zeitlin, A. (2019). *The Demand for Insurance under Limited Trust: Evidence from a Field Experiment in Kenya* (No. 2019-06). Centre for the Study of African Economies, University of Oxford.

Devarakonda, S. (2016). Insurance penetration and economic growth in India. *FIIB Business Review, 5*(3), 3–12.

Dorfman, M.S. & Adelman, S.W. (2002). An analysis of the quality of internet life insurance advice. *Risk Management and Insurance Review, 5*, 135–154.

Dusuki, A.W. & Abdullah, N.I. (2007). Maqasid al-Shariah, Maslahah, and corporate social responsibility. *American Journal of Islamic Social Sciences, 24*(1), 25.

Emamgholipour, S., Arab, M., & Mohajerzadeh, Z. (2017). Life insurance demand: Middle East and North Africa. *International Journal of Social Economics, 44*(4), 521–529.

Farooq, S.U., Chaudhry, T.S., Alam, F.E., & Ahmad, G. (2010). An analytical study of the potential of takaful companies. *European Journal of Economics, Finance and Administrative Sciences, 20*, 54–75.

Fauzi, P.N.F.N.M., Rashid, K.A., Sharkawi, A.A., Hasan, S.F., Aripin, S., & Arifin, M.A. (2016). Takaful: A review on performance, issues and challenges in Malaysia. *Journal of Scientific Research and Development, 3*(4), 71–76.

Guiso, L. (2012). Trust and Insurance Markets 1. *Economic Notes*, *41*(1–2), 1–26.

Haron, H., Razali, N.N.S.M., & Mohamad, F. (2019). Factors influencing financial planning retirement amongst employees in the private sector in east coast Malaysia: Literature review and research agenda. *KnE Social Sciences*, 1115–1129.

Hassan, H.A. & Abbas, S.K. (2019). Factors influencing the investors' intention to adopt Takaful (Islamic insurance) products. *Journal of Islamic Marketing*, *11*(1), 1–13.

Hassan, R., Salman, S.A., Kassim, S., & Majdi, H. (2018). Awareness and knowledge of takaful in Malaysia: A survey of Malaysian consumers. *International Journal of Business and Social Science*, *9*(11), 45–53.

Henry, R.A., Weber, J.G., & Yarbrough, D. (2001). Money management practices of college students. *College Student Journal*, *35*(2), 244–244.

Hsee, C.K. & Kunreuther, H.C. (2000). The affection effect in insurance decisions. *Journal of Risk and Uncertainty*. 20, 141–159. 10.1023/A:1007876907268

Htay, S.N.N., Sadzali, N.S., & Amin, H. (2015). An analysis of the viability of micro health takaful in Malaysia. *Qualitative Research in Financial Markets*, *7*(1), 37–71.

Husin, M.M. & Ab Rahman, A. (2013). What drives consumers to participate into family takaful schemes? A literature review. *Journal of Islamic Marketing*, *4*(3), 264–280.

Husin, M. M., Ismail, N., & Ab Rahman, A. (2016). The roles of mass media, word of mouth and subjective norm in family takaful purchase intention. *Journal of Islamic Marketing*, *7*(1), 59–73.

Husniyah, A.R., Norhasmah, S., & Amim, O.M. (2017). Assessing predictors for health insurance purchase among Malaysian public sector employees. In *Regional Studies on Economic Growth, Financial Economics and Management* (pp. 91–107). Springer, Cham.

Ishak, N.H.I. (2017). Concept paper: Customer satisfaction in Malaysian takaful industry. *International Journal of Academic Research in Business and Social Sciences*, *7*(3), 380–391.

Ismail, F. & Tan, Y.Y. (2018). *Global Takaful Report 2017 Market Trends in Family and General Takaful*. Retrieved from www.milliman.com/en/insight/global-takaful-report-2017-market-trends-in-family-and-general-takaful

Jamshidi, D. & Hussin, N. (2016). Forecasting patronage factors of Islamic credit card as a new e-commerce banking service: an integration of TAM with perceived religiosity and trust. *Journal of Islamic Marketing*, *7*(4), 378–404.

Kamil, N.M. & Nor, N.B.M. (2014). Factors influencing the choice of takaful over conventional insurance: The case of Malaysia. *Journal of Islamic Finance*, *176*(3192), 1–14.

Kaur, J. (2015). Insurance penetration and density in India. *International Journal of Business Management*, *2*(1), 765–770.

Keese, M. (2010). Who feels constrained by high debt burdens? Subjective vs. objective measures of household indebtedness (February 1, 2010). *Ruhr Economic Paper*, 169.

Kjosevski, J. (2012). The determinants of life insurance demand in central and southeastern Europe. *International Journal of Economics and Finance*, *4*(3), 237–247.

Kotler, P. & Keller, K.L. (2016). *Marketing Management* (15th ed). Pearson.

Kunreuther, H. (1996). Mitigating disaster losses through insurance. *Journal of Risk and Uncertainty*, 12, 171–187.

Lahsasna, A. (ed.) (2016). *Risk and Takaful Planning*. Kuala Lumpur, Malaysia: IBFIM.

Lea, S.E., Webley, P., & Walker, C.M. (1995). Psychological factors in consumer debt: Money management, economic socialization, and credit use. *Journal of Economic Psychology*, *16*(4), 681–701.

Lee, J. (2009). Understanding college students' purchase behavior of fashion counterfeits: Fashion consciousness, public self-consciousness, ethical obligation, ethical judgment, and the theory of planned behavior (Doctoral dissertation, Ohio University).

Li, D., Moshirian, F., Nguyen, P., & Wee, T. (2007). The demand for life insurance in OECD countries. *Journal of Risk and Insurance, 74*, 637–652.

Liebenberg, A.P., Carson, J.M., & Dumm, R.E. (2012). A dynamic analysis of the demand for life insurance. *Journal of Risk and Insurance, 79*(3), 619–644.

Lim, C.C. & Haberman, S. (2004, June). Modelling life insurance demand from a macro-economic perspective: The Malaysian case. In Research Paper: *The 8th International Congress on Insurance, Mathematics and Economics*, Rome, 3–9.

Lim, J. (2019, March 11). Malaysia's 2019 takaful growth to stay moderate. *The Edge Financial Daily*, Retrieved from www.theedgemarkets.com/article/malaysias-2019-takaful-growth-stay-moderate

Lin, C., Hsiao, Y.J., & Yeh, C.Y. (2017). Financial literacy, financial advisors, and information sources on demand for life insurance. *Pacific-Basin Finance Journal, 43*, 218–237.

Lo, A.Y. (2013). The role of social norms in climate adaptation: Mediating risk perception and flood insurance purchase. *Global Environmental Change, 23*(5), 1249–1257.

Loewenstein, G.F., Weber, E.U., Hsee, C.K., & Welch, N. (2001). Risk as feelings. *Psychological Bulletin, 127*(2), 267.

Loke, Y.J. & Goh, Y.Y. (2012). Purchase decision of life insurance policies among Malaysians. *International Journal of Social Science and Humanity, 2*(5), 415.

Lovelock, C. and Wirtz, J. (2001), *Services Marketing: People, Technology, Structure* (5th ed.). London, UK: Pearson.

Lusardi, A., Mitchell, O., & Curto, V. (2010). Financial literacy among the young. *Journal of Consumer Affairs, 44*(2), 358–380.

Mahdzan, N.S. & Victorian, S.M.P. (2013). The determinants of life insurance demand: A focus on saving motives and financial literacy. *Asian Social Science, 9*(5), 274–284.

Manaf, A.W.A. & Amiruddin, N. (2019). Fintech and the challenge of digital disruption in takaful operation. *Asia Proceedings of Social Sciences, 4*(1), 1–3.

Masud, M.M., Rana, M.S., Mia, M.A., & Saifullah, M.K. (2019). How productive are life insurance institutions in Malaysia? A malmquist approach. *The Journal of Asian Finance, Economics and Business, 6*(1), 241–248.

Mayfield, C., Perdue, G., & Wooten, K. (2008). Investment management and personality type. *Financial Services Review, 17*(3), 219–236.

Md. Taib, F.M., Ramayah, T., & Razak, D.A. (2008). Factors influencing intention to use diminishing partnership home financing. *International Journal of Islamic and Middle Eastern Finance and Management, 1*(3), 235–248.

Milevsky, M.A. (2006). *The Calculus of Retirement Income: Financial Models for Pension Annuities and Life Insurance*. Cambridge University Press.

Modigliani, F. & Tarantelli, E. (1975). The consumption function in a developing economy and the Italian experience. *The American Economic Review, 65*(5), 825–842.

Nash, R., Bouchard, M., & Malm, A. (2018). Twisting trust: social networks, due diligence, and loss of capital in a Ponzi scheme. *Crime, Law and Social Change, 69*(1), 67–89.

Nesterova, D. (2008). Determinants of the demand for life insurance: Evidence from selected CIS and CEE countries: National University—Kyiv-Mohyla Academy Master's Program in Economics of Uncertainty. *Journal of Finance, 35*, 1155–1172.

Noland, M. (2005). Religion and economic performance. *World Development, 33*(8), 1215–1232.

Nowotny, H., Scott, P.B., & Gibbons, M.T. (2013). *Re-thinking Science: Knowledge and the Public in an Age of Uncertainty*. John Wiley & Sons.

Othman, N., Mohamad, A.M., & Ismail, N. (2018). Predicting factors affecting Muslims' family takaful participation: Theory of planned behaviour. *Global Business and Management Research, 10*(3), 1054.

Pradhan, R.P., Arvin, B.M., Norman, N.R., Nair, M., & Hall, J.H. (2016). Insurance penetration and economic growth nexus: Cross-country evidence from ASEAN. *Research in International Business and Finance, 36*, 447–458.

Ab Rahim, F. & Amin, H. (2011). Determinants of Islamic insurance acceptance: An empirical analysis. *International Journal of Business and Society, 12*(2), 37.

Rahman, M., Azma, N., Masud, M., Kaium, A., & Ismail, Y. (2020). Determinants of indebtedness: Influence of behavioral and demographic factors. *International Journal of Financial Studies, 8*(1), 8.

Rao, M. (2019, August 22). Buying life insurance is a sound investment. *The Malaysian Reserve*, Retrieved from https://themalaysianreserve.com/2019/08/22/buying-life-insurance-is-a-sound-investment/

Raza, A., Farhan, M., & Akram, M. (2011). A comparison of financial performance in investment banking sector in Pakistan. *International Journal of Business and Social Science, 2*(9), 72–81.

Raza, S.A., Ahmed, R., Ali, M., & Qureshi, M.A. (2019). Influential factors of Islamic insurance adoption: An extension of theory of planned behavior. *Journal of Islamic Marketing*. https://doi.org/10.1108/JIMA-03-2019-0047

Redzuan, H., Rahman, Z.A., & Aidid, S.S.S.H. (2009). Economic determinants of life insurance consumption: Evidence from Malaysia. *International Review of Business Research Papers, 5*(5), 193–211.

Richter, A., Schiller, J., & Schlesinger, H. (2014). Behavioral insurance: Theory and experiments. *Journal of Risk and Uncertainty, 48*(2), 85–96.

Saleh, I. (2012). Islamic televangelism: The Salafi window to their paradise. *In Global and Local Televangelism* (pp. 64–83). Palgrave Macmillan, London.

Savvides, S. (2006). Inquiry into the macroeconomic and household motives to demand life insurance: Review and empirical evidence from Cyprus. *Journal of Business and Society, 19*, 37–79.

Schanz, K.U., Alms, H., & Company (2019). *ASEAN Insurance Pulse 2019*. Retrieved on May 16 2020 from https://anziif.com/~/media/files/pdfs/members%20centre%20 pdfs/2019%20whitepapers/asean%20pulse%202019%20final.pdf

Shafii, Z., Abiddin, Z., & Ahmad, A.R. (2009). Ethnic heterogeneity in the Malaysian economy: A special reference to the ethnic group participation in financial planning activities. *Journal of International Social Research, 2*(8), 394–401.

Shectman, R.G. (1982). New concepts in life insurance planning: Universal life. Cumberland Law Review, *13*, 219.

Shen, N.M. (2018). *Insurance Sector's Consolidation Is Not Easy*. Retrieved from https://themalaysianreserve.com/2018/10/15/insurance-sectors-consolidation-is-not-easy/.

Sherif, M. & Hussnain, S. (2017). Family takaful in developing countries: The case of Middle East and North Africa (MENA). *International Journal of Islamic and Middle Eastern Finance and Management, 10*(3), 371–399.

Sherif, M. & Azlina Shaairi, N. (2013). Determinants of demand on family takaful in Malaysia. *Journal of Islamic Accounting and Business Research, 4*(1), 26–50.

Shukor, S.A. (2020). Trust in takaful agents: Antecedents and consequences. *Journal of Islamic Accounting and Business Research,* 11(6), 1161–1174. https://doi.org/10.1108/JIABR-01-2018-0013

Siang, L.C. & Weng, L.K. (2011). Factors affecting non-Muslim consumers towards intention to use Islamic banking products and services. In *Las Vegas International Academic Conference*. Las Vegas, NV.

Skinner, J. & Dubinsky, A.J. (1984). Purchasing insurance: Predictors of family decision-making responsibility. *Journal of Risk and Insurance*, 51(3), 514–523. http://dx.doi.org/10.2307/252483

Soualhi, Y. & Al Shammari, A.A.R. (2015). Indicators of takaful awareness among Kuwaitis. *Journal of Islamic Banking and Finance*, 3(2), 75–89.

Souiden, N. & Jabeur, Y. (2015). The impact of Islamic beliefs on consumers' attitudes and purchase intentions of life insurance. *International Journal of Bank Marketing*, 33(4), 423–441.

Souiden, N. & Rani, M. (2015). Consumer attitudes and purchase intentions toward Islamic banks: The influence of religiosity. *International Journal of Bank Marketing*, 33(2),143–161.

Swiss Re (2019). *The 2019 Financial Condition Report "From risk to resilience"*. Retrieved from www.swissre.com/dam/jcr:db66b5d2-a7e0-4c99-b731-50704201afb6/2019-swiss-re-financial-condition-report.pdf

Tan, H.B., Wong, M.F., & Law, S.H. (2009). The effect of consumer factors and firm efficiency on Malaysian life insurance expenditure. *International Journal of Business and Society*, 10(1), 59–73.

Truett, D.B. & Truett, L.J. (1990). The demand for life insurance in Mexico and the United States: A comparative study. *Journal of Risk and Insurance*, 321–328.

Tversky, A. & Kahneman, D. (1973). Availability: A heuristic for judging frequency and probability. *Cognitive Psychology*, 5(2), 207–232.

Tversky, A. & Kahneman, D. (1979). Prospect theory: An analysis of decision under risk. Econometrica, 47(2), 263–291.

Wahid, S.N.S., Azemi, S.N.A.N., Rashid, S.A., Hilmi, Z.A.G., Razak, M.R., & Ab Ghani, P. (2019). Malaysian life expectancy by gender and ethnic group: A comparative study. In *Proceedings of the Regional Conference on Science, Technology and Social Sciences (RCSTSS 2016)* (pp. 339–345). Springer, Singapore.

Wakker, P., Thaler, R., & Tversky, A. (1997). Probabilistic insurance. *Journal of Risk and Uncertainty*, 15(1), 7–28.

Zakaria, Z., Azmi, N.M., Hassan, N.F.H.N., Salleh, W.A., Tajuddin, M.T., Sallem, N.R., & Nor, J.M. (2016). The intention to purchase life insurance: A case study of staff in public universities. *Procedia Economics and Finance*, 37(16), 358–365.

Zhang, L., Zhu, J., & Liu, Q. (2012). A meta-analysis of mobile commerce adoption and the moderating effect of culture. *Computers in Human Behavior*, 28(5), 1902–1911.

Zick, C.D., Smith, K.R., Mayer, R.N., & Botkin, J.R. (2000). Genetic testing, adverse selection, and the demand for life insurance. *American Journal of Medical Genetics*, 93(1), 29–39.

6   Summary and strategic recommendations

6.0 Summary

As consumers who actively engage in today's complex financial environment, individuals are vulnerable in various aspects of their finances. This book deliberated on four main attributes of consumer finances – namely issues related to borrowing, saving, investing, and protection – and how people are prone to making mistakes that would adversely influence their financial positions and ultimately affect their financial well-being. It is therefore the general aim of this book to discuss these issues in detail and to position Malaysian consumers in a setting that would then facilitate the exploration of psychological and behavioural factors affecting their decisions and actions in the aforementioned attributes of personal finance.

Chapter 1 delineated the four main objectives of this book. The *first objective* is to examine the current state and trends of various consumer financial vulnerabilities in Malaysia, namely, over-indebtedness (Chapter 2), retirement savings inadequacy (Chapter 3), fraudulent investment victimisation (Chapter 4), and underinsurance (Chapter 5). The discussions in Chapters 2 to 5 also aimed to achieve the second and third objectives of the book, which are to explore the causes of consumer financial vulnerabilities from the perspective of behavioural and psychological theories (*second objective*) and to discuss the various policies that have already been implemented to influence consumer financial behaviour (*third objective*). Lastly, the *fourth objective* of this book is to propose strategies to policymakers on ways to nurture and nudge consumers in the recommended ways of managing their finances, which is the focus of the present chapter (Chapter 6).

Chapter 2 of this book discussed the providers of debt to households in Malaysia and thereafter evaluated the state of household indebtedness in the country. With the highest level of household debt-to-GDP ratio in Asia, that is in excess of 80% of GDP for the past decade, household indebtedness in Malaysia has become an issue that has dominated public discourse in recent years. The problem of over-indebtedness arises when a household finds that servicing their debt takes up a disproportionately large percentage of their household income. This may lead to stress, not only from the perspective of mental health but also from the perspective of financial health as there will be competing needs from the household budget. In order to understand the incidence of over-indebtedness, this chapter will go on to discuss the issues from psychological perspectives such as the lack of self-control on the part of the borrowers, as well as behavioural factors such as materialism and trying to keep up certain social norms as being drivers of over-borrowing. Financial regulators such as Bank Negara Malaysia (BNM) and the Securities Commission (SC) can implement more effective policies by teaming up with industry bodies and NGOs to drive the message on financial literacy to ensure a better understanding of household budgetary commitments. Financial literacy programmes that inculcate positive money management should also be imbued from a young age and incorporated within the school syllabus or external activities.

Chapter 3 discussed how the Malaysian population is transitioning into becoming an aged population whereby the percentage of the elderly will exceed that of the youngest age group. Life expectancy is also increasing, whereby as of 2017, males are expected to live till 74 and females till 78 years. Malaysia's evolvement into an aged population will therefore have significant consequences on the nation's future economy and social security system. The national savings rate shows that Malaysia has the second lowest savings rate among the ASEAN-5 countries, which is also on a declining trend. In addition, statistics from the Employees' Provident Fund (EPF) provide evidence that the average level of retirement savings available for retirees will deplete in less than five years, leaving them extremely vulnerable in their golden years. Chapter 3 also outlined the factors obstructing proper retirement planning among Malaysians. From a psychological perspective, people generally seem to lack the sufficient knowledge to plan for their retirement, prefer to live in the present moment rather than think about future uncertainties, fail to set long term financial goals, and neglect to plan for their finances. These failures stem from the broad psychological domains of *cognition* (financial illiteracy and financial planning), *motivation* (goal setting), and *disposition* (time preference).

Chapter 4 examined the issue of financial frauds and scams in Malaysia. Statistics show that financial frauds and scams have become a prevalent and damaging problem for Malaysian consumers. A total loss of RM1.94 billion was reported by the Commercial Crime Department of Royal Malaysian Police in 2017. The chapter also highlighted the modus operandi and persuasion techniques used by fraudsters and scammers for consumers to better understand different and sophisticated fraud techniques that are used. Self-control, diffusion, agency, and routine activity theories were argued as theories behind consumers' susceptibility to deceptive sales practices or frauds. Factors such as financial illiteracy, risk-taking, personalities, over-trust, greed, overconfidence, third parties' incentive, low reporting, and online activities, on the other hand, are said to be the factors that explain why there are still many Malaysians falling victims to financial frauds and scams even after warnings and information have been disseminated. The chapter also highlights current financial awareness efforts and initiatives committed by relevant government ministries, institutions, and other key stakeholders to combat financial frauds and scams from spreading. Finally, several recommendations and measures were proposed to better protect consumers and the society from any type of financial frauds and scams.

Chapter 5 deliberated on the issue of underinsurance in Malaysia. According to the 2017 ASEAN Insurance Pulse report, Malaysia's life and non-life real insurance premium growth is lower than the average real premium growth of ASEAN countries. In addition, a report by BNM shows that the current life insurance penetration rate fell far short of the national targeted penetration rate to reach 75% by 2020 and failed to close the insurance and family takaful protection gap. Chapter 5 also highlighted that the low level of national awareness about insurance, low households' disposable income, and lack of technological advancement among insurance/takaful service providers are the reasons behind the insurance and takaful industry's low penetration rate. The chapter identifies major factors that demotivate Malaysian households from possessing insurance/ takaful policies such as complexities in insurance/takaful contracts, overpriced average premium per policy, and low return in investment-linked policies. An individual's behaviour does not always conform to the notions of economic theories, yet the theory of risk aversion, life-cycle hypothesis, behavioural life-cycle hypothesis, availability bias, and prospect theory have been found to be useful in explaining the issue of underinsurance in Malaysia. Psychological factors such as worry and fear, risk perception, trust, religious belief, social norms, and financial literacy are among the factors influencing individuals' insurance/takaful purchasing behaviour. Finally, it is proposed that the government should enhance continuous nationwide insurance awareness campaigns and introduce a mandatory contribution for the national healthcare system, while insurers should offer more affordable premium per policy together with advanced digital services to significantly reduce the protection gap for Malaysian households.

6.1 Psychological domains influencing consumer financial vulnerabilities

Throughout Chapters 2 to 5, various factors influencing consumer financial vulnerabilities were highlighted and reviewed. In this section, those factors are grouped under three broad domains from the field of psychology, which are *cognition*, *motivation*, and *disposition*, to guide the discussion on factors that influence financial vulnerabilities. This will be further discussed in the following subsections.

6.1.1 Cognition

Cognition is defined as "the mental action or process of acquiring knowledge and understanding through thought, experience, and the senses" (Colman, 2015, p. 141). According to Lang (1985), cognition refers to "the symbolic (or conceptual) processing of information that is required for the central representation and organised expression of a response." Meanwhile, Allaire and Masiske (2002) suggested that daily cognition is derived from a set of underlying basic abilities and is the combination of abilities that may influence cognitive performance in daily contexts as opposed to any single basic ability (Allaire & Marsiske, 1999; Marsiske & Willis, 1998). Cognition entails various components of intellectual functions such as "memory, association, concept formation, pattern recognition, language, attention, perception, action, problem solving, and mental imagery. attention, the development of knowledge, memory and working memory, judgement and evaluation, reasoning and computation, problem-solving and decision-making, comprehension and the production of language" (Wang & Gloor, 2018).

As discussed in Chapters 2 to 5 of this book, *financial literacy*, which falls under the broad psychological domain of cognition, has profound effects on various types of consumer financial vulnerabilities including over-indebtedness, saving behaviour, investment, and insurance protection. Financial literacy, which is an amalgamation of financial awareness, knowledge, skill, attitude, and behaviour, can be viewed as a cognitive factor that influences consumers in their financial behaviour. In making financial decisions, individuals will mentally process the knowledge that they have in regards to cost and benefits, and risk and returns, in order to make evaluations and judgements regarding various aspects of personal finance including spending, saving, investing, and protecting their assets. Individuals who have higher financial literacy are found to have higher retirement savings, less likely to be over-indebted, have a lower tendency to invest in fraudulent investments, and are more likely to protect themselves using insurance or takaful. Therefore, it is evidently crucial for financial literacy levels among consumers to be increased to overcome their financial vulnerabilities and to ultimately achieve higher levels of financial well-being.

Other factors related to cognition that are discussed in this book are *financial planning* and *money management*. In Chapter 3, it was found that people who had conducted some form of financial planning would have higher retirement wealth and outcomes than those who did not have the opportunity to do so. According to Hershey, Jacobs-Lawson, and Austin (2013), individuals would need to have the capacity, willingness, and opportunity to conduct financial planning for retirement. Meanwhile, in Chapter 5, it was argued that individuals who took the effort to manage their money have a higher tendency to protect their wealth using insurance and takaful. Hence, it is clear that financial behaviours that are driven by cognitive processes are more likely to produce positive financial outcomes among individuals.

Another factor under cognition that has an effect on consumer finances is *religious belief*. Regardless of religion, people with religious faiths generally believe that there is life after death. Throughout their lives, people's behaviour and actions are guided by their acquisition of religious knowledge and practices. Due to their belief that there is life after death, there is sometimes a misconception among people that their fate is in the hands of their Creator which would then render 'planning' for the event of demise, such as through insurance and takaful, unnecessary. However, in a country such as Malaysia where the majority of people are Muslims, this misconception is gradually changing since the introduction of takaful in year 1984 which gave Muslims the conviction that preparing for unexpected contingencies in life is encouraged and compliant with Islamic Shariah principles. Efforts must be made to continue encouraging Muslims and Malaysians in general to plan for contingencies and protect their income and wealth via insurance and takaful plans, through interventions that would alter their cognitive behaviour.

6.1.2 Motivation

Research on consumers' finances has demonstrated the importance of several key motivational factors that influence financial vulnerabilities. In particular, social norms, fear, and goal clarity have been repeatedly highlighted. Motivation is a theoretical concept developed to explain human behaviour. One's motivation is what leads individuals to act in order to achieve a goal or to fulfil a need or expectation (Maslow, 1943). Motivation entails three major components, namely activation, persistence, and intensity. Activation will initiate a behaviour, while persistence will ensure that the behaviour is continued, and intensity will make someone concentrate and focus towards pursuing a goal (Hockenbury & Hockenbury, 2010).

Social norm has been identified as one of the motivational factors that influence over-indebtedness and underinsurance among Malaysians. Social norm is referred to one's attitude towards a behaviour that is triggered by social pressure or guidance. Individuals tend to follow the norm that has been primed within the society, although it is against rational behaviour. This kind of attitude is also called a social dilemma (Biel & Thøgersen, 2007). D'Alessio and Iezzi (2013) found that a household is motivated to take more and more debt when its existing and expected resources are not sufficient to meet living standards set by the society. This type of motivation has also been identified by Abraham, Sheeran, and Johnston (1998) and Sommer and Dumont (2011). Similarly, other groups of individuals appear to be more motivated to subscribe to insurance services once they receive pressure from the society (Amron, Usman, & Mursid, 2018; Husin, Ismail, & Ab Rahman, 2016). Therefore, it has been shown that social norms' behavioural component can help to control the problem of over-indebtedness and underinsurance.

Retirement savings inadequacy, on the other hand, appears to be relatively more motivated by *goal clarity* (Hershey, Jacobs-Lawson, McArdle, & Hamagami, 2007; Neukam & Hershey, 2003). Most often, an individual's motivation to have retirement savings is a translation of well-defined retirement goals that are originated from thoughts about how life will be during retirement (Stawski, Hershey, & Jacobs-Lawson, 2007). The thoughts would finally be manifested through the actions of aggressive saving or proper engagement in a retirement plan (Hershey et al., 2007; Topa, Lunceford, & Boyatzis, 2018). As an example of the latter, Neukam and Hershey (2003) found that the strength of financial goals positively influenced retirement savings contributions.

Previous studies have demonstrated the importance of *worry and fear* in motivating individuals to insure themselves and loved ones. This explanation was proposed by Baron, Hershey, and Kunreuther (2000) who view worry as a primary motivating factor for individuals to engage in more protective behaviour like subscribing to insurance. This behaviour will indirectly support the efforts of the government to reduce the number of citizens who are underinsured. Other studies have also found that the vast majority of individuals are willing to insure themselves against any risky situation as a result of fear they experienced in connection with a particular risk (Loewenstein, Weber, Hsee, & Welch, 2001).

Based on the above discussion, this book provides evidence that motivational factors such as *social norm*, *goal clarity*, and *worry and fear* are relevant to consumer financial behaviours. These factors may help to overcome over-indebtedness, retirement savings inadequacy, and underinsurance.

6.1.3 Disposition

The third psychological domain discussed in this section is disposition, which refers to the traits that individuals are born with and develop over time (Mischel & Shoda, 1998). This is also defined as an internal attribution that always (or mostly) causes an event to occur or reflects in one's behaviour. The dispositional domain identifies routes of differentiating individuals from one another. Wright and Mischel (1987) suggested that the dispositional domain should be analysed to understand how people behave in situations (if-then propositions) instead of merely looking at generalised behaviour. It is also considered as a key aspect of personality construct. Studies on financial vulnerabilities have identified several related factors like overconfidence, self-control, materialism, time preference, trust, greed, and risk perception. These factors can be grouped under the dispositional domain.

Overconfidence is one of the factors that cause Malaysian households to hold excessive debts and engage in fraudulent investment activities. Grohmann, Menkhoff, Merkle, and Schmacker (2019) found that individuals who anticipate higher income in the future are more inclined to take up debt. It is also noticed that in many occasions, one's overconfidence increases the likelihood of falling into various investment scams (Fischer, Lea, & Evans, 2013; Gamble, Boyle, Yu, & Bennett, 2013). Hence, it can be viewed that overconfident individuals are more likely to be over-indebted, have higher chances of falling into fraudulent investments and less likely to protect themselves using insurance or takaful, and as such, end up falling into disastrous financial positions.

Many researchers also claim that the high incidence of bankruptcy among Malaysian youth due to excessive borrowing and spending is largely a result of high levels of materialistic behaviour to increase their perceived social status. Studies have positively linked *materialism* to compulsive buying behaviour and negatively linked to savings behaviour and self-control which in turn make people financially vulnerable. Azma, Rahman, Adeyemi, and Rahman (2019) found that in Malaysia, people who have a high level of materialism tend to save less and have low levels of self-control, making it one of the possible contributing factors for insufficient retirement savings among Malaysian households.

It is also argued that retirement savings inadequacy in Malaysia can be explained by another factor under the dispositional domain, namely *time preference*. Studies have identified that people in general prefer instant returns over higher returns in future dates (Hastings, Mitchell, & Chyn, 2011), and thus this tendency may discourage people to be involved in early retirement planning. *Self-control* is another dispositional factor that influences both over-indebtedness and fraudulent investment activities. Lack of self-control causes an individual to spend excessively disregarding rational behaviour, leading to over-indebtedness and possible defaults in repayment obligations. It is claimed that people who have low levels of external locus of control or low levels of emotional stability are more likely to fall into financial scams and cyber-frauds (Van de Weijer & Leukfeldt, 2017; Whitty, 2019).

Trust and *greed* have also been identified as important dispositional factors causing individuals to fall into fraudulent investments. Many have suggested that any over-trust reduces doubt and increases the possibility of engaging in scams (e.g. Laroche, Steyer, & Théron, 2019). It is argued that people who easily trust others are more likely to fall into the trap of the scammers. However, this is not always the case, as in many occasions, people become greedy and put their money in suspicious investments despite knowing the risk of loss. *Greed* influences individuals towards making biased judgement, allowing themselves to be easily scammed (Baker & Puttonen, 2017).

Trust is one of the important determinants that influences consumers' decisions in purchasing goods and services. As such, the level of consumers' trust in agents and insurers plays an important role when it comes to buying insurance or takaful policies. In general, customers may be reluctant to buy insurance/takaful if they have doubts about getting back the compensation claim. In other words, the lack of trust in agents and the insurers may make the protection plan unpopular. Therefore, it is very important to build and enhance trust between consumers, insurers, and insurance agents to reduce the existing insurance and takaful protection gap in the Malaysian society.

Finally, the last factor under the dispositional domain is *risk perception*, which indicates how people position risk while making decisions. Past studies have documented that people with low risk perceptions are less likely to invest in low probability events. Individuals with low risk perceptions tend not to buy insurance or takaful considering the low probability of unexpected events (e.g. critical disease, accident, etc.). On the other hand, perceived risk about insurance or takaful has negative influence on the demand for insurance/takaful policies. It means that, when individuals believe that insurance or takaful involves some form of risks, they would less likely purchase the scheme. In line with this argument, Raza et al. (2019) documented that perceived risk of insurance/takaful has a negative influence on the intention to purchase takaful schemes in Pakistan.

Based on the above discussion, it is noticed that some factors from the dispositional domain are related to each other, hence making the decision-making process more complex. It is therefore crucial for individuals to assess and understand their existing dispositional factors to avoid themselves from making sub-optimal financial decisions in order to achieve higher levels of financial well-being.

6.2 Strategic recommendations

Having discussed the psychological domains related to the four consumer financial vulnerabilities, this section provides strategic recommendations for policymakers and the relevant stakeholders on ways to nudge consumers in the right way to manage their finances. These recommendations are mapped to the five strategic priorities of the Malaysian National Strategy of Financial Literacy 2019–2023 that were presented earlier in Chapter 1 (Section 1.4). The recommendations are mapped to each of the strategic priorities and consumer financial vulnerabilities that were the focus of this book, as summarised in Table 6.1.

6.2.1 SP1: Nurture values from young

The very first strategic priority (SP1) of the MNSFL is to "*Nurture values from young*". Developing a strong value system that incorporates financial education and introducing it at the early stages of life is the key to achieve a sustainable financial well-being. This value system is recommended to inculcate a better understanding of financial numeracy, which ultimately assists individuals to control their emotions and uphold rational borrowing and spending behaviours. Therefore, it is proposed that the Ministry of Education should include financial education into the curriculum and co-curricular activities of pre-school, primary schools, secondary schools, and tertiary education. A compulsory financial education from pre-school to university will help individuals to develop a solid foundation in managing and monitoring their borrowing and spending activities over their lifetime by lowering the likelihood of default and delinquency. Knowing the alarming fact that about 65 thousand youths in Malaysia have been declared bankrupt since 2013, BNM, SC, and the Credit Counselling and Debt Management Agency (AKPK) should organise more customised financial education programmes for children and youth to enhance their understanding on the problem of over-indebtedness. To arrest this bankruptcy problem, families and communities should also play a more active role in inculcating financial education in early childhood as the financial education process should begin at home and continue in educational institutions, community, society, and the workplace. Parents must show good spending and borrowing behaviours to set an example for their children and constantly take steps to instil this behaviour in them. What is also needed are massive continuous awareness campaigns and programmes in schools and universities by BNM, SC, and AKPK to enhance the understanding of bankruptcy and its consequences.

Savings and money management habits can be exercised from schools to universities through courses and co-curricular activities. Educational institutions can play an active role in providing various savings plans such as monthly savings scheme for a year-end school event to enhance their money management skills.

Table 6.1 Mapping of strategic priorities to consumer financial vulnerabilities

MNSFL Strategic priority (SP)	Recommendations	Agency/institution responsible	Factors	Actions by individuals
PANEL A: OVER-INDEBTEDNESS				
SP1: Financial literacy in schools	Inculcate better understanding of financial numeracy from a young age.	BNM, MOE, SC	Financial literacy Self-control	Increase knowledge on consumption smoothing and budgeting
SP2: Fintech awareness campaigns	Promote use of technology to better manage and monitor financial position.	BNM	Financial literacy	Search for better credit choices
SP3: Financial education for lower income households	Equip the employed and self-employed with financial knowledge to encourage financial sustainability.	BNM, SC	Overconfidence Self-control Social norms	Avoid over-commitment and overspending
SP4: Innovative financial planning guides and tools	Provide accessible and affordable financial planning services.	AKPK. MFPC	Self-control Materialism	Plan for adverse financial shocks and to have financial slack
SP5: Bankruptcy awareness campaigns	Increase awareness of incidence and consequences of bankruptcy.	AKPK, BNM, CTOS	Materialism Social norms	Seek assistance for debt counselling and repayment plans to avoid a default
PANEL B: RETIREMENT SAVING				
SP1: Financial education through curriculum and co-curricular activities	Cultivate the habit of saving and money management among school children.	BNM, SC, EPF	Time preference Financial literacy	Set a good example for the younger generation in terms of financial behaviour
SP2: Nationwide outreach campaigns	Intensify promotions on the role of financial planners and make financial services more affordable and accessible, particularly to the deprived segments of society.	MFPC, financial planners, and community leaders	Financial planning Goal setting	Seek the help of trusted professional financial planners for retirement planning

SP3: Financial education at the workplace	Integrate financial education at the workplace as a value-added benefit for employees.	Employers and financial institutions	Financial literacy Goal setting Time preference	Actively engage in financial education programmes
SP4: Innovative tools to seek professional advice for long-term financial planning	Promote the use of digital finance to encourage long-term retirement planning. Reinforce the value of financial planning services.	BNM, SC, MFPC	Goal setting Financial planning	Use financial related apps to keep track of own retirement savings goals
SP5: Innovation of savings products	Disseminate information on the latest financial products in the market that are tailored to one's risk attitudes and retirement goals.	BNM, SC, and financial institutions	Financial planning Goal setting	Keep updated on savings products available in the market

PANEL C: FINANCIAL FRAUD VICTIMISATION

SP1: Financial literacy education	Expand financial literacy curriculum beyond financial facts and information.	Schools and Universities	Financial literacy Self-control	Gain more knowledge on fraud activities
SP2: Public awareness and education campaigns	Use social media and other financial technology tools.	MCMC	Financial literacy Trust	Confirm with the relevant authorities
SP3: Community-based activities in consumerism security	Sharing and spreading information via community-based activities.	Community leaders	Trust Personalities	Address consumerism security concerns
SP4: Accessible information on legal investment platforms.	Educate Malaysians to subscribe only to legal and recognised platforms.	BNM and SC	Greed Self-control Personalities	Avoid unrecognised and doubtful investment entities
SP5: Cohesive policy between different sectors	Establish a better crime control policy.	MDTCA, BNM, and SC	Overconfidence Trust	Follow relevant authorities' suggestions and advice

(*continued*)

Table 6.1 Cont.

MNSFL Strategic priority (SP)	Recommendations	Agency/institution responsible	Factors	Actions by individuals
PANEL D: UNDERINSURANCE				
SP1: Holistic religious education	Boost holistic religious views on purchasing insurance among children and youth.	Schools and Universities	Religious belief Financial literacy	Learn and share holistic religious view of having protection with children
SP2: Nationwide public awareness and education campaigns	Highlight the importance of the role of insurance agents and provide a clear picture on the purpose of various insurance products.	BNM, LIAM, MITBA, MTA	Fear and care Risk perception Trust in insurance agents	Attend awareness programmes and seek advice from trusted people about insurance agents
SP3: Money management and positive perception development	Boost positive perception of purchasing protection plan and money management through community-based activities.	LIAM, Community and worship place leaders	Social norms Money management Religious belief	Learn about protection from the community
SP4: Digitalised services and diversified investment options	Advances technological support to promote online-based insurance services.	BNM, NAMLIFA, MFPC, MITBA, MTA	Worry and fear Risk Perception Trust	Learn to use digital devices to have better access to insurance products
SP5: Wealth accumulation and preservation	Educate the benefits of wealth accumulation and simplify the insurance plans policies.	BNM, insurance, and takaful companies	Money management Worry and fear Religious belief Risk perception	Learn the importance of wealth accumulation and consequences of underinsurance

Financial regulators such as BNM and SC should work together with EPF to offer various exciting educational activities related to savings and retirement savings in educational institutions. The regulators can support commercial banks to offer and promote various savings schemes tailored to the youth to encourage savings. It is also highly recommended for guardians to start educating their children at home in creating their savings by setting an example. Such efforts are aimed to address households' inadequate savings and retirement savings problem. If the saving concept is not taught well nor exercised from childhood, it will result in a serious decline in the standards of living in old age due to insufficient retirement savings in Malaysia. Consequently, there might be an increase in social problems and fraudulent schemes involving young people.

Extended financial literacy curriculum that contains awareness about scammers and their persuasion techniques should be introduced in schools and universities with the aim of creating awareness that would improve their investment behaviours. The youth are more vulnerable to financial frauds and scams that take place on social media; hence, educational institutions can use their official websites and verified social media pages such as their Facebook page to enhance awareness apart from including it in various co-curricular activities. Most importantly, parents must share various information about fraudulent schemes with their children and advise them to carefully study and consult the relevant authorities before making any investment decisions. Besides, guardians should motivate and support their children to attend financial literacy and awareness programmes in order to gain more knowledge on commercial fraud activities. In addition, the Malaysian Communications and Multimedia Commission (MCMC) and any other relevant bodies should work together with educational institutions to create awareness programmes among the youth about various new scams and their persuasion techniques. Such efforts are highly recommended to tackle the dynamic consumer commercial frauds and scams in Malaysia that are on an increasing trend.

Additionally, to address the misconceptions about purchasing insurance and takaful plans, a holistic religious view can be included into the curriculum and co-curricular activities of schools and tertiary education. Educating children and young adults at the early stages of their lives about the importance of buying adequate insurance and takaful plans will help to reduce the insurance protection gap and avoid future uncertainties. Entities such as the Life Insurance Association of Malaysia (LIAM), National Association of Malaysian Life Insurance Fieldforce and Advisers (NAMLIFA), Malaysian Takaful Association (MTA), and Malaysian Financial Planning Council (MFPC) should work closely with schools and universities and offer joint courses or provide resource persons to teach insurance courses. Besides, the above entities may organise various exciting educational activities on insurance and takaful for the youth in a community through worship leaders and residents' associations. Finally, parents should create awareness and clear the air about the misconceptions of insurance and takaful to their children through sharing the benefits of having insurance to protect themselves against various risks and preserving wealth.

6.2.2 SP2: Increase access to financial management information, tools, and resources

The second strategic priority (SP2) of the MNSFL is to "*Increase access to financial management information, tools and resources*". At the very foundation, the Malaysian government desires to benefit from its financial technology and advancement to become a country with citizens that are less stressed about their financial situations and have high financial well-being. This can be achieved when financial management information, tools, and resources are easily accessible by the society. In line with this strategy, it is proposed that BNM should introduce an app that can provide consumers with all the information required in managing their finances. This app may also help consumers in managing and monitoring their borrowing activities, advise them on the level of their debt service ratio, and inform them on the ability to service their debts based on their current financial conditions. This will ensure that the over-indebtedness problem will be minimised. BNM could also discourage consumers from going to illegal moneylenders or loan sharks by introducing a couple of credit or loan alternative providers via Fintech. In addition, financial technology campaigns and financial education initiatives should also aggressively be conducted in every state or locality with the aim of increasing financial awareness and literacy among consumers on the usage of technology in financial activities. The consumers should play their role in carefully scrutinising different types of credit choices through the application software or technology proposed by BNM.

In recent years, more and more information on financial management techniques is available for consumers. Nevertheless, it is reported that retirement savings is still inadequate among Malaysians. This issue can be addressed via the help of professional financial planners. The awareness on the usage of financial planners or advisors in planning for retirement is still low among Malaysians. It is also questionable whether financial planning services offered are affordable and accessible. Therefore, bodies such as the MFPC, financial planners' association, and community leaders should give more attention in promoting financial planning services' initiatives through nationwide outreach campaigns. The campaign should intensify awareness on the role of financial planning services and make the services more affordable and accessible. Free financial advisory service to the society could also be offered as a community service to Malaysians, in urban as well as in rural areas, particularly those in the lower income bracket. Such efforts are aimed to address the problem of retirement savings inadequacy among Malaysians and to improve certain psychological traits that may influence saving behaviour such as financial planning and goal-setting behaviours. It is also believed that through the help of professional financial planners, an individual can have better financial planning and a clearer goal setting.

Consumer commercial frauds and scams in Malaysia are increasing, and the dynamic shift or changes in fraud techniques and strategies have further endangered consumers in the country. Consequently, many of them are falling into different types of fraudulent schemes. Public awareness and education campaigns on commercial frauds could be implemented in order to protect the vulnerable group of society from these frauds. One of the most effective way to intensify financial awareness and education campaigns is through social media and other financial technology tools. The MCMC and any relevant bodies, for example, could guide consumer on how to identify illegal financial schemes via different access to financial management information, tools, and resources. This effort will help consumers with low financial literacy to carefully study and check with the relevant authorities before participating or falling prey to any type of financial frauds or scams.

Similar public awareness and nationwide education campaigns on the importance of basic insurance or takaful plans for every household could also be run to address the issue of under-protection among Malaysians. This campaign should highlight the significant role of insurance agents and provide a clear picture on the purpose of various insurance and takaful products. This will further help Malaysian consumers in managing their financial risk through more access to financial management information, tools, and resources related to insurance or takaful. Entities such as the BNM, Malaysian Insurance and Takaful Brokers Association (MITBA), LIAM as well as insurance planners could make a collaborative effort to help Malaysians increase their understanding on the true risks involved in natural hazards and threats to their health, life, and the life of their loved ones. On the part of consumers, apart from attending the suggested awareness campaigns, they should put some efforts in researching about insurance products and pricing as well as seeking advice from trusted people to find reliable and trustworthy insurance agents.

6.2.3 SP3: Inculcate positive behaviour among targeted groups

The third strategic priority (SP3) of the MNSFL is to "*Inculcate positive behaviour among targeted groups*". In line with this strategy, it is recommended that financial education programmes be offered to specific target groups, particularly the low- and middle-income household groups, as well as self-employed individuals, to foster good money management practices. Since these groups appear to be most vulnerable in regards to being over-indebted, it is crucial that this group of society be equipped with sufficient financial knowledge and skills to encourage long-term personal financial sustainability. BNM and SC should play a more active role in providing financial education programmes such as through roadshows and carnivals at specific rural and urban areas that would attract these targeted crowds. Such efforts are aimed to tackle the problem of over-indebtedness among the vulnerable group of people and to address the improvement of certain psychological traits that may adversely influence debt-taking behaviour, for example, the issue of lack of self-control and being overconfident of their financial position. With proper financial knowledge and skills, it is hoped that the groups of people who are vulnerable to debts can improve their understanding and skills related to borrowing behaviour.

Financial education can also be targeted to employees at the workplace with the aim of promoting financial knowledge and skills that would improve saving behaviour. Employers should collaborate with representatives of financial institutions such as bankers, unit trust consultants, and insurance services providers to integrate financial education at the workplace as a value-added benefit for employees. Retirement planning services could also be offered to new employees, whereby the financial advisors could offer services such as computation of retirement needs and the minimum required savings per month that should be allocated into savings plans. The financial advisor or financial planner should introduce to the employees the various savings plans offered in the market such as the Private Retirement Scheme (PRS), unit trusts funds, insurance plans, and other financial products. Employees should take the opportunity to actively engage in financial education programmes offered not only at the workplace, but also courses and seminars that are offered outside the workplace such as those organised by financial institutions and private financial planning companies.

In addition, community leaders can also take the initiative to provide community-based activities in consumerism security to tackle the issue of financial fraud victimisation. One way to promote this activity is to educate Malaysians through programmes that would promote the sharing of experience and spreading information related to financial frauds and scams through community-based communication tools like group chats, websites, and social media. These efforts are aimed to tackle the issue of being too trusting of financial fraud scammers. On the part of consumers, they can play a role by sharing information about fraudulent investment schemes with friends and family to address the consumerism security concerns among the community. By sharing information with family and friends, awareness of the various types of financial fraud can ultimately be increased in the society as a whole.

Finally, to address the issue of under-protection among Malaysians, the strategy that could be undertaken requires collaborative efforts of various entities such as the LIAM, NAMLIFA, community leaders, worship leaders, and residents' associations. To inculcate positive behaviour among targeted groups, as outlined in SP3 of the MFSFL, the entities mentioned above should organise programmes that promote money management skills and enhance positive perceptions about the importance of insurance and takaful protection plans. This can be done by boosting perceptions of insurance and takaful through community-based activities such as sharing with family, friends, and neighbours on the benefits of having insurance to protect against various personal risks such as death, disabilities, illnesses, and other health problems. Community-based communication via WhatsApp, Telegram, and Facebook pages are some examples of tools that can be used to disseminate useful information regarding the importance of protecting personal wealth and assets through insurance and takaful. This strategy aims to address the issue of following social norms among the Malaysian society. Since there are still negative perceptions regarding insurance and takaful in the mindsets of Malaysians, and because Malaysians are inclined to behave according to social norms, it is suggested that positive perceptions of insurance and takaful can be enhanced through these community-based activities.

6.2.4 SP4: Boost long-term financial and retirement planning

The fourth strategic priority (SP4) is to "*Boost long-term financial and retire-ment planning*" of households. This is especially essential for households in the lower income group. Although they do not have such high levels of debt, their debt burden is harder for them to manage compared to those in the higher income group. Accessible and affordable financial planning tools and guides will be useful in assisting the B40 households to improve their money management skills. Usage of simple application softwares and distribution of online poster guides can be utilised at a relatively low cost. AKPK can play a role in educating the public on good money management skills as this will lead to lower incidences of bankruptcies. All households will also benefit from better financial planning skills as it will help them improve their ability to plan for adverse financial shocks to either income or expenses and to work towards building up financial slack (in other words, extra savings for precautionary purposes). Adverse financial shocks can occur due to sudden loss of income or unexpected expenses caused by job loss, illness, or disability. Having some extra savings for such rainy days will help households feel less distressed.

Introducing and promoting the use of digital finance via mobile applications can also be used to encourage long-term retirement planning for Malaysians of all walks of life. These innovative tools allow individuals and households to access professional advice and search for suitable retirement savings plans at a relatively low cost. These digital finance tools are able to reach large numbers of households compared to traditional in-person consultations. The use of these digital finance apps will also allow individuals and households to keep track of their retirement savings goals, as just encouraging savings without clear goals will likely lead to withdrawals for some intermediate need or want. Nonetheless, there is also a need to reinforce the value of financial planning services by profes-sionally certified financial planners to assist in retirement planning for those with more complex assets or those that need tailor-made arrangements. Both financial regulators, BNM and the SC, should collaborate with industry bodies such as the MFPC on this front to ensure a simple and consistent message is put across all the financial and retirement planning platforms.

Educating the Malaysian public to make long-term investment and retirement plans only via legal and recognised investment platforms is also essential in com-batting the rise of investment fraud cases. BNM and the SC should continue public engagements and enhance their messaging on the need to avoid unneces-sarily high-risk investments and to enforce the message that one should not be engaging with unrecognised bodies or institutions. Updates on blacklisted invest-ment vehicles should be continuously highlighted via traditional and social media to keep the public better informed. There should also be constant reminders to be mindful of phishing tactics of fraudsters on digital platforms, and the public must be made aware of how to protect themselves from such exposure.

More advanced digital finance platforms and tools will also enable the intro-duction of innovative insurance products that are more affordable and attractive to the public. Information on assurance products that offer diversified investment and savings options in insurance plans can be made available on these online platforms. The public should be encouraged to access various websites and mobile apps to compare the various insurance plans available on the market and the benefits that each of them offers. BNM together with MFPC and MITBA can play a role to ensure information is collated and continuously updated, and that these are communicated in a simplified manner that the public can easily understand. The use of legalistic terms should be kept to a minimum. Nonetheless, awareness on the benefits of seeking professional advice from insurance agents should also be promoted as standardised insurance plans may not fit everyone's circumstances.

6.2.5 SP5: Building and safeguarding wealth

The important message that households need to build their wealth and also safeguard what they have is the focus of the final strategic priority "*Building and safeguarding wealth*" (SP5). For individuals who are over-indebted, the first step towards safeguarding their assets is to avoid going into bankruptcy. The consequences of being a bankrupt can lead to being stripped of all the assets and wealth that have accumulated over one's lifetime, and restrictions imposed on bankrupts in Malaysia make it difficult for one to move out of that situation and can remain so for life until all outstanding debts are cleared. Hence, it is imperative that over-indebted individuals seek debt counselling and work out affordable repayment plans with their creditors to avoid getting into default. Developing and distributing information as well as campaigns to increase awareness of bankruptcy in traditional and social media can be effectively employed through collaboration between government agencies and industry associations such as AKPK and CTOS.

In order to encourage investment for retirement, information on the latest financial products and services available in the market can be disseminated via online platforms. This is where the collaboration between BNM, SC, and financial institutions is essential to provide timely and accurate information. Individuals and households should also work to increase their own financial literacy by keeping informed and updated on retirement savings products that are offered by financial institutions. Financial literacy is an important skill that will allow one to better select products that match one's risk attitudes and retirement goals.

To protect the public from squandering away their hard-earned savings on fraudulent investment schemes, a financial crime control policy established with the collaboration of the Ministry of Domestic Trade and Consumer Affairs, BNM and the SC can help reduce the rate of commercial and financial frauds and scams. Individual policymaking by each agency and regulator can lead to policy loopholes that will be taken advantage of by these fraudsters. The public can play a proactive role by following the advice and suggestions from the relevant authorities before handing over their money or assets to others. A realistic expectation on current investment returns will also enable one to avoid committing to high-risk ventures.

Educating the public on the benefits of accumulating and preserving their wealth via insurance awareness programmes should be an ongoing exercise in promoting investment literacy. Awareness campaigns by BNM with the collaboration of insurance and takaful companies can be made accessible and interactive via various public engagements activities. This will open up opportunities for the public to attend financial protection and awareness programmes to get a better understanding on the importance of wealth accumulation and the consequences of being under-protected. There is also a need for insurance providers to simplify the policy document relating to sophisticated insurance plans to allow the public to better understand what they are putting their money into. A clearer understanding of insurance contracts will enable individuals and households to select policies that will be suitable for themselves.

6.3 Conclusion

This book examined four personal finance issues that can be a cause of financial vulnerability among consumers in Malaysia, namely over-indebtedness, retirement savings inadequacy, financial fraud victimisation, and underinsurance. This book has provided relevant and timely information that can be the basis of increasing financial knowledge through thorough understanding of the financial vulnerabilities typically faced by consumers. It is hoped that the information from this book will help to expand financial education for all Malaysians in general and the readers of this book in particular.

Despite all the changes and dynamism of consumerism practices, the ultimate goal in financial education has not changed, that is, to improve financial well-being. This book is written with the needs of consumers in mind, and it is expected to deliver the resources that the consumers need to succeed in practicing good financial behaviour and making prudent financial decisions. Therefore, another goal of this book is to further assist educators, researchers, parental groups, government agencies, and the community to heighten awareness and intensify financial education initiatives among the society through a detailed discussion on the factors influencing financial vulnerability. A combination of behavioural and psychological factors highlighted in this book will help to promote responsible behaviour and rational attitudes among individuals in making sound financial decisions.

This book also aspires to elevate the levels of financial literacy of its readers. The topics discussed in this book should provide guidance for people to plan for their future through short-term and long-term financial planning. This will ensure that they have sufficient funds to meet their future financial needs, including sufficient income during retirement. It is also hoped that this book will help consumers to differentiate between legitimate financial products and fraudulent schemes. In addition, with basic financial knowledge on issues in consumer finances, individuals should be able to find appropriate financial products and make informed financial choices.

Finally, this book offers suggestions for actions and policies to address the financial vulnerabilities challenges facing consumers. The suggestions and recommendations provided are expected to elevate the levels of financial well-being of Malaysians and promote healthy financial behaviour. Good financial well-being and behaviour can promote economic growth and hence, increase the livelihood of people.

References

Abraham, C., Sheeran, P., & Johnston, M. (1998). From health beliefs to self-regulation: Theoretical advances in the psychology of action control. *Psychology and Health, 13*(4), 569–591.

Allaire, J.C. & Marsiske, M. (1999). Everyday cognition: Age and intellectual ability correlates. *Psychology and Aging, 14*(4), 627.

Allaire, J.C. & Marsiske, M. (2002). Well- and ill-defined measures of everyday cognition: Relationship to older adults' intellectual ability and functional status. *Psychology and Aging, 17*(1), 101.

Amron, A., Usman, U., & Mursid, A. (2018). The role of electronic word of mouth, conventional media, and subjective norms on the intention to purchase Sharia insurance services. *Journal of Financial Services Marketing, 23*(3–4), 218–225.

ASEAN Insurance Pulse (2017) *A Market Survey*. Switzerland: Dr. Schanz, Alms & Company. Retrieved on 27 December 2019 from https://faberconsulting.ch/files/faber/pdf-pulse-reports/ASEAN_Insurance_Pulse_2017.pdf

Azma, N., Rahman, M., Adeyemi, A., & Rahman, M. (2019). Propensity toward indebtedness: Evidence from Malaysia. *Review of Behavioral Finance, 11*(2), 188–200.

Baker, H.K. & Puttonen, V. (2017). *Investment Traps Exposed: Navigating Investor Mistakes and Behavioral Biases*. Emerald Group Publishing.

Baron, J., Hershey, J.C., & Kunreuther, H. (2000). Determinants of priority for risk reduction: the role of worry. *Risk Analysis, 20*(4), 413–428.

Biel, A. & Thøgersen, J. (2007). Activation of social norms in social dilemmas: A review of the evidence and reflections on the implications for environmental behaviour. *Journal of economic psychology, 28*(1), 93–112.

Colman, A.M. (2015). *A Dictionary of Psychology*, 4th edition. Oxford University Press, Oxford United Kingdom.

d'Alessio, G. & Iezzi, S. (2013). Household over-indebtedness: Definition and measurement with Italian data. *Bank of Italy Occasional Paper*, 149.

Fischer, P., Lea, S.E., & Evans, K.M. (2013). Why do individuals respond to fraudulent scam communications and lose money? The psychological determinants of scam compliance. *Journal of Applied Social Psychology, 43*(10), 2060–2072.

Flores, S.A.M. & Vieira, K.M. (2014). Propensity toward indebtedness: An analysis using behavioral factors. *Journal of Behavioral and Experimental Finance, 3*, 1–10.

Gamble, K.J., Boyle, P., Yu, L., & Bennett, D. (2013). Aging, financial literacy, and fraud. Netspar Discussion Paper DP11/2013–066. Retrieved on 21 November 2019 from https://pdfs.semanticscholar.org/3575/e931ea339b9d7b78398d8bfdbfd180715fa5.pdf

Grohmann, A., Menkhoff, L., Merkle, C., & Schmacker, R. (2019). Earn More Tomorrow: Overconfident Income Expectations and Consumer Indebtedness. SFB Rationality & Competition, Discussion Paper, 152.

Hastings, J., Mitchell, O.S., & Chyn, E. (2011). Fees, framing, and financial literacy in the choice of pension manager. *Financial Literacy: Implications for Retirement Security and the Financial Marketplace*, 101.

Hershey, D.A., Jacobs-Lawson, J.M., & Austin, J.T. (2013). Effective financial planning for retirement. In M. Wang (ed.), Oxford library of psychology. *The Oxford Handbook of Retirement* (p. 402–430). Oxford University Press.

Hershey, D.A., Jacobs-Lawson, J.M., McArdle, J.J., & Hamagami, F. (2007). Psychological foundations of financial planning for retirement. *Journal of Adult Development*, *14*(1–2), 26–36.

Hockenbury, D.H. & Hockenbury, S.E. (2010). *Psychology*. New York: Worth Publishers.

Husin, M.M., Ismail, N., & Ab Rahman, A. (2016). The roles of mass media, word of mouth and subjective norm in family takaful purchase intention. *Journal of Islamic Marketing*, *7*(1), 59–73.

Lang, P.J. (1984). Cognition in emotion: Concept and action. *Emotions, Cognition, and Behavior*, 192–226.

Lang, P.J. (1985). Cognition in motion: Concept and action. In C.E. Izard, J. Kagan, & R.B. Zajonc (eds.), *Emotions, Cognition, and Behavior*, 192–226. Cambridge University Press.

Laroche, H., Steyer, V., & Théron, C. (2019). How could you be so gullible? Scams and over-trust in organizations. *Journal of Business Ethics*, *160*(3), 641–656.

Loewenstein, G.F., Weber, E.U., Hsee, C.K., & Welch, N. (2001). Risk as feelings. *Psychological Bbulletin*, *127*(2), 267.

Marsiske, M. & Willis, S.L. (1998). Practical creativity in older adults' everyday problem solving: Life-span perspectives. *Creativity and Successful Aging: Theoretical and Empirical Approaches*, 73–113.

Maslow, A.H. (1943). A theory of human motivation. *Psychological Review*, *50*(4), 370–396. https://doi.org/10.1037/h0054346

Mischel, W. & Shoda, Y. (1998). Reconciling processing dynamics and personality dispositions. *Annual Review of Psychology*, *49*(1), 229–258.

Neukam, K.A. & Hershey, D.A. (2003). Financial inhibition, financial activation, and saving for retirement. *Financial Services Review*, *12*(1), 19.

Raza, S.A., Ahmed, R., Ali, M., & Qureshi, M.A. (2019). Influential factors of Islamic insurance adoption: An extension of theory of planned behavior. *Journal of Islamic Marketing*. https://doi.org/10.1108/JIMA-03-2019-0047

Sadkhan, S.B. (2018). "Cognitive and the future", *2018 International Conference on Advance of Sustainable Engineering and its Application (ICASEA)*, Wasit, 2018, pp. 269–270.

Sommer, M. & Dumont, K. (2011). Psychosocial factors predicting academic performance of students at a historically disadvantaged university. *South African Journal of Psychology*, *41*(3), 386–395.

Stawski, R.S., Hershey, D.A., & Jacobs-Lawson, J.M. (2007). Goal clarity and financial planning activities as determinants of retirement savings contributions. *The International Journal of Aging and Human Development*, *64*(1), 13–32.

Topa, G., Lunceford, G., & Boyatzis, R.E. (2018). Financial planning for retirement: a psychosocial perspective. *Frontiers in Psychology*, *8*, 2338.

Van de Weijer, S.G. & Leukfeldt, E.R. (2017). Big five personality traits of cybercrime victims. *Cyberpsychology, Behavior, and Social Networking, 20*(7), 407–412.

Wang, X. & Gloor, P.A. (2018). Wuity as Higher Cognition Combining Intuitive and Deliberate Judgments for Creativity: Analyzing Elon Musk's Way to Innovate. In F. Grippa et al. (eds), *Collaborative Innovation Networks, Studeis on Entrepreneurship, Structural Change and Industrial Dynamics*. Retrieved on 20 March 2020 from https://doi.org/10.1007/978-3-319-74295-3_14

Whitty, M.T. (2019). Predicting susceptibility to cyber-fraud victimhood. *Journal of Financial Crime. 26*(1), 277–292.

Wright, J.C. & Mischel, W. (1987). A conditional approach to dispositional constructs: The local predictability of social behavior. *Journal of Personality and Social Psychology, 53*(6), 1159–1177.

Index

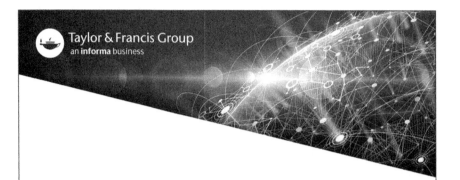